Creative Arts for Early Childhood

Sinéad E. Kelly

GILL EDUCATION

Gill Education
Hume Avenue
Park West
Dublin 12
www.gilleducation.ie

Gill Education is an imprint of M.H. Gill & Co.

© Sinéad E. Kelly 2014

978 07171 5974 1

Design and print origination by O'K Graphic Design, Dublin
Printed by GraphyCems, Spain
Index by Adam Pozner

For permission to reproduce photographs, the author and publisher gratefully acknowledge the following:

© Alamy: 16, 129; © Shutterstock: 2, 13, 25, 26, 28, 34, 39, 44, 50, 54, 62, 66, 71, 75, 82, 87, 95, 102, 106, 111, 122, 127, 134, 138, 140, 146, 185, 186, 188, 190, 198, 200, 203, 204, 206, 221, 228.

The author and publisher have made every effort to trace all copyright holders, but if any has been inadvertently overlooked we would be pleased to make the necessary arrangement at the first opportunity.

The paper used in this book comes from the wood pulp of managed forests. For every tree felled, at least one tree is planted, thereby renewing natural resources.

All rights reserved. No part of this publication may be copied, reproduced or transmitted in any form or by any means, without written permission of the publishers or else under the terms of any licence permitting limited copying issued by the Irish Copyright Licensing Agency.

A CIP catalogue record is available for this book from the British Library

For Fionn

This book has been inspired by the imaginative, fun-filled personalities that I have encountered while working in the field of early childhood care and education. Each day working with children, families, students and like-minded professionals is more exciting than the last.

Contents

How to Use this Book	v
Chapter 1 Introduction	1
Chapter 2 The Creative Environment and Play Partnerships	9
Chapter 3 Planning, Implementing and Assessing Activities	19
Chapter 4 Creative Play and Developmental Stages	32
Chapter 5 Exploring and Creating	60
Chapter 6 Exploring and Creating: The Outdoor Play Space	117
Chapter 7 Creative Play and Positive Mental Health	174
Chapter 8 Unlocking the Adult's Creativity	193
Chapter 9 Creative Safe Environments	214
Chapter 10 Creative Arts Assessment	228
References and Resources	238
Index	244

How to Use this Book

This book aims to guide the reader through the process of designing a creative arts curriculum for young children using a multi-strategy, child-centred approach. Each chapter offers the reader a variety of learning goals to explore. At the beginning of each chapter there is a list of learning outcomes for that chapter. These learning outcomes are taken from the NFQ Level 5 component specifications in Creative Arts for Early Childhood (awarded by Quality and Qualifications Ireland (QQI)). The learning outcomes (LO) covered in this book are:

- LO 1: Examine a variety of creative media opportunities with young children.
- LO 2: Summarise the benefits of exploration and participation in creative arts for the child.
- LO 3: Explore the role of the adult in creating an environment in which children feel secure and confident enough to take risks and explore new situations.
- LO 4: Plan opportunities for consultation with children to plan and engage in creative arts experiences.
- LO 5: Test open-ended materials and natural items for creative arts, in both indoor and outdoor environments, appropriate to different stages of children's development.
- LO 6: Explore challenges for adults in respecting choices and decisions of children.
- LO 7: Employ developmentally appropriate creative arts activities which promote the holistic development of the child.
- LO 8: Reflect on one's own role and responsibilities when engaging in creative arts activities with children (being mindful of health and safety).

You will notice that the learning outcomes overlap between chapters. This is because many of the learning outcomes are intertwined in a variety of ways. It is important to reflect on how chapters link with each other and begin to recognise where these correlations happen when working with young children. The NFQ Level 6 component 'Early Childhood Arts and Culture', leading to a Level 6 award in Early Childhood Care and Education (ECCE) (awarded by QQI), also uses a set of learning outcomes that are intended to build on the learning achieved in the Level 5 component. This textbook introduces the following concepts from the Level 6 learning outcomes 3, 4, 5, 6, 7, 8 and 10.

3. Provide artistic and cultural experiences that support the holistic development of the child.
4. Guide children to use their own values and artistic skills to explore, think about and communicate with their environment.
5. Assess a range of resources to support children's creative and cultural development.
6. Use appropriate space and materials to plan arts- and culture-based experiences that engage children in a supportive way.
7. Lead appropriate observations to evaluate the child's artistic and cultural development.
8. Appraise one's own range of specialised skills and those of colleagues in meeting the creative and cultural needs of the child in the ECCE setting.
10. Manage tasks within the parameters of professional conduct including relations with parents, guardians, children and colleagues.

Each chapter of this book aims to provide the reader with a mixture of theory, practice, national policy and guidelines. It would be ideal to read this book in collaboration with other aspiring early years practitioners or established early years professionals, which could be organised in an educational setting or a workplace.

In the 'Over to You' sections in each chapter the reader is offered a space to put new ideas into action using a variety of means, including:
- case studies
- debates
- designing creative arts programmes, play spaces and presentations
- designing, implementing and evaluating arts displays
- group discussions and practical tasks
- internet-based research
- reflective learning journal
- linking equipment and materials with play opportunities
- linking play with Aistear Themes
- observation
- planning, implementing and reviewing creative arts activities
- visualisations.

The chapters in this book are divided as follows:
- **Chapter 1** introduces the reader to the underlying philosophies of the book, putting forward a method of child-centred, process-oriented play in the creative arts curriculum.
- **Chapter 2 The Creative Environment** focuses on setting the scene and outlines how to encourage creativity to flourish in early childhood environments. Using a 'SPICE' framework, as outlined by Brown (2003), we focus on the child's social, physical, intellectual, creative and emotional space. We also look at the three Fs – fun, freedom and flexibility.
- **Chapter 3 Planning, Implementing and Assessing Activities** looks at the journey of planning, implementing and assessing a creative arts activity with an individual child, a pair of children and groups of children. This chapter is closely linked with the ethos of Síolta (CECDE 2006) and Aistear (NCCA 2009) as well as the 2006 Child Care (Pre-School Services) (No. 2) Regulations (DoHC 2006a).
- **Chapter 4 Creative Play and Developmental Stages** explores different developmental stages with young children in terms of their creative abilities. We address play behaviours of the young child, look at examples of creative arts activities for specific age groups and address the role of the adult in facilitating learning.
- **Chapter 5 Exploring and Creating** addresses how creative arts activities can be incorporated into spontaneous and planned play activities. Looking specifically at the music centre, the small world area, the discovery centre, the table-top area, the arts and crafts centre, the messy play area, the book corner, the construction area, the writing centre and the home corner, we address materials, equipment and types of activity that could be accommodated in these areas.
- **Chapter 6 Exploring and Creating: The Outdoor Play Space** discusses how to facilitate the creative arts in an outside space. In this chapter we also look at bringing creativity on outings with young children and using alternative materials in the early years environment to promote the creative arts curriculum.
- **Chapter 7 Creative Play and Positive Mental Health** focuses on promoting mental wellness in the early years environment. In this chapter we address adults' role in ensuring that children's rights are upheld as well as looking at creative arts as a therapeutic tool, using current and established research as a discussion point.
- **Chapter 8 Unlocking the Adult's Creativity** looks at how the practitioner's creativity can be nurtured using a series of creative arts activities designed specifically for adults. We discuss how an individual's creativity may be 'lost' as they move through childhood into the adult years and how to recapture some of the creative freedoms experienced in our youth.

- **Chapter 9 Creative Safe Environments** deals with how to balance safety with fun, looking specifically at Irish legislation relating to safety in the early years environment and focusing on the Childcare Act 1991, the Child Care (Pre-School Services) (No. 2) Regulations (DoHC 2006a), the Safety, Health and Welfare at Work Act 2005 and the Safety, Health and Welfare at Work (General Application) Regulations 2007. Chapter 9 also looks at the recommendations proposed for early years settings in Síolta Standard 9: Safety and Welfare.
- **Chapter 10 Creative Arts Assessment** is designed for the aspiring early years practitioner moving through the Level 5 component, Creative Arts for Early Childhood (awarded by QQI). It addresses the 'Collection of Work' and 'Project' and discusses how learning can be demonstrated in the Creative Arts for Early Childhood assessment framework.

Introduction

Working with young children is one of the most fun, challenging and exciting professions one can undertake. Each day brings with it new possibilities for learning, playing and creating. This book aims to offer the aspiring early years practitioner a chance to reflect on the use of creative arts when designing play programmes for young children.

Creative arts in the early years can be categorised as active play opportunities in the fields of drama, movement and dance, visual arts and music. When it comes to encouraging creativity and creative thinking with young children, it is acknowledged that creative play is more than what is found in the arts curriculum: creative thinking can also be found in areas such as science and the humanities.

Before we begin our creative arts journey, it is important to distinguish between *creativity* and *creative learning*. Ronsen (2010), in his foreword to the *Born Creative* project, puts forward the idea that when individuals engage in at least one of the four pillars of creative learning – investigating, discovering, inventing and co-operating – the learning can be described as 'creative'.

Creativity differs from creative learning because creativity is concerned with an individual's imagination and with bringing to life images, thoughts and feelings. According to Fumoto *et al.* (2012), creativity and creative thinking are best fostered in an environment where:

- Thinking or behaving using one's imagination is founded on solid social fields through nurturing relationships with peers and adults.
- The child's cognitive abilities are fostered through having a purpose in play as there is a planned objective to achieve.
- The child views the play as valuable and worthwhile, which builds strong emotional foundations in the child.
- The process generates something original and new for the child, motivating them to continue in their endeavours.

When we observe young children participating in the creative arts, we can see that the possibilities for them to use their imagination are endless. When young children engage with the creative arts a two-part creative process unfolds for them.

The first part of the creative process can be described as the 'incubation' period, in which young children gather ideas and hold them in their minds. During this stage children are becoming aware that they want to create something. This incubation process can take a long time to develop as children form new concepts in their minds, learn about the world around them and test ideas.

When the child feels comfortable with their idea the second part of the process emerges. This can be described as the 'creation' phase. During this period the child puts their idea into action through sounds, words and behaviours. The child may feel uneasy trying out this new experience and you may find that many creative thoughts are lost if the child feels uncomfortable or uneasy with the experience. The majority of young children's creations are designed around a variation of a particular theme they may know well. Creations can also emerge through repetition of the same actions over and over again. Read the following anecdote and reflect on the questions below.

A CREATIVITY STORY

Clayton is four years old and has been attending his sessional preschool for eight months. He started in September and he will be finishing in June. Each morning Clayton's key worker, Julia, has asked him where he would like to play, and every day for the last eight months Clayton has said 'in the car corner'. Julia has introduced different activities into the car corner with Clayton, such as books about cars, houses and mini figures, construction materials, arts and crafts experiences; she even made another 'car corner' in the gardening space outside. One morning at the end of May, as Julia was asking each child where they wanted to play, she turned to Clayton, expecting his usual response, when he suddenly said, 'With the paint.' The room went quiet as Julia and the other children watched as Clayton walked over to the arts and crafts centre, put on a smock and started to paint ... a car.

QUESTIONS FOR REFLECTION

- What do you think might have inspired Clayton to go to the arts and crafts area that morning?
- Was Clayton able to be creative in the car corner?
- Thinking about creativity as a two-part process, how long did Clayton's incubation phase last?
- What might influence the length of time of an individual's incubation phase?
- How did Julia gently prompt Clayton's creativity?

Isbell and Raines (2007) remind us that it is an exciting time to be an early years educator. With advances in technology, as well as an increased respect for childhood, we have fantastic insights into how young children learn. With greater knowledge of how the brain develops, of the impact of relationships with young children, and the understanding that young individuals acquire dispositions, skills and knowledge through active participation with their environment, the early years practitioner is at an advantage when designing a child-centred curriculum. Over the last two hundred years, early childhood pioneers such as Rousseau, Montessori, Pestalozzi, Owen, Froebel and Steiner, and more contemporary educationalists, among them Weikart, Bruce and Hayes, have promoted the use of play to foster children's curiosity and meaning-making skills. These early childhood advocates have shaped the way we work with young children and their families in Ireland today.

It is interesting to note that despite the knowledge we have about how people learn it is well documented that creativity and the arts have been in a steady decline globally. The Irish education system has shadowed this global downturn in creative arts appreciation and moved away from promoting creativity, individual learning and inspiring children to have new and innovative ideas. Looking at the Junior Certificate as an example, we can wonder whether the focus on learning gives priority to exam results rather than the quality of learning. In 2012 changes in the Irish education system were introduced with the aim of moving away from the rote learning system encouraged in state examinations such as the Junior Certificate. It is proposed that over the next number of years the format of the Junior Certificate will change to focus on a process-based approach using a variety of assessment methods such as assignments, projects, case studies, performances, oral activities, written pieces and different kinds of test as well as incorporating ICT to enhance the learning experience. A process-based approach can be described as a journey that emphasises how learning is undertaken or 'done'.

You will observe that active learning occurs when children engage in activities using their senses and movements (Bruce 2004). This active process employs the use of intellectual abilities such as thoughts and decision-making skills as well as overcoming a variety of holistic challenges that are initiated in the action. When children participate in play in an active and meaningful manner you may notice a 'learning product' forming. This learning product is a display of how children demonstrate their new knowledge. The role of the educator is to recognise the many varieties of ways in which children choose to demonstrate how they learn, and to celebrate these achievements with the child. This ability to understand children's learning is eloquently described in the Reggio Emilia approach as the 'hundred languages of children'. In Irish early education, process-based education is a practice that has been advocated for many years. Process-based learning is a useful tool when ensuring that children's rights are upheld in the education system.

Taking Aistear, the Early Childhood Curriculum Framework (NCCA 2009), as an example, we can see how process-based learning is actively promoted in early education in Ireland. This framework celebrates early childhood as a time of being, a time of enjoying and learning from experiences as they unfold. Aistear (which is the Irish word for 'journey') acknowledges the importance of solid early learning foundations, as they have a significant impact in later life experiences. The Aistear guide highlights to the educator that young children learn best through respectful, loving and trusting relationships with the adults and children in their lives. Aistear also promotes the use of play, exploration and collaborative discussion in the early years environment. Using twelve child-centred principles in conjunction with four integrated Themes – Well-Being; Communication; Identity and Belonging; and Exploring and Thinking – the educator is equipped with a framework to design personal learning plans for children that focus on process-based play and learning. Throughout this book we will be using the principles and themes of Aistear, as well as the ethos of Síolta, to underpin ideas for the early years creative arts curriculum.

Play and exploration are especially important for the creative arts curriculum as active learning is central to creativity. Isbell and Raines (2007) remind us that the creative arts have held an important place in human civilisation throughout history. Painting, singing, dancing and playing have been constant personal and interpersonal communication tools across countless generations. Creative arts inspire children to think in innovative ways, find out new ideas about themselves and the world around them as well as offering opportunities to challenge themselves in fun and original ways. Wright (2010) highlights that our imagination reaches its peak in the early years and gradually declines as we grow into middle childhood and beyond. Encouraging children to place high value on the arts in the early years can promote the ongoing development and nurturing of their imagination in its declining years. Sir Ken Robinson, in his February 2006 TED Talk on creativity, maintained that for children to be successful in their lives their imaginations must be nurtured. In his presentation he emphasised that in the formal schooling system creativity is as important as literacy and should be given the same status. This idea is interesting because in the field of early education it is recognised that the creative arts curriculum is a fantastic medium for encouraging the development of other modalities such as language, movement, science, mathematics and countless others. Robinson puts forward the intriguing thought that as children grow older educators start to move learning away from bodies and focus their efforts towards the brain, specifically the left-hand side of the brain, which aids logical thinking, analysis and accuracy. The role of the early years educator is to ensure that young children are offered a solid and balanced foundation of active play experiences which engage minds, bodies and hearts. We have a duty to refocus our values so that the creative arts are viewed as an educational philosophy rather than simply a set of 'activities'.

In this book we categorise the arts into four main areas: dramatic play; movement and dance; visual arts; and music. Using the National School Curriculum (DES 1999) in conjunction with Aistear: the Early Childhood Curriculum Framework, let us now look at what each of these categories encompasses.

Dramatic play

Young children begin acting out the world around them from a very young age. Traditionally, drama is associated with the theatre, television shows, films, performance, costumes, setting and stages. With young children, drama comes in the form of socio-dramatic play. This type of play allows children to make sense of their environment and the people they interact with, and to make meanings out of the unknown. Socio-dramatic play gives children the chance to test out 'what if' situations, experience new and different feelings in a safe space and make their imagination come alive. You can observe socio-dramatic play taking these forms:

- improvisation through 'making' up fantasy scenes or recreating real-life situations
- embodying other personalities and creating new situations
- re-enacting life issues, new or old pieces of knowledge or themes in a role-play fashion
- communicating a message to other people
- 'living' a story, or making the story up as they go along; this also involves solving problems in both the real world and fictional worlds and can include co-operation with peers or/and adults
- reflecting on and conversing about events in life so that the outcome of the play reflects the child's perception of their world.

Movement and dance

From the moment young children are born their movements are innate. Movement is a primal force in the human body and most of the body's movements are unconscious and unscripted. In early years education we try to capture these natural movements and intertwine them with everyday learning. Dance can be described as the 'art of motion' and it is the action that is involved in dance that allows us to explore our body movements in new and creative ways. Through dance we can discover:

- the movements the body can create
- the dynamics of bodily movement
- how a body moves in a particular space
- the relationships that develop when the body interacts with other people or objects.

These discoveries can be labelled the 'principles of movement' and through dance you may notice that children explore:

- their movements in response to a noise, tempo, theme or idea
- how they choose movements to express ideas, thoughts and feelings they are experiencing
- how to create a simple movement sequence in response to an idea, theme, sound, etc.; and they may development this sequence into a dance.

Visual arts

The visual arts allow for artistic expression and communication through the medium of concrete images. This form of creative arts gives the young child the opportunity to create tangible links between their imagination and the real world. The medium of visual art allows the child to reflect, organise and express their life experiences, wonderings and feelings in a physical form. Visual arts can take shape in many ways:

- mark making/drawing
- painting and use of colour
- printing
- cutting/tearing and pasting (collage)
- dough/clay sculpture
- construction
- fabric and fibre creations
- photography.

As we can see, visual arts can be created using a two- or three-dimensional format and the young child should be offered balanced opportunities across the different types of visual artistic form. A well-integrated visual arts curriculum in the early years will enable the child to:
- develop personal aesthetic responses to art and beauty in their environment
- explore and develop an awareness of line, shape, colour, tone, texture, pattern, spatial organisation as well as three-dimensional qualities of form
- communicate messages with a sense of fun and purpose.

In addition, the child will:
- depending on their age and stage of development, be able to play in a spontaneous, imaginative and structured way with a variety of materials, such as paints, paper, crayons, chalks, pencils, ink, dough, clay, fabric, fibre, papier mâché and construction materials. They will begin to include focused design and planning in their visual art work
- begin to apply particular skills and techniques in their visual art work and demonstrate awareness of particular elements in their artwork
- begin to look at other artists in their environment with curiosity and openness
- begin to identify a variety of visual arts media in their world and imagine the creative processes involved in their fruition
- become astute in describing their artistic processes and be able to discuss specific elements in their work that hold personal importance
- be able to critically reflect on their artwork and that of their peers
- show an interest in responding to visual arts experiences in a variety of imaginative ways, such as recreating a visual arts piece through another artistic medium such as dramatic arts, dance, music, etc.

Music

Music is an art form that is deeply rooted in the psyche. It is a medium in which messages, thoughts, feelings and actions can be shared in a unique and evocative way. Each person is born with an innate and individual relationship with music and with their own individual musical abilities. Music is embedded in one's culture and heritage. In the early years setting it can be employed as a valuable medium for learning. When introducing the musical arts to young children we should employ three main strands:

1. **Listening and responding:** When young children are given the opportunity to listen to a piece of music they are transported to a different world. Musical listening should include a range of different types of music, from classical to contemporary and everything in between. While listening to music young children will engage in responses that engage both their senses and abilities in an active and purposeful manner.
2. **Performing:** Young children are not burdened by the constraints of inhibitions and a fear of societal judgement. It is a wonderful event when a child performs a song or piece of music using their voice and/or a musical instrument. When performing, the child actively experiences musical concepts such as rhythm, pitch, tempo, beat, melody, harmony, intervals, etc. In addition, musical performance elicits a sense of accomplishment that brings with it a specific type of confidence and joy.
3. **Composing:** Young children will instinctively make repetitive sounds and sound patterns. We can hear this in the cooing of very young babies and it continues throughout early childhood. In the early years setting this innate ability can be fostered and developed through encouraging the child to compose and record their own pieces of music and song. This act of composition channels the child's creativity in a very unique way and provides a medium for reflective self-expression.

OVER TO YOU

Create a learning journal. Use this personal log to write and reflect on any ideas, reflections and activities that inspire you when reading this book. If you begin to feel lethargic or if your mind wanders while you're reading, put the book down, take a break and come back to it when you are able to focus! Note these concentration lapses in your journal and reflect on what may be distracting you. Remember to allow your creativity to flourish during your journey through this text and keep a record of your personal discoveries. A note to remember at this point: if you are completing your Level 5 component in Creative Arts for Early Childhood (awarded by QQI), a learning journal will serve you well when it comes to completing your assessments.

The Creative Environment and Play Partnerships

This chapter explores aspects of the following Learning Outcomes:

- LO 2: Summarise the benefits of exploration and participation in creative arts for the child.
- LO 3: Explore the role of the adult in creating an environment in which children feel secure and confident enough to take risks and explore new situations.
- LO 4: Plan opportunities for consultation with children to plan and engage in creative arts experiences.
- LO 6: Explore challenges for adults in respecting choices and decisions of children.

> *Creativity has to be nurtured: it does not happen on its own.*
> (Essa 2010:257)

In Chapter 1 we discussed what creativity is and where it can be observed in an early childhood arts curriculum. In this chapter we will look at the practitioner's role in developing the creative environment in order to encourage children to engage with the arts curriculum in a meaningful way. We will also look at how to bring the environment past the preschool walls and discuss how to involve your local community in the young child's creative development.

The 'non-threatening' environment

The practitioner's role in designing and maintaining the creative environment is of vital importance. The environment you design is the medium in which the child's learning can occur. Curtis and O'Hagan state that 'when children are offered a safe and non-threatening environment they will communicate the depth of their feelings through play. Children do not talk about their concerns and problems, they play them out' (2003:112–13).

But how do we create environments in which children can feel safe enough to make friends, play and learn? To design an early childhood environment that promotes creativity we can look to the SPICE framework (Brown 2003). SPICE stands for Social, Physical, Intellectual, Creative and Emotional. The following reflection points help us understand the meaning behind the SPICE acronym.

> **QUESTIONS FOR REFLECTION**
>
> **S** – How do you want **social** interactions to happen in the early years service?
> **P** – What will be **physically** around the child in the early years environment?
> **I** – What types of **intellectual** stimulation will be available for the child in their environment?
> **C** – How will **creativity** be actively encouraged in the environment?
> **E** – How are the child's **emotional** needs met in the programme?

The social environment

In an early years service we often forget to look at all the social interactions that happen throughout the day as being part of the creative arts curriculum. In a positive social environment children can feel comfortable and confident enough to speak openly about their views. The practitioner needs to be mindful about their role modelling communication. Are you speaking with the child at their level? Are you talking with the child, listening to and responding to what they say? A child will feel more comfortable communicating in an early years service if they feel that they are welcome and cared for, and that they belong there. Have you ever walked into a room where you don't know anybody? This feeling of the unknown brings with it a sense of being an 'outsider'. This 'outsider' feeling can cause us to become shy and quiet, almost invisible. In an early years setting we want children to feel part of the service, and simple planning for your social environment can help with this.

> **QUESTIONS FOR REFLECTION**
>
> Ask yourself the following questions about the social environment.
> - Do the adults play with the children during free play/work time, activity time, outside play time, etc.?
> - Do the adults plan activities based on the child's interests and abilities?
> - At mealtimes does everybody (adults and children) sit together and have relaxed conversations while eating?
> - Are children given the opportunity to choose their own activities?
> - If a problem arises with a child, are they given the opportunity, with support, to solve it themselves?
> - Are the children given times throughout the day to converse with each other in pairs, in small groups, in larger groups?
> - Do the different age groups get to mix, talk and play with each other?
> - Are there policies in the service that discuss how to interact with children?
> - Does each child get to choose who they play with, when and how they will play?

The Aistear Framework describes the Theme of Identity and Belonging as being 'about children developing a positive sense of themselves as they are, and feeling that they are valued and respected as part of a family and community' (NCCA 2009). New and Cochran (2007) describe the social environment as one that promotes conversations, dramatic play, sharing, co-operation and an acceptance of diversity. In addition to this, the Síolta Standards of 'Rights of the Child', 'Environment', 'Interactions', 'Play' and 'Communications', among others (CECDE 2006), give practitioners signposts for reflection on how to prioritise the social environment.

Moving beyond the early education setting, we can look to community services and initiatives to enhance the child's creative learning opportunities in a social way. The practitioner has an important role in organising visits to local art galleries, musical and dramatic societies; going on walks in the community and viewing any environmental art work that is on show. Look around – there is a wealth of art and design on offer! What are the designs of the buildings? How would you construct the swings and slides in the park? What posters are in shop windows? Are there any graffiti on walls? Get information from your county childcare committee, county council, local library, local schools, etc. to help you plan exciting events for young children to visit. These types of creative outing also help develop children's aesthetic interests. (We shall discuss outings in more detail in Chapter 6.)

The physical environment

Standard 2 in the Síolta manual looks specifically at 'Environment'. It asks the practitioner to ensure that play environments, 'both indoor and outdoor (including materials and equipment)' are enriching, 'well-maintained, safe, available, accessible, adaptable, developmentally appropriate, and offer a variety of challenging and stimulating experiences'.

The physical environment, both indoor and outdoor, should offer a variety of creative learning opportunities to the child in the form of play-based activities. In Chapters 3, 5 and 6 we will look at how to design different play areas in an early childhood setting that can encourage both spontaneous and planned creative activities.

QUESTIONS FOR REFLECTION

When thinking about the physical environment the practitioner might ask themselves the following questions:

- Is the environment up to standard and in line with national legislation?
- Does the environment reflect (through pictures, books, materials, equipment, music, food, etc.) the diversity of the children it is accommodating?
- Is the environment organised to suit different learning levels, abilities, skills and interests?
- Are there defined areas to play, rest, eat, store materials, clean up?
- Do the equipment, materials and fixtures suit the people who are using them? (Equipment and materials for both adults and children, e.g. chairs.)
- Are there measures in place for children who have additional mobility requirements? (Walking/transport aids such as wheelchairs, etc.)
- Are the different types of play accommodated in different interest areas such as home corner, construction corner, art area, etc.?
- Does the outdoor space have defined interest areas?
- Is the children's work displayed at child's eye level?
- Is there information, photos, etc. about the children's families in the environment?
- Are children's names displayed?
- Do the children have their own personal space to store items?
- Are the environments clean and well maintained?
- Is the environment bright and lit with natural light where possible?
- Is there enough space to play and move in the environment?
- Are the colour schemes in place suitable for the environment?

The *Síolta Research Digest* on Environment (CECDE 2007) highlights that when these spaces are designed in a considered manner they become a place where a child's 'initiative is encouraged, their competence is nurtured, and their curiosity is aroused'. When physical spaces are designed with the creative arts curriculum in mind, one can observe children exploring independently and/or with their peers in the environment. A well-designed physical space gives children the opportunity to make play decisions and carry out these thoughts and feelings in action. We can also assess whether a play space is of high creative quality when children are enabled to engage in meaningful active learning experiences that offer opportunities for problem solving and negotiation.

OVER TO YOU

With permission, visit an early childhood service and assess the environment using the questions for reflection above. Reflect on your answers. What messages do they send to you about the ethos of the service, how the management and the staff value the children in their care and their families, and how creativity is fostered through the physical environment?

The intellectually stimulating environment

Children receive intellectual stimulation through both spontaneous and planned activities that are available in the early years environment. The practitioner aims therefore to provide 'experiences, materials and encouragement that help children to become curious explorers of their world' (Martin & Fabes 2009:288). Being in environments, both indoor and outdoor, that are visually stimulating goes a long way towards motivating children to engage with creative play. This play should offer 'a range of developmentally appropriate, challenging, diverse, creative and enriching experiences for all children' (Síolta Component 2.5). In addition to providing interesting and fun materials, best practice reminds the practitioner to make opportunities available for parents and families to become involved in daily routines and activities (Síolta Component 3.2). Having a daily routine displayed in the early years environment gives children, parents and caregivers a chance to take ownership of their activities and plan what they want to become involved with. Displaying the routine/curriculum in pictures or photographs at child's eye level gives an added depth to the adult–child learning partnership (Síolta Components 7.1 and 7.3). We will look at how to plan individual, pair, small group and large group activities in Chapter 3.

> **OVER TO YOU**
>
> The early years practitioner has a responsibility to look very closely at the curriculum approach they employ in the setting. Have a discussion with an early years practitioner and ask:
> - What curriculum is currently in use in the service?
> - Does the curriculum in place utilise the twelve principles outlined in the Aistear Framework?
> - How do practitioners keep themselves up to date with any national and international changes in the curriculum? (The Síolta Standard 'Curriculum' looks at this question specifically in Component 7.2.)
> - Does the service employ the Síolta guidelines?
>
> After having this discussion, reflect on your own practice and think about what type of values you would employ to ensure a high-quality intellectual environment.

The creative environment

Promoting a creative environment means a lot more than providing paint and paper! Research conducted by Saracho (1990, 1992) suggests that a creative environment should be psychologically and physically safe, include interesting activities, allow children the time to create and play and ensure that negative judgement is not passed on children's ideas. This contributes to a space in which children feel able to imagine and share their ideas without fear of ridicule. Looking at the Síolta Standard 'The Rights of the Child' (Component 1.1), we can see that in the Irish context children's choices and decisions should be heard and respected in the setting.

Following on from the idea of idea of sharing imaginative ideas we can look to the Síolta Standards of 'Play' (Component 6.5) and 'Interaction', specifically Component 5.4. In these Components the practitioner uses play as a means to allow creativity to flourish. High-quality play focuses on the process of the activity rather than the finished product, as discussed in Chapter 1. Sometimes adults have their own ideas of what children should be learning or doing – 'They should know their colours', 'They should know how to write their name', etc. – but the creative practitioner allows the child to 'go with the flow' and follow their own needs and interests. This relaxed space allows learning to happen in an organic manner, which reinforces creative thinking. Talking and listening, offering responses and encouraging the child to expand their language skills using developmentally appropriate challenges all promote a positive creative environment.

OVER TO YOU

Try a role play with one of your colleagues. Take it in turns to be Person A and Person B.

Person A begins to draw a cat. Person B tells them it does not look like a cat, it looks like a dog, etc., making generally negative/critical comments until person A states that the picture is finished. Time how long Person A takes to draw the cat.

Now begin the sequence again. Person A starts drawing a cat, but this time Person B gives positive reinforcing comments such as, 'I see you're trying to draw a cat', 'Its ears look fluffy', etc. See how long Person A takes to draw the cat when positive comments are made.

After the two cats are drawn Person A reflects on both experiences and describes what it was like to have their creativity criticised and then promoted.

Now repeat the role play with Person B drawing the two cat pictures.

What does this exercise tell you about the impact of criticism on an individual's creativity?

The emotional environment

Hyson (2004) describes three key aspects to building a secure emotional environment for young children. One of these aspects is predictability. Predictability helps children to know how people are going to behave and what will happen in their day. In an early education setting we need to be mindful of transition times in children's lives, for example moving to a different room or a change in practitioner. Having consistent key relationships with practitioners (Síolta Component 13.1) helps the child to form a strong bond and attachments. A key worker system could be useful when developing emotional environments. Beaver *et al.* (2001) describe a key worker system as one in which one staff member takes responsibility for a group of children. The practitioner in the key worker role is able to form a close relationship with each child in their care, get to know their interests and abilities, forge a strong partnership with the child's parents/caregivers, and in turn is able to plan relevant activities for the child.

The second key aspect of developing an emotionally secure environment as described by Hyson (2004) is that the child is warmly accepted into the setting. The following questions for reflection take a look at how a child and family can feel welcome in an early years service.

> **QUESTIONS FOR REFLECTION**
>
> Ask yourself:
> - Do you call each child and their parent/caregiver by their name when you greet them?
> - Are the children's names and/or photos displayed over coat hooks, on chairs, etc.?
> - Are there pictures of the child and their family displayed in the room?
> - Is the child's creative work displayed in the room?
> - Does the practitioner take time to speak with the child throughout the day and to their parents/caregivers as the child is leaving each day?
> - Are the other children encouraged to greet their peers using their names?

Simple gestures in the setting can have a huge impact on the emotional environment and can go a long way towards making a child and their families feel happy and secure. The Síolta Standard of 'Identity and Belonging' (Component 14.1) reminds us to value children's sense of belonging in the setting through written policies and procedures which are reflected in practice.

The third aspect is responsiveness. This means that the emotional focus of the early childhood setting shows the child 'that they matter, that their actions have consequences and they can make a difference in what happens in the world' (Hyson 2004:39). Ensuring that children have daily interactions with the outside world offers fantastic opportunities to teach about action and consequence. Activities that can be incorporated into the creative arts curriculum include plant and animal care, scientific activities such as playing with water or sand, musical activities such as playing instruments and practical activities, for example baking. These activities demonstrate consequence and difference in active and fun ways. For example, listening to and identifying different sounds in nature offers children a wider perspective of the world they live in while also developing their aesthetic abilities and their ability to discriminate differences.

THE CREATIVE ENVIRONMENT AND PLAY PARTNERSHIPS

> **OVER TO YOU**
>
> Think about the three phrases used by Hyson in regard to showing children that:
> - they matter
> - their actions have consequences
> - they can make a difference in what happens in the world.
>
> Discuss each of these phrases. What impact would a child's belief in the truth of each of these phrases have on their overall wellbeing and ability to be creative?

In addition to the SPICE framework, three more words that were added to the Playwork philosophy (Brown 2003) fit very well when describing a creative environment:

Fun

Fun is an essential element in any early years setting. When a child is having fun they are given the opportunity to take safe risks, challenge themselves and be entertained. Think about being with a person or in a place you really enjoy, that you find fun. What is it about that person or place that makes you smile and laugh? Is it exciting there? Is it love? Do you feel wanted and respected? That fun feeling of joy is what we want to recreate in the early years environment!

Freedom

Freedom is something we sometimes take for granted as adults. As adults we choose what to wear every day, what time to get up in the morning, what to eat, what to do. Imagine being a child and all those decisions being made by somebody else. A child can be in a very powerless position. An early years environment that promotes creativity and the creative arts should aim to give children a sense of freedom and control over their lives. If children know the rules in the room they can then test these rules or boundaries to see what happens if they break them! This means that the rules should come with a set of consequences if broken. In a democratic environment (one where everybody's voice is heard), the children and adults devise the rules and consequences together, as partners. Children can also be offered power and control in the early years environment by choosing what and when they want to play, having developmentally appropriate equipment and materials at the child's level and allowing children to take part in decision making in activities. An example of this decision making could be asking the child/children what book/s they want to hear at story time or which music they would like to hear at snack time.

Having a balance between structure and freedom in the early years environment is supported in practical ways described by Saracho (2012:307):
- asking open-ended questions
- accepting vague answers
- modelling creative thinking and behaviours
- encouraging exploration play and persistence in activities
- praising unexpected answers.

Flexibility

In a creative environment the daily routine should be flexible and offer opportunities for the child to explore, experiment and investigate. This can be a challenge for the practitioner if child/adult ratios are high. A balance can be struck by managing the early years setting in a manner that understands that each child in your care has different wants, likes and needs. As a practitioner we are in a position of power and this power should be used to allow children to play and learn in ways that suit the child, rather than what suits us as adults.

> **QUESTION FOR REFLECTION**
>
> Imagine that it is winter and it's snowing. The practitioner generally does not bring their group of children outside until after snack time, but the children are asking to go outside now. What could the practitioner do?

Chapter summary

This chapter looked at the practitioner's role in planning a creatively focused environment using a SPICE framework (Brown 2003). By focusing on the social, physical, intellectual, creative and emotional aspects of the early childhood setting, practitioners can create a space where children feel safe and supported to explore ideas and create fun play adventures.

> **OVER TO YOU**
>
> Imagine you are going to design your own play space for a group of children. Taking one or more of the age groups 0–1, 1–2, 2–3, 3–4 and 4–6, imagine how you would incorporate all the SPICE ideas with the ethos of Fun, Flexibility and Freedom! Research the Child Care (Pre-School Services) (No. 2) Regulations (DoHC 2006a) for child/space ratios and child/adult ratios to get an idea of how many children and adults can be in an early years room.

Planning, Implementing and Assessing Activities

This chapter explores aspects of the following Learning Outcomes:
- LO 3: Explore the role of the adult in creating an environment in which children feel secure and confident enough to take risks and explore new situations
- LO 4: Plan opportunities for consultation with children to plan and engage in creative arts experiences
- LO 7: Employ developmentally appropriate creative arts activities which promote the holistic development of the child
- LO 8: Reflect on one's own role and responsibilities when engaging in creative arts activities with children (being mindful of health and safety).

Planned activities

What are 'activities' with young children? Activities are planned and unplanned events that occur during the child's day. Examples of planned activities might be planting seeds in the garden or going on a nature walk. Unplanned activities happen spontaneously, for example when a child looks out of the window, spots a butterfly and decides to draw a picture about it; or comes across an acorn in the garden and decides to explore what it is. Unplanned activities make up a large portion of the child's day and this type of 'incidental learning' (Campbell & Jobling 2012) is very important to the child's overall development. Unplanned activities can also be called 'self-initiated learning' and are essential for the development of intrinsic motivation within the young child. We will discuss planned and unplanned activities more in Chapters 5 and 6.

One of the major daily tasks of the early years practitioner is planning a series of individual and group activities for the children they are working with. Activities can be planned for individual children, for children in pairs, for small groups of children or large groups of children. They can be planned for most times of the day, for example during circle time, during outdoor play time, at dinner time, etc. One of the key challenges for the early years educator is to plan activities that are fun and offer active learning opportunities for the child. Planning activities gives the practitioner an opportunity to conduct 'active research' in the early years environment.

> **OVER TO YOU**
>
> In the online resource Google Books one can access a preview of a number of textbooks. Using this facility, research the topic 'Active Research in Early Childhood Education' and think about how you could incorporate this approach into your day-to-day routine.

Planning activities is a key component for compliance with Regulation Five of the Child Care (Pre-School Services) (No. 2) Regulations, which addresses the 'Health, Welfare and Development of the Child'. This regulation states:

> A person carrying on a pre-school service shall ensure that each child's learning, development and wellbeing is facilitated within the daily life of the service through the provision of the appropriate opportunities, experiences, activities, interactions, materials and equipment having regard to the age and stage of development of the child and the child's cultural context. (DoHC 2006a)

This section of the pre-school regulations legally obliges the preschool practitioner to dedicate time to designing developmentally appropriate activities for young children. The Síolta Standards Curriculum, Legislation (Components 7.5 and 15.1) and Planning and Evaluation (Components 8.1, 8.2 and 8.3) support this area. We will now look at an example of how to design activities using a three-step approach which is adapted from the High/Scope ethos: Plan, Do and Review.

Step 1: Planning – if you fail to plan you plan to fail!

What are the child's interests?

When planning activities we need to start with what the child's interested in. We can find out what a child's interests are in many ways, for example by observing them, speaking with them and asking their parents/caregivers. When we establish what the child likes to do, we can start to plan the activity. For example, if we observe a child or group of children who enjoy playing with blocks we can begin to plan our activity in the block/construction corner.

What is the aim?

When you have established what the child/group of children would enjoy doing, the next stage is to develop an aim. An aim can be defined as a desired outcome, i.e. what you would like the children to learn from the activity. The Aistear Themes of Identity and Belonging, Communication, Exploring and Thinking, and Well-being give us a great framework when developing aims for activities. For example, if you have observed during dinner time a pair of children, Sarah and Ross, having difficulty sharing, you could plan an activity with the aim of encouraging sharing and communication skills. The Síolta Standards of Play and Communication (Components 6.7, 7.6 could apply here). Once you have your aim figured out you can move on to the 'nitty gritty': the objectives.

What are the objectives?

Objectives of activities are a 'to do' list that you put in place before the aim is reached. Imagine that you are standing at the bottom of a staircase; the objectives are all the steps that you must take to reach the top. When planning objectives for an activity you need to consider the following points:

- What are the child/children's observation records telling me about the child's likes, dislikes, interests and abilities?
- What do other people working with the child/children think would be a good way to meet the aim? By including others in the decision-making process, while being respectful of confidentiality, you are using a best practice approach outlined in the Síolta Standards of Consultation and Organisation (Components 4.1 and 10.5).
- What resources (equipment, materials, finances, time, space, etc.) are available to me? (See the Resources section below.)
- What are the child's/children's and parents'/caregivers' ideas around the activity plan? Having these conversations with families strengthens the partnership between practitioner and the child's home as well as complying with the Síolta Standards Parents and Families, and Communication (Components 3.1 and 12.2).
- What are the child/children's views about the activity plan? When working with children we enter into a play partnership in which children have a right to be involved in decisions that concern their lives.

- Are there any additional needs/different abilities that I need to consider? How will I plan for these variations in paired and group activities?
- How does the activity plan link with the Aistear Themes of Well-Being, Identity and Belonging, Exploring and Thinking, and Communicating?
- After reading up on childhood activities, what ideas does my research (from books, articles, websites, etc.) offer for improving my plan?
- What form of assessment will I use to evaluate this activity? (See Step 3: Reviewing the Activity at the end of this chapter for some ideas.)

Resources: what do I need for the activity?

When planning an activity it is a good idea to organise the resources you will need and have them prepared and ready before the activity begins – a bit like getting ready to bake a cake and having all of the ingredients ready to go. Consider the following points:

- **Equipment:** 'Equipment' can be defined as items that are long-lasting and durable. These could be tables, chairs, aprons, paint brushes, floor mats, gardening tools, musical instruments, etc. Before planning an activity you must check what equipment is already in your facility, assess whether it is suitable to use and decide whether any additional equipment is needed.
- **Materials:** Materials are items that are used in the activity and are generally not reused, for example paint, flour, paper, felt, flower seeds, etc. It is a good idea to have a store of materials in the service, organised for easy access for both the child and adult. This is discussed more in Chapters 5 and 6.
- **Personnel:** When planning activities you need to think about whether you can complete them alone or whether you need a second or third practitioner/volunteer to help you. Do you need help setting up the activity, managing it or tidying up afterwards? Do you need a second adult available when you are completing your observation of the activity? Be mindful that if your planned activity is an outing, such as a walk to the local park, the adult/child ratios will need to be in line not only with the Child Care (Pre-School Services) (No. 2) Regulations (DoHC 2006a) but also with your service's insurance agreement. Remember that your plan needs to be fun for the child/children and this means that you must be available to support them throughout the activity, so ask yourself: Do I need a second pair of hands?
- **Safe spaces:** As well as possibly needing a second practitioner to help facilitate the fun, a second adult can also help to make the activity safer. (We will look at risk assessments when planning activities in Chapter 9.) The first stage in planning for safety is deciding where the activity will take place. Will it be in the home area? The art area? The outside play area? Will you be going on an outing? Remember,

planning for safety is aimed not only at keeping the children in the service safe, but the adults too! Here are a few considerations in relation to safety.

- *Transport hazards* – think about accidents/incidents that might occur when coming into contact with vehicles. Do the children need to get to a new area in the service or to somewhere outside the service? If you are walking, what are the risks in relation to encountering vehicles? Do you need to cross the road? Are there safe paths to walk on? Are there traffic lights? If you will be getting a taxi or a bus, is it properly insured and does it have seatbelts, etc.?
- *Human hazards* – think about accidents/incidents that might occur when coming into contact with other people. How are you going to pair/group children together? Do they like each other? Is there a possibility that one child might frighten/intimidate another child? How can you overcome these issues?
- *Chemical hazards* – think about accidents/incidents that might occur when coming into contact with chemicals such as ingredients in paint, glue, etc. Have you checked that everything you are planning to use is non-toxic? Have you checked with parents/caregivers for any allergies to materials the child/children may have? How will you protect clothes and skin from any chemical spills? How will you reduce the risk of children swallowing harmful chemicals? Do you know who the first aid officer is in your service if a child swallows any of the materials? Is there a policy in your service that covers safe chemical use?
- *Physical hazards* – think about accidents/incidents that might occur from physical causes, such as slipping, tripping, falling, etc. Is the play area free from obstructions that the child/children could fall over? Is there a possibility the child could swallow and choke on any of the items you are using? Are 'non-slip' items used where possible (on chair feet, floor mats, etc.)? How are you ensuring that the environment is free of physical safety hazards?
- *Biological hazards* – think about possible transmission of viruses, bacteria and fungi between people. Is there somewhere close and convenient for children and adults to wash their hands after the activity? Is there warm running water with soap and individual hand towels/air dryer in line with the pre-school regulations (DoHC 2006a) requirements? How will you prevent-cross contamination of materials/equipment that may have been in a child's mouth? What is the service's policy on illness?

- **Finance**: As the saying goes, 'nothing in life is free', and this also applies to planning your activity!

> **QUESTIONS FOR REFLECTION**
>
> When costing the activity ask yourself the following questions to assess your costs:
> - Will extra staff be needed and how will they be sought?
> - What materials will be used?
> - How much are these materials per child?
> - Is extra equipment needed? If so, how much does it cost?
> - Do we need transport? If so, how will we pay for it?
> - Do I need to budget for extra food?
> - If we are going to be out of the building, do we have credit on phones in case of emergency?
> - How will clothes be protected?

- **Time:** How much time will this activity take? Activity time frames will differ depending on a number of factors. Consider the following:
  - the age and stage of the child
  - the interest the child has in the activity
  - what the activity is
  - how many children are taking part
  - what is happening in the child's vicinity that might distract them from the current activity
  - the time of day
  - what has happened directly before and is due to happen directly after the activity.

It is important to remember that even though you have planned the activity, one or more of the children may not want to engage in it! If a child or even a number or children do not want to engage in the plan you should ensure that there are other play options the child/children can avail of. The best type of play allows the child to choose themselves if they want to participate or not.

Activities happen in three parts – setting up, doing and tidying up – so make a rough estimate of how much time you need to allocate to each part. We sometimes focus so much on the activity itself we forget to plan for how to tidy it up afterwards!

Well done! Now your plan is prepared the next step is to put it into action.

PLANNING, IMPLEMENTING AND ASSESSING ACTIVITIES 25

Step 2: 'Doing' the activity – bring on the fun!

Now you have planned the activity, you know:

- what the activity is
- the reason you designed it
- the child/children who will be participating
- the input there will be from parents/caregivers and other relevant staff
- the child's views on the activity
- how you will be recording the activity (observation, samples of the children's work, taking photographs or video, etc.)
- how the activity links with Aistear and other literature
- when the activity will happen
- where the activity will happen
- what resources you will need
- safety considerations
- what secondary activity a child can do if they choose not to take part in the planned activity.

Before the activity

Remember that even the simplest of activities will require some setting-up time.

> **QUESTIONS FOR REFLECTION**
> - Have you informed any co-workers in the room that you are beginning the activity and you may not want to be disturbed?
> - Do you have a pen and notepad/paper or other recording device ready to complete observations?
> - If your activity is outside, are children and adults wearing suitable protective clothing (rain jackets, hats, scarves, etc.)? Has sun cream been applied if it is a sunny day?
> - Has everybody used the toilet, had their nappy changed, etc.?

Depending on your activity it can take a short time to set up or a longer time to prepare. If the children in your group are of suitable age and stage of development they may be able to assist or take the lead in setting up activities. By encouraging the child to help prepare and tidy up you are enabling them to feel a sense of ownership over the task while offering opportunities to develop a sense of independence. Allocating these 'jobs' in fun ways, such as pulling names out of a hat, will make setting up activities extra exciting!

During the activity

Now you are ready to call the child/children over to the activity. Introduce the activity by telling the child/children about the activity and any simple rules that are involved. Check whether they want to take part. If any child is reluctant, allow them to leave the activity and let them know that they are welcome to return at any point. Remember Brown's (2003) three Fs – Fun, Freedom and Flexibility. You have planned this activity for the child/children; let them make it their own and enjoy it! During the activity you get a great opportunity to play with the child/children, talk and reflect with them about the process, getting a sense of, among other things, the children's likes, dislikes and abilities. Take observations, photographs and video recordings (where appropriate). Keep samples of work for your Síolta evidence folder and to share with the children and families.

Tidy-up

Now for the dreaded tidy-up time! This chore can be transformed into an exciting game by giving the children their own tasks to complete. Using a method such as a 'job wheel', you can make the tidy-up experience fun and enriching, as well as saving time. If the child/group of children choose not to tidy up, their choice should be respected. In a well-organised environment tidy-up time becomes 'child's play' when the children – through picture labelling, etc. – have a clear understanding of where materials and equipment belong.

PLANNING, IMPLEMENTING AND ASSESSING ACTIVITIES

> **OVER TO YOU**
>
> Have a look at how a High/Scope early years environment uses labelling for equipment to make tidy-up time more efficient. Make some labels yourself and think about how this 'labelled' approach can aid a young child's learning.

Step 3: Reviewing the activity – a time to think

The review is an aspect of planning and completing activities with young children that is often overlooked. The review is important for future planning and to check whether you are content with how you are organising learning opportunities. In the review stage you need to give yourself time and space to reflect and think.

Giving yourself this space to reflect develops your professional practice and gives you a greater understanding of not only the children in your care but also how you as the practitioner work with them. Reviews also offer space not just to look at what may have gone 'wrong' in an activity but to praise ourselves for the good work we have done in planning and completing an activity. Allowing the time to reflect and record the outcomes of activities works with the Síolta Standard of Organisation. In addition to this the Síolta Standard of Professional Practice (Components 11.3 and 11.4) notes the importance of reviewing activities. The Síolta guidelines give some fantastic signposts for review in their manuals (www.siolta.ie/access_manuals.php) and these can be a great starting point when reflecting on your creative arts programme.

Aistear highlights five different types of assessment we can consider to gain a detailed perspective on the child's learning:

1. **Self-assessment:** This involves children thinking about their own learning and development and looking at what they have done and achieved. Ask the child about the activity and continue the conversation using open-ended questions. Remember to note the child's response; you will gain an invaluable insight into the child's development.
2. **Conversations:** Conversations are a fantastic way to support the assessment process. Invite the child into conversations by using questions or by thinking aloud. Open conversations with statements such as 'I'm wondering what would happen if …', or 'That looks exciting.' When engaging in conversation, give the child time to think about what you have said or asked and then respond; and respond to what the child is saying. You may even choose to use props such as pictures, books or pieces of work to encourage conversation.

3   **Observations:** Observation involves watching and listening to the children and recording what we see and hear. Observations should take place on an ongoing basis and are recorded in a child's individual file in line with the service's policies. Best practice would insist on observations being conducted in partnership with the child's parents/caregivers. By completing and keeping records of observations in line with the service's policy on observations you are also working in line with the Síolta Standard Parents and Families (Components 3.3, 3.4) as well as the Child Care (Pre-School Services) (No. 2) Regulations (DoHC 2006a).

4   **Setting tasks:** This may involve setting a task or activity specifically to assess an aspect of a child's learning or development, for example in the home corner asking a child to pick out the yellow fruit from the press to assess if they are aware of the colour yellow, or setting up an obstacle course to get an understanding of a child's gait.

5   **Testing:** This type of assessment uses a set of tasks and/or questions to collect information about a child's learning and development. These tests are usually standardised tests based on developmental age-range norms (milestones).

When assessing any planned activity it is good practice to look at the assessment in two overlapping parts: the adult's role; and the benefits for the child.

The adult's role in the activity

The relationships between the child and adult in the early childhood setting are central to the assessment of early learning and development (NCCA 2009). Assessment is interactive. This means it can only happen if the practitioner is interacting, playing and engaging with the child/group of children in their care.

> **QUESTIONS FOR REFLECTION**
> - During the activity, did you get involved?
> - What was your role in the play? Leader? Partner? Follower?
> - Did you carefully watch and observe?
> - Did you listen to and talk with the child/group of children?
> - If your activity occurred at meal time, for example, did you sit with the children, partaking in the social activity of eating and talking together?
> - Did you get the opportunity to discuss this activity with other people in the child's life, such as other practitioners, their friends and parents/caregivers?

By reflecting on your role in the learning process you can see the child/group of children in context, with their environment giving a deeper perspective on the play event.

It is important to ensure that assessments occur naturally and authentically, that they are informal and ongoing, carried out over a period of time, and in the context of the child's interactions with real-life situations. Look at Gibbs' reflective cycle and think about how this framework could aid adult reflections.

Assessing progress with an individual child

During your planning stage you drew up an aim for the activity and a list of objectives to meet this aim. When reviewing the activity, one danger is that we can sometimes focus so strongly on what we want to see that we inadvertently ignore some fantastic learning that may have happened. For example, if you planned an activity to develop a child's physical wellbeing, specifically their gross motor movement, when assessing you might be so focused on the child's physical movements that you missed the new communication skills they used with their peers. In its 2004 document *Towards a Framework of Early Learning*, the National Council for Curriculum and Assessment (NCCA) outlined that assessments are holistic in nature (NCCA 2004). This means that learning does not happen in isolation. If a child's wellbeing is the aim of the activity, it is the adult's role to assess what additional learning was also identified in areas such as communication, exploring and thinking, and identity and belonging. The Aistear framework recommends that a child-centred assessment focuses on the strengths the child has shown during the activity as well as identifying aspects of learning that need further development (NCCA 2009).

Planning for future learning: extending activities

> Good plans are flexible, allowing children's changing interests and responses to learning to be incorporated over time. This type of planning takes time and comes from knowing children well – their interests, needs, cultures, backgrounds and abilities. Assessment information is, therefore, at the heart of planning. (NCCA 2009)

Now that you have successfully planned, done and reviewed the activity, you can complete this learning cycle by using the assessment to develop future activities for the child/group of children.

Day-to-day activity planning involves short-term plans. This type of planning looks at what activities the child has previously engaged in and gives us an opportunity to plan the next step in the child's learning process. For example, if you are working with Chloe, who is three years and four months, and she has completed all the five-piece jigsaws, your future plans for Chloe could include encouraging her to move on to a six-piece jigsaw. In documenting this ongoing daily plan in Chloe's files you would be compiling what Aistear (NCCA 2009) would call a 'Personal Learning Plan' (PLP). Collecting this type of information in an ongoing and consistent manner, and ensuring that it is stored safely, links with the Síolta Standard of Communication (Component 12.1).

Chapter summary

This chapter looked at how to devise a play activity for a young child, a pair of children or a group of children. Here's a brief review.

Step 1: The plan
- What are the child's interests?
- What is the aim?
- What are the objectives?
- What resources do I need?
- Safety considerations.
- Finance.
- Time.

Step 2: 'Doing' the activity

- Setting up.
- Doing the activity.
- Tidying up.

Step 3: Reviewing the activity

- Give yourself time.
- Give yourself space.
- Decide what to reflect on. (What questions about the activity do you want to answer?)
- Decide how you want to reflect. (What type of assessment method will you be using?)
- Decide who you will reflect with (children, staff and families).
- Plan for future learning opportunities.

OVER TO YOU

Now it's your turn!

Plan, implement and review an activity for a child you know using the framework outlined above. Take into consideration the child's interests and abilities, their likes and dislikes and what they will find fun. Remember to consult with the child and other people in the child's life, such as early years practitioners and parents/caregivers.

In your assessment use the information in this chapter as well looking specifically at the learning goals outlined in the Aistear framework (NCCA 2009).

Evaluate the strengths and weaknesses of your planning and make detailed suggestions for improvement. (Chapter 10 gives examples of questions to use when evaluating implemented activities.)

4 Creative Play and Developmental Stages

This chapter explores aspects of the following Learning Outcomes:

- LO 1: Examine a variety of creative media opportunities with young children.
- LO 2: Summarise the benefits of exploration and participation in creative arts for the child.
- LO 3: Explore the role of the adult in creating an environment in which children feel secure and confident enough to take risks and explore new situations.
- LO 4: Plan opportunities for consultation with children to plan and engage in creative arts experiences.
- LO 5: Test open-ended materials and natural items for creative arts, in both the indoor and outdoor environments, appropriate to different stages of children's development.
- LO 7: Employ developmentally appropriate creative arts activities which promote the holistic development of the child.

In this chapter we look at how to plan for play in the creative arts curriculum, taking into consideration children's different ages, stages and play behaviours from birth to six years. We look at the creative arts curriculum through dramatic arts, movement and dance, visual arts and musical arts.

This chapter is designed to spark the reader's imagination; as you are reading, note in your reflective journal some of your own ideas for activities. This chapter also looks at the adults' roles when working with and supporting young children. As well as planning, implementing and assessing activities, the adult takes on an important role as advocate and supporter of the child's progress. This advocacy role aids in developing the child's confidence and nurtures the creativity that lies within each child.

Aistear's principles, themes and guidelines

Before we begin looking at developmental stages with young children, let us reflect on the Aistear principles, themes and best practice guidelines which underpin Irish practice when working with young children (NCCA 2009).

Principles

1. Equality and diversity
2. Relationships
3. Parents, family and community
4. The adult's role
5. The child's uniqueness
6. Children as citizens
7. Play and hands-on experiences
8. The learning environment
9. Communication and language
10. Holistic learning and development
11. Relevant and meaningful experiences
12. Active learning

Themes

1. Wellbeing
2. Identity and Belonging
3. Communicating
4. Exploring and Thinking

Guidelines for good practice

1. Building partnerships between parents and practitioners.
2. Learning and developing through interactions.
3. Learning and developing through play.
4. Supporting learning and development through assessment.

A practitioner using the Aistear framework in combination with Síolta and the Child

Care (Pre-School Services) (No. 2) Regulations (2006) is guided towards high-quality personal learning plans for young children.

> **OVER TO YOU**
>
> Research *Aistear: The Early Childhood Curriculum Framework* (NCCA 2009) and *Síolta: The National Quality Framework for Early Childhood Education* (CECDE 2006) and note their similarities and differences. Reflect on how knowledge of these two documents could influence how you play and interact with young children.

The following sections of this chapter reflect on age groups between birth and six years and focus on how the practitioner can work with children in a developmentally appropriate manner.

Birth to 12 months

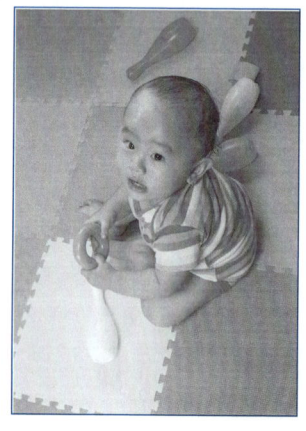

Vygotsky put forward the view that during play a child's thinking becomes more sophisticated than at any other time. Play allows the child the freedom to explore and experiment without fear or embarrassment. In play the child is 'a head taller than himself' (Vygotsky 1978:103). We have referred to the term 'active learning' previously; it is important to note that active learning and play are intertwined experiences. French and Murphy (2005) describe a child's play as the intrinsic motivation to explore and engage with their environment, an inherent ability to seek and gain knowledge, the 'highest form of learning in early childhood' (NCCA 2004:44). Play is how children acquire skills and abilities. They learn best through exploring, investigating, discovering, experimenting and practising. High-quality play should promote the healthy development of physical, social, emotional, cognitive and language skills.

In babies aged 0–12 months we can see that their play is mainly 'sensorial' – that they are exploring the sights, smells, tastes, touch and sounds in their world. In this first year a baby moves through an amazing growth spurt in which they learn to support their own head, sit, crawl, stand and sometimes even walk. In addition, the baby is learning about communication and emotion as well as recognising who they want to be close to. The baby's brain develops rapidly in the first year and this is encouraged through high-quality human attachment with a person or people the baby trusts and loves. Hugs, kisses and smiles are so important for babies' development. As an early years professional, displaying genuine affection should become part of your disposition; without this the quality of attachments between child and adult will be greatly affected.

Stage of development and play behaviour

From birth until approximately three months of age, play with objects is minimal as the majority of learning occurs when babies are exploring their reflexive actions – kicking, grasping, sucking, etc. Infants will use their sight and auditory senses when beginning to explore. Research has found that newborn babies focus best approximately eight inches from their face. This sight range increases over time and by three months of age they may even be able to see as far as a few feet away. This knowledge can guide the adults in a young baby's life in how best to place objects within visual fields. It has been observed that small babies respond best to bright colours, such as reds and yellows, and objects with a high pattern contrast, such as black and white stripes. Above all, young babies respond most to the human face and will prefer to watch faces over objects and toys. In addition to this you may notice that small babies begin to turn their heads in the direction of sounds they can hear. Small babies generally prefer sounds that are 'low impact' and gentle on their auditory senses. In these early months babies' play will mainly consist of exploring their bodies. As young babies have a limited ability to grasp objects for any length of time, it is best practice to introduce materials that are soft, lightweight and safe for the baby to hold. At three months you may notice the baby beginning to reach for objects that are slightly out of their grasp, such as on a mobile or 'baby gym'. Child safety mirrors are a great addition to the child's play environment at this stage.

By approximately four months of age the baby is beginning to actively engage with their environment in a myriad of ways. As their vision is now enhanced you will notice that the baby can observe objects moving with efficient and fluid eye movements.

Hughes (2010) describes how young children aged from five to 10 months first want to make sense of objects in their world by mouthing them. This mouthing action allows the child to discern the characteristics of objects. Also at this stage babies are beginning to roll onto their back and may even start to push up onto their hands and knees. These abilities, as well as the mastery of grasp, allow the child to engage in more active forms of exploratory play such as reaching, grasping, pulling, pushing, slapping, shaking and squeezing. As the child's abilities progress you may observe them beginning to sit by themselves at approximately six to seven months of age. This new-found independence increases possibilities for play as the baby can now easily manipulate objects within a reachable area. You will notice that in addition to mouthing objects the baby will explore them by passing them between their hands in a repetitive fashion. Moving closer to eight months of age the baby is gaining an ability to recognise words that are repeated often in their presence. You may notice that at eight months a baby may have begun to crawl and will try to stand up with support. It is also at this stage that the baby starts to understand the concept of 'object permanence'. This means that they are now able to recognise that when an object or person is out of sight they have not disappeared; they will in fact return. At this age baby may begin to show an interest in brightly coloured books with vivid illustrations.

As the baby becomes that bit older, 10–20 months, they begin to engage in functional play. At this point they are figuring out what an object can do; their mouthing and exploring actions can be called heuristic play. This is a time of exciting possibilities for creativity. The young child's physical abilities are becoming more advanced and they will use objects to see how their bodies can adapt to them. The pincer grip will begin to develop rapidly as the child reaches their first year milestone, and you will notice their interest growing in small objects that they can pick up between their thumb and fingers. Around this stage, it is useful to introduce an abundance of sensorial activities that aid an understanding of the concept of cause and effect. As children move though this stage they will also begin to imitate words, intonations and gestures they hear often.

Goals for the creative arts curriculum

At approximately five to six months, when a child can sit by themselves, we can introduce a treasure basket to promote heuristic play. A treasure basket can be made using a range of natural materials and household objects, for example:

- paper/cardboard objects – notebooks, sturdy cardboard tubes, greaseproof paper
- wooden objects – small bowl, egg cup, curtain rings, coaster
- various textiles – small knitted toys, bean bags, a piece of flannel, bags of herbs, a bag of lavender, coloured ribbons
- rubber objects – a ball, a bath plug with securely attached chain, a soap holder
- metal objects – egg cup, measuring spoons, tea strainer, whisk, bells
- natural objects – a lemon, orange, other fruits and vegetables, pumice stone, loofah, shells, pine/fir cones
- brushes – a small scrubbing brush, pastry brush, baby's hair brush, nail brush (unused), make-up brush, paint brush
- other objects such as hair rollers, small mirror, scent bags, ceramic bowl.

Treasure baskets provide wonderful opportunities for babies and young children to use their senses to discover, explore, investigate and examine new materials, shapes, colours, tastes, textures, sounds, weights and quantities. They can also help develop

cognitive skills, while promoting open-ended play. It is important to note that safety must be a priority:
- Babies should be supervised when engaging with the treasure basket.
- All items in the basket should be non-toxic and cleaned between each baby's use.
- Check for any allergies before placing any potentially harmful items in the basket.

Be mindful that the essence of play is risk taking as the young child explores their limitations in the world around them. Your role is to intervene if this risk taking turns into a potential hazard.

> **OVER TO YOU**
>
> Develop a treasure basket and assess its learning potential using the Aistear Themes of Identity and Belonging, Communication, Wellbeing, and Exploring and Thinking. Research Goldschmied and Jackson (2004) as part of your development.

Exploration and participation in creative arts

Dramatic arts

As we have seen, up to 12 months of age, children engage mainly in sensorial play and functional play. At this stage of development young children are not able to communicate through play what they are imagining. One way of aiding a baby's dramatic play abilities is with books. Looking at books together is a great way of having some enjoyable cuddle time with the young child. Books offer a great opportunity for learning new language skills and knowledge and also help develop the special relationship between the child and the caregiver. Choose a book that has bright, colourful illustrations and very few words. Go through the pages slowly and follow the child's pace. If the child wants to linger on a picture after you have finished reading the words on the page, look at the picture with the child. If they want to turn the pages, allow then to do so. Story time should be an enjoyable and relaxing time for you and baby.

Movement and dance

Did you know that the movement babies feel when in the arms of an adult becomes the basis for when they will later walk, run, jump and skip? Put some music on, hold the baby firmly in your arms – and dance! Waltz, jive, salsa, rumba or a general freestyle around the floor – just go for it. This type of spontaneous fun is what creativity is all about. Encourage baby to move to the beat by dancing with them, clapping along to music and playing music with a variety of different tempos in the baby's environment.

Remember, babies' hearing can be very sensitive, so keep the volume of the music at an appropriate level.

Visual arts

It is important to introduce colour to the young child. Babies can see colour from birth, but colour is fuzzy until approximately two to three months. At this age babies will generally show a preference for primary colours – red, yellow and blue. Colours can be introduced through illustrated picture books such as *Colour Me Happy!* by Shen Roddie and Ben Cort, as well as through flash cards and paintings. It is not advisable to introduce paints, crayons or colouring pencils with babies as the young child is still at the 'mouthing stage' and will want to investigate these new items by putting them in their mouth.

Musical arts

Percussion instruments are a great learning tool for babies. Did you know that a rattle is a musical instrument? Observing with baby the different sounds instruments make, from loud to soft and everything in between, is a fantastic beginning to an individual's musical development. Sing with baby and play a variety of music. Motivate them to respond by clapping or tapping your hands. Baby may even wave their own hands, clap, screech and move with the music. Encourage this through positive tones in your voice, smiling and cheering baby on!

Role of the adult

Babies' play is described as solitary. This means that during play they can be totally engrossed in the activity and may not notice other individuals. The adult's role is to sit close to the baby while they are engrossed in play. By sitting close to the baby one is offering emotional support and security through reassuring messages such as smiles, gestures and sounds that remind the baby that their caregiver is close by as they explore new objects and possibilities.

The adult has an important role in providing new and safe challenges for baby in a fun and secure way. Babies love exploring their world; they are curious to find out how things work and what they are for. Your role is to facilitate them in this exploration.

The adult provides a role model for the baby and their growing mind. If you want baby to dance and sing, you will need to dance and sing. If you want baby to explore the treasure basket, you sit on the floor with them and explore the treasure basket. More fun equals more learning!

One major role of an early years practitioner working with babies is to love them. The love you show will support the attachment between baby and you and when baby feels a secure attachment they will feel happy in their play and creative exploration. Remember, smiles, hugs and kisses are all part of a baby's day!

> **OVER TO YOU**
>
> A major theory in the field of child development is 'attachment theory'. Research this concept in relation to learning and think about how you can ensure that a young child feels attached to you when you work closely with them.

One to two years

At one to two years of age a child will generally begin to speak some words and become mobile; and their play will now reflect this new-found freedom and independence. You will see that their gross and fine motor skills are developing at a rapid rate, so they need plenty of opportunities to strengthen their muscles in fun, challenging and stimulating ways. Having a lot of space to move around – both inside and outside – is important at this age as the toddler loves to run and jump, climb and tumble. Create a safe space where this type of rough and tumble play is encouraged rather than halted.

The young child at this point of their development can be described as being in a 'solitary play stage'. You will observe this as the child plays alone, usually unaware that others are playing around them. This 'solitary play' stage is important for a child's development as it allows the young child the freedom to explore their own capabilities without interference or interruption from other children's play. As the toddler moves closer to two years of age they will be progressing into a 'parallel stage of play'. You will notice this happen when they begin to take a keen interest in what other children are playing with, they will position themselves to play alongside other children and sometimes you may even notice the toddler copying the other person's actions.

> **OVER TO YOU**
>
> Think about a child you know who is around this age (one–two years). What types of activity do they love doing? If you could plan any activity for this toddler, what would you plan?

As the young child becomes more confident in walking, you will notice that they will begin to explore their physicality by, for example, running, jumping and balancing. They will start to pull toys behind them and investigate how to get on and off furniture, up and down stairs. Some children may at this age begin to become interested in kicking footballs, etc. The young child at this stage of development becomes quite concerned with order and grouping and may enjoy sorting objects into categories. You will notice language emerging in the form of simple phrases and active words such as 'up', 'down', etc.

Stage of development and play behaviour

The child at this age will actively explore their environment, figuring out what things do, what fits where and how things work. This can be referred to as 'functional' play or 'epistemic' play (Hutt 1979). You will notice this stage easily as the toddler is busy and productive. They are becoming concerned with problem solving and discovering the world around them. It is an exciting and fun time, not only for the child but also for you, the adult who is aiding in the child's fast-paced play.

The young child is watching the adults and other children in their life very closely. They learn from what they see, and copy simple actions. Social learning theory comes into play here. This theory shows us that children learn what they see.

> **OVER TO YOU**
>
> Go to YouTube, search for the Albert Bandura's 'Bobo doll experiment' and think about how social learning theory might impact on your practice with young children.

At this stage of development the young child has learned through conditioning that certain actions will result in attention from adults. They will repeat any actions that gain attention; and these actions can be either positive or negative! How are you reacting to the child when they are doing something well? Are you praising them and rewarding them with your time? How are you reacting if a child does something that may be seen as negative, such as throwing a tantrum? Remember, try to ignore any negative behaviours, unless they are hurting either the child themselves or somebody else.

At this stage the child's behaviour will veer between being 'clingy' and wanting their independence. They still need loads of love and cuddles, especially at times when they might be feeling a bit emotional, such as when they are hungry, tired or feeling a bit ill. Be available for love and hugs – they are just as important as any other activity in the day.

At this point you will notice that the young child will have no concept of sharing or ownership, so have enough toys, materials and equipment to go round!

Goals for the creative arts curriculum

At this stage of development the child may be moving towards being able to play alongside other children (parallel play) and begin to carry out simple one-sentence instructions, e.g. can you find your bag? Can you get the dolly? The toddler may be able to carry out simple instructions but they may choose not to! This is fine; remember, your job is to motivate in a positive way and if you model the behaviour you want the child to do they will, eventually, do it too!

Exploration and participation in creative arts

Dramatic arts

At this age the young child is beginning to model the behaviours of the people they see and love most in their world. If they see their mum on the phone, they will want to talk on a phone. If they see dad pushing a buggy, they too will want a buggy to push. Link closely with the young child's parents/carers and find out who the child likes to pretend to be at home. It is important to supply props to support this pretend play. Having pictures of each child's family posted in the home corner will encourage children to re-enact family memories while they are in your care. Remember that pets are part of the family too and it is important that children's dogs, cats, goldfish, etc. are also represented in family photos. You may even notice the young toddler pretending to act like the family pet! The adult can aid in the child's dramatic representations through playing with the child. Simple games like pretending to feed the dolly or pretending to fall asleep help develop the young child's imagination.

Movement and dance

As we mentioned above, toddlers need a lot of space in which to move about. One way to encourage this in the early education environment is through movement and dance activities. Dance is a fantastic way of communicating with children who are not yet verbal. This full body movement expresses vital messages such as emotion and is also a great learning tool. Think of the choreographed song, 'Head, Fingers, Knees and Toes'. How can you make this simple tune into a great movement and dance activity for the young child? Consider the points we addressed in Chapter 3 regarding planning, implementing and reviewing an activity. What other simple movement songs are available for one- to two-year-old children? You could even make up a new one yourself!

Visual arts

At this age the young child will be interested in mark making for the 'cause and effect' action. It is at this age that you can introduce painting in a relaxed and process-based manner. The young child will generally not be concerned about what the painting will look like at the end: they are more interested in the colours, the feeling of the paint on their hands and the effect of putting it on paper or canvas. It is important that you explore the process of painting with the child – 'What does the paint feel like?', 'Oh, you chose the colour red', 'You mixed red and yellow – well done' – rather than focusing on the finished product. It might be an interesting activity for you to do some finger painting for the experience of choosing the colours, placing them on the page and mixing them without the pressure of 'making something'. Try it with your colleagues and reflect what it is like to paint without having to produce 'a painting'.

At this stage of artistic development the child's painting may not be representational, but that does not mean that the child is not expressing themselves through their visual art work. Take the following case study as an example.

CASE STUDY

Maurice, aged 23 months, is sitting with his key worker Áine. Maurice has been playing with the service's pet rabbit, Thumper, and is now using paint on paper. Áine says to Maurice, 'I see you're making dots on the page; your hand is making dots.' Maurice runs to the window, points with the paint brush to the rabbit hutch, then jumps back to the painting. Áine looks at Maurice and at the painting and says, 'It looks like Thumper is jumping on your page.' Maurice smiles and nods.

In this study we can see that although Maurice is not at the stage of visually representing Thumper he has communicated his interest in Thumper's movements through visual art work. Áine was able to recognise this form of communication through talking with, closely observing and checking with Maurice.

Musical arts

It is a good idea for toddlers to be exposed to music at different times of the day. Music can accompany parts of a daily routine and can provide comfort through repetition. For example, a piece of music can be used to signify a transition time such as tidy-up time. Think about the following times of the day and choose a type of music that could be used:

- snack time
- rest/sleep time
- tidy-up time.

In addition to music being part of the daily routine, toddlers can take ownership of music by creating their own. Having musical instruments available, at the child's level, and modelling how to play them will give the child the opportunity to create new sounds and express themselves in a new way. Provide instruments such as bells, castanets, xylophones and maracas so that the child can play freely and spontaneously with them. These instruments could be home-made or 'real'. Encourage the child to use them through modelling, praising the young child when they use them and dancing along with the music they create. If you get the opportunity, record a piece of the child's music, using audio or video (in line with your facility's policy on observations) and keep this with the child's personal learning plan.

Role of the adult

At this exploration stage the child will need a lot of high-quality supervision as they are testing out their world and do not understand the dangers around them. The best way to do this is to be down at the child's level playing with them.

The adult should provide different play activities that encourage active learning as the child will lose concentration easily. Distraction will help here to stop any unwanted behaviour.

OVER TO YOU

Think about distraction. How can it help with a possibly conflictual situation such as a disagreement over sharing a toy such as a set of maracas?

Awarding regular praise displays to children how to get attention through positive means. An example of this positive reinforcement would be 'I am very proud you shared the paint brush with me.' Remember, when praising children, be specific and praise the behaviours rather than saying a general 'Good girl' or 'Good boy'.

OVER TO YOU

Think about the difference between being specific about praising behaviour – 'I can see you put a lot of work into your painting; well done. The colours you chose are beautiful' – and a general praise statement such as 'Good girl'.

We used the term 'social learning theory' earlier. Children learn what they see, and one of the most important jobs of the adult is to be a positive role model. If you want a child to share, show them how to share. If you want a child to engage with the creative arts, you must also engage with the creative arts. You are responsible for showing children how to be during play.

> **OVER TO YOU**
>
> Think of a child or a small group of children aged one to two years of age and plan the following activities, taking into consideration the framework in Chapter 3:
> 1. dramatic play activity
> 2. movement and dance activity
> 3. visual arts activity
> 4. music activity.

Two to three years

At between two and three years of age the young child is noticing other children at play and beginning to play alongside others as they concretely move into the 'parallel' stage of play. You will notice that the child's language is expanding and their play begins to change from functional/epistemic play into ludic/pretend play. In ludic/pretend play the young child begins to use their imagination, engaging in role play activities, for example enacting simple functions such as being asleep or feeding a doll. You will also notice that at this stage of development the child's play is defined by repetition and exaggeration. When they are pretending to be mammy or daddy they will be very dramatic in their re-enactment of that person, often amplifying actions that they may have seen. Can you remember when a toddler you know engaged in dramatic play, for example pushing a buggy with a baby, or talking on the phone? Reflect on this and think about what type of actions the child had to perform to recreate this scene. Did they use their brain to remember? Did they use their gross motor or fine motor skills to carry it out? Did they use any language skills? It is amazing how far a child's development has come in such a short amount of time.

CREATIVE PLAY AND DEVELOPMENTAL STAGES

OVER TO YOU

Note down the developmental differences between a 12-month-old putting a phone to their ear in dramatic play fashion and a two-year-old carrying out the same action.

At this age the child is beginning to gain confidence in their physical abilities and they love playing outside. Remember, the child can easily get frustrated and their concentration span is usually less than 10 minutes per activity. It is so important to offer active opportunities for the toddler to be independent. Provide plenty of toys, materials and equipment at the child's level, as sharing is difficult.

As the child progresses to the age of three years you may begin to notice that they have started to move towards the 'co-operative' play stage. In co-operative play the child will join with another child or a group of children and share their play through communication and negotiation, for example 'You be mammy and I'll be daddy and we'll push the baby.'

Stage of development and play behaviour

You may notice that the young child can become easily frustrated and may have tantrums. This can be due to the frustration of wanting to communicate but just not having the words to do so. Imagine if you were in a country where they speak a different language from yours. How would you feel if you were thirsty and wanted to order a glass of water but nobody could understand you? How would this inability to communicate make you feel? Another way to role play feelings of frustration is through a game of charades with your colleagues. Feel what it is like to try to communicate through actions alone. How long does it take before you begin to feel impatient or frustrated? Be patient with the toddler in play as they may be trying to communicate.

At this age the toddler is becoming less easily distracted. This means that they can focus on activities for a little longer than before. Encourage this through motivation and praise when you notice that they have remained in a play frame for a period of time.

You will notice that the young child will be watching and mirroring the actions of others. This could be the actions of their family, the actions of their friends or the actions of you, the early years educator.

The child can also get quite possessive of people they love. They may dislike other children receiving your attention. Remember to share your love, hugs and attention equally. The young child does not yet understand the reason they have to wait and frustration may happen if there is a delay. Remember here that the best way to prevent this impatience is prevention. Planning activities in advance and following a well-designed and child-centred daily routine will help prevent unnecessary delays. Toddlers can find sharing difficult. As we have seen, they do not like delays and compromise is too much for a child at this egocentric stage of development. Imagine that you are really hungry and you have just been handed an individual portion of your favourite food and you are then expected to turn to the person next to you and give them half. Your initial reaction might be 'No'. The toddler at this stage says 'No' to sharing, and we should respect this choice as much as possible.

You will notice that toddlers are active and become restless if they get bored. Plan a lot of energetic activities, both indoors and outdoors, make sure the child has water to keep them hydrated and plan regular intervals to serve healthy food to keep them energised and growing.

Goals for the creative arts curriculum

When we hear the word 'toddler' the image of the 'terrible twos' often comes to mind. This idea of the young child as 'terrible' is a misrepresentation of their inquisitive nature. Think of any challenging behaviour the young child might be displaying as a learning opportunity yet to be explored. The creative arts curriculum is a fantastic medium for facilitating these new learning opportunities. If the young child is having difficulty waiting for their needs to be met, plan fun play activities around waiting. For example, consider the song 'Row, Row, Row Your Boat':

Row, row, row your boat
Gently down the stream,
Merrily, merrily, merrily, merrily
Life is but a dream.

Row, row, row, your boat
Gently down the stream,
If you see a crocodile
Don't forget to ... Scream!

Using the pause in the last line of the song to demonstrate what it is like to wait is a safe and fun way to demonstrate patience with young children!

Sharing is another learning opportunity that can be supported. Think about what types of fun activities can model sharing. It is important at this point to motivate young children to say 'please' and 'thank you' and to begin introducing basic manners into their vocabulary.

CREATIVE PLAY AND DEVELOPMENTAL STAGES

OVER TO YOU

Look at the following 'challenging behaviours' that young children sometimes demonstrate. Think about how you can make these into learning opportunities using the creative arts curriculum:

- refusing to eat a snack
- grabbing toys from other children
- hitting others
- shouting at inappropriate moments
- throwing equipment

Have you observed any behaviour by young children that could be used as a learning opportunity?

Exploration and participation in creative arts

Dramatic arts

At this age the young child is using their imagination more and more in their dramatic play. Their play has moved from remembering to creating. To encourage this creativity, provide props such as dress-up clothes, real-life home objects and books which have simple stories and high-quality illustrations. The child's environment should reflect the move from functional play to imaginative play, with designated areas that provide a variety of opportunities for the child to re-enact the world around them. Think about what questions one should ask of a child's family when trying to figure out what props would be needed to support their play.

At this age the young child is now able to begin construction play, building simple walls and towers. Promote this development through providing a space for construction to happen, include construction-based equipment and materials and above all else make your support and encouragement readily available.

Movement and dance

The toddler's physical abilities have developed rapidly in a short time. They now have fantastic gross and fine motor movements, allowing them to challenge themselves in energetic and complicated ways. They can balance, jump, hop; even simple tumbles and somersaults are attempted. You may notice an increased interest in equipment like ride-on cars and tricycles. In addition to this the young child's vocabulary has increased and so too has their ability to repeat simple songs and actions. Encourage this by displaying pictures of songs you repeat often and get children to choose which tunes they want to sing and dance to. You can extend this by providing families with a recording of the songs and a copy of the words and actions that can be used at home.

> **OVER TO YOU**
>
> Think of a simple song that a two- or three-year-old you know enjoys. Design an image for it, record the song and write out the words and actions for it as a template for a 'family song pack'. Remember, the movement and dance moves are just as important as the song!

Visual arts

Children at the age of two to three years enjoy the process involved with visual arts activities. They are focused on the sensation of their arm movement and the feeling of the brush and paint/colouring pencil/crayon on paper. Only later do they discover that through this activity the paint can make marks, colours can be mixed and shapes can be created. As hand–eye co-ordination improves, children intentionally create lines and shapes that were earlier produced unintentionally.

As the toddler begins to understand that pictures in books represent objects in the real world they use this knowledge when scribbling. As the child moves closer to three years of age the pictures become more representational. As visual art is still process-based at this age, the young child is focused on the colours and materials used during the task. Two-year-old children are described as being at the 'scribble' stage of artistic development. You will find that initially their markings will be 'disordered': they are uncontrolled; they are either dark or light depending on the context of the child when they are drawing them. As the child gains more control over their hand and arm movements you will notice that their scribbling becomes 'longitudinal'; it contains patterns indicating controlled repetition of motions. You will observe the child becoming visually aware of what they are drawing, but above all they enjoy the process – the kinaesthetic movements. A circle might be the first shape to be made and this usually occurs as the child reaches their third year.

Musical arts

Using music as a comfort tool is as important for the two–three-year-old as it is for the younger child; continue to use it in your daily routine. A music area can be designed in the layout of the room. Having a child-sized shelf with home-made as well as 'real' instruments is important, allowing children access to music throughout the day. Children of this age should also be encouraged to sing using a wide range of tones and pitches! We often hear adults say, 'I can't sing', but we want to encourage children to sing as much as they want without the critical word 'can't' ringing in their ears! Singing and music gives children a fantastic insight into language through repetition, beat and rhythm. The adult has the opportunity to introduce concepts such as high, low, fast, slow, loud and soft through singing with the child. Gently tapping out the rhythm of songs on the child's back or hand as they sit on your knee while singing adds an extra dimension to the music activity. It is important to note that although CDs and recordings are a great resource in a music corner, nothing can rival a real-life performance from an adult, so don't be shy and remove the words 'I can't sing' from your vocabulary!

Role of the adult

It is important to maintain high-quality supervision at this age as the young child does not yet understand what is safe and what is dangerous. Try to anticipate any possible frustrations. While young children are trying to be independent, they also lack some of the physical and cognitive skills necessary to complete tasks. Play close by them; observe how challenging an activity might be for them. Intervene, support and help where necessary.

The importance of praise cannot be over-emphasised. Just as with one- to two-year-old children, it is important to continue to praise positive behaviour and ignore any challenging behaviours where possible. Try a rule of 1:2; for every comment you made about challenging behaviour, follow it up with a minimum of two positive comments about a child's actions. Role-play this with your colleagues: in pairs, spend one hour observing and commenting on each other's positive behaviours. Notice how many simple actions would have been overlooked if you had not been watching out for them!

The adult has a really important job in being a consistent enforcer of boundaries for children of this age. Children aged two–three years are beginning to test boundaries and see what they are and are not allowed to do. Remember that this testing is a natural part of life and rules should be enforced in a positive manner. Think back to Chapter 2, where we discussed the ideas around nurturing creativity in the early years environment. Rules and boundaries will encourage creativity if enforced in an encouraging and nurturing way. I want you now to reflect on a time when you tested the boundaries/broke the rules: was the situation dealt with in a constructive way in which you felt supported or in a way that made you feel silenced and shamed?

OVER TO YOU

Think of a child or a small group of children aged two–three years of age and plan the following activities, taking into consideration the framework in Chapter 3.
1. **dramatic play activity**
2. **movement and dance activity**
3. **visual arts activity**
4. **music activity.**

Three to four years

As the young child reaches the age of three to four years, they begin to co-operate and enjoy playing together in pairs and small groups. A majority of the play can be classed as 'pretend' at this stage. You will begin to notice that the three- to four-year-old demonstrates symbolic behaviour, enjoys physical activities, is developing fine motor skills and begins to reflect on their world in picture form.

OVER TO YOU

Research and discuss in a small group how you would observe 'symbolic behaviour' and how this knowledge might impact on your professional practice.

You will notice that at this age the child has become interested in creating concrete items which have a finishing point, such as making a cake, planting a seed and watching it grow into a plant, etc. The child is also beginning to express themselves through painting and drawing. You will also observe how competent they have become in their physical abilities, that they like to use these skills in play and are confident when running and climbing.

Stage of development and play behaviour

At this age the young child is able to follow single rules and this is evident as they enjoy imitating others in play. You may notice this occurring when the young child engages in repetitive activities with set structures, such as action songs and rhymes.

The child's concentration span has increased as they continue to grow. This is evident in their increasing ability to wait for a short time. Waiting can still be difficult for the three- to four-year-old, especially when it comes to sharing, and group play needs to be supported by the adult. It is important to note that each child has their own concentration span and limits of patience. How might you be able to establish how long an individual child can maintain concentration in play? How would you track their day-to-day progress?

The young child at this age, generally speaking, has become quite social and enjoys being with other children, as they have now entered a co-operative stage of play. When planning activities it is important to take the child's stage of play into account. Carry out observations that aim to answer questions such as: Does the child have friends to play with? Which children generally play together? How can you encourage a child to mix with children who are not in their immediate circle of friends?

At this age children generally enjoy helping adults. It is good practice to try to give each child daily opportunities for responsibilities in the environment. Create a 'chore board' with pictures of different tasks such as wiping the tables, sweeping the floor, handing out snacks, etc. Allow the children to place their own picture beside the task they would like to do; this gives the child a sense of ownership and independence in the early years environment.

Goals for the creative arts curriculum

As we have learned, a creative environment is one in which a child feels loved, safe and secure. Routine, security and loving attachments will nurture a child's creative instincts. At the age of three to four years we should aim to help the child follow simple child-centred rules, for example saying 'please' and 'thank you', taking turns and sharing, following adults' instructions and helping to tidy up after play. The child at this stage should be involved in developing these rules as they are now verbal and have a right to be given an equal voice in the environment in matters that affect their life. The creative arts curriculum can facilitate this, acting as a springboard for these experiences.

OVER TO YOU

Taking into consideration the United Nations Convention on the Rights of the Child, think about how you can ensure that the child's voice is heard when planning a creative arts curriculum.

Exploration and participation in creative arts

Dramatic arts

At the age of three to four the child's imaginative play has become increasingly sophisticated and you will notice that it develops at a rapid pace. The child will generally enjoy taking on the personas of people they meet in the real world or through media such as television, action figures, the internet, etc. Promote this type of reflection and creativity where possible. Be mindful, however, that not all images that children try to recreate at this age are positive. It is a good idea to consult closely with families around any dramatic play that could be perceived by the adult or other children as scary or violent. The child may not realise that the play they are recreating could be intimidating others. Think about a dramatic play activity you have observed a child playing that could be perceived as 'harmful'. How could you in this case promote a different type of play without stifling the child's creative ability?

Dramatic play can be extended into many areas of the preschool environment at this age. Chapters 5 and 6 identify the different types of play that can occur in a range of interest areas.

Movement and dance

The concepts of fast/slow, high/low and loud/soft can be introduced through a variety of different music styles. Now that children are able to carry out simple instructions, it can be a great opportunity to introduce linking the tempo of music to one's physical movements. Listen to the following pieces of music (available on YouTube) and think how you might move differently to each of them.
- 'Mahna Mahna' – *Muppet Show*
- Beethoven's Symphony No. 6 – Disney's *Fantasia*
- 'Happy Silly Song' – Mark Andrew Hanson
- 'All I Want is You' – Barry Louis Polisar

A great idea when designing a movement soundtrack for your early years environment is to link with families and find out what music they listen to at home. Bringing this music into the preschool creates a fantastic opportunity for creating different types of movement that are based on children's individual cultures.

Visual arts

As the young child's hand–eye co-ordination increases you will notice that they begin to have an awareness and interest in what marks they are making. The young child begins to explore specific qualities of line, shape and colour and they become interested in some of the following graphic elements:
- big and little
- shapes touching and not touching
- filled shapes and empty shapes
- shapes with marks inside and outside
- irregular shapes
- colour mixing.

At the age of three to four years you will notice that the child is exploring repetition and variation, repeating similar scribbles all over the paper. The child's awareness of their mark making continues to be refined as they grow and they become quite expert when working within the boundaries of the paper, beginning to place shapes in different locations. It is important to offer a variety of materials – different brush sizes and shapes, different colours and sizes of paper – as these differences encourage active exploration of the visual arts medium. The child's scribble becomes quite 'circular' at this stage before moving on to a 'naming' phase of scribble development. The child may even start telling stories about the scribble they have produced. In a relatively short space of time the child's artistic development moves from focusing specifically on kinaesthetic thinking – motion – to imaginative thinking – pictures. This development can be encouraged throughout the scribble stage of development by asking a child, very simply, to 'Tell me about your picture.' When this stage of development is observed, celebrate it! Carefully write down what the child has described and display this description and the child's name with the picture in your art area. This type of display is described in more detail in the next chapter.

Musical arts

As we have seen, the three- to four-year-old child is engaging in pretend play and they are beginning to co-operate with their peers, with adult guidance. Listen to the pieces of music listed in the movement and dance section above and think about the range of emotions that these songs evoke. A great way for children to express these emotions is through the use of colour. Play a song and encourage the child to paint while the song is playing. Each time the mood changes in the piece of music, encourage the child to change the colour of their paint.

OVER TO YOU

Try out this activity yourself using the Elizabeth Mitchell version of the song 'You Are My Sunshine' (available on YouTube). Think about other ways in which you could encourage children to identify and express emotions through music.

Role of the adult

At this age young children are actively seeking reinforcement from the adults in their lives. Give plenty of praise and encouragement as this builds confidence and makes children more likely to feel safe in their creativity. Remember to 'catch' the child being good, and offer positive comments on specific behaviours.

If you are implementing activities such as the music activity listed above, it is vital to explain the rules of the game clearly! Children are more likely to remember rules they understand. Use simple language, speak slowly and demonstrate with actions what you would like to happen. If the child does not want to play the game/complete the activity the way you want them to do it, that's perfectly fine. In these cases the child should be complimented on creating their own activity! Use phrases such as, 'Wow! I see you've created your own game. What are the rules of your activity?' to make it clear that you are encouraging the child's independent thinking skills.

Young children will continue to require high-quality adult supervision. You will find that most of the time children can play together without conflict or frustration, but disagreements and difficult moments will occasionally occur. It is your responsibility to be available at all times to support children through these challenges and offer yourself as a positive role model.

At this age young children should be supported, with the aim of empowering them to resolve their own dilemmas. Think of the support you can give a child when they say, 'I can't draw a cat – will you do it?' How could you support the child in a way that offers them the opportunity to solve the problem of drawing a cat themselves?

OVER TO YOU

Think of a child or a small group of children aged three to four years of age and plan the following activities, taking into consideration the framework in Chapter 3.

1   dramatic play activity
2   movement and dance activity
3   visual arts activity
4   music activity.

Four to six years

As the child progresses in their development to the age of four to six years you will notice that they become increasingly interested in the details and boundaries that come with games and activities. This period has been referred to as the 'games with rules' stage. At this point you will notice that they are rapidly developing co-operation skills and learning how to negotiate rules to form a 'game'.

Dramatic activities become a focus of the young child's play, with make-believe scenarios becoming increasingly adventurous and fantastic! As the child is now firmly rooted in the co-operative play stage they have developed the ability to extend imaginative play from their peers'  play themes and to co-ordinate roles and actions during play. Complex re-enactments, storylines and plot developments appear in entertaining and informative play scenes. Until the age of four or five you may notice that the young child does not yet understand the difference between fantasy and reality, for example believing that characters from television shows are real. In addition to this, during play children will often 'become' people or animals that they want to understand more about, such as a doctor, a hairdresser, a garda or a polar bear.

As motor skills develop the four- to six-year-old child will challenge their physical abilities and if given opportunities and support will continue to try new physical experiences. The four-year-old child's finger dexterity and hand–eye co-ordination is at a point where they can handle a computer keyboard with reasonable ease. As the child grows, so too does their ability to negotiate computers, tablets and handheld devises.

Stage of development and play behaviour

The child is beginning to master co-operative play and is generally able to engage with others in pairs and small groups without adult help. You will find that at this age young children are able to create their own activities, once they are offered the appropriate resources to do so. Closely observe each child to find out what they are interested in and what will need to be provided to facilitate spontaneous play.

The four- to six-year-old has a good grasp of language and you will find that they are able to communicate feelings, hopes and wishes verbally. This ability will reduced the number of frustrations that may have peppered their earlier childhood; but challenges may still be present – the world is still a new place. It is important to seek out the child's opinions on matters that affect their lives and implement any suggestions, where possible, that the child puts forward. This active response to the child's opinion demonstrates how much you value their input.

At this age the child not only appreciates the need for rules but embraces these rules – if they make sense to them. It is a great idea to create rules with children as this gives them an understanding of the reasons behind the rules as well as an understanding of any consequences if the rules are broken. Under Regulation Nine: 'Behaviour Management', the Child Care (Pre-School Services) (No. 2) Regulations (DoHC 2006a) highlights that any behaviour management techniques enforced in the preschool must be documented through written policies and must be respectful to the child's rights, while taking into account their age and stage of development.

Goals for the creative arts curriculum

The creative arts curriculum is a fantastic resource for developing basic social skills. At this age the child should be actively encouraged to ask permission to use equipment, toys and materials that another child may be using. A 'use your words' approach can be taken in the environment in which children are supported to verbalise any wants they have. Children can also be offered the opportunity to comfort a distressed playmate – if they observe a peer who is sad or frustrated during play, for example.

> **OVER TO YOU**
>
> Look at the learning goals addressed in the Aistear themes of Wellbeing, Identity and Belonging, Exploring and Thinking, and Communication. How could the creative arts curriculum be utilised to promote these goals for children aged from four to six?

Exploration and participation in creative arts

Dramatic arts

Imaginative activities take up a high proportion of the four- to six-year-old's play. Observe the children in your care and find out what type of imaginative play they are most interested in. You can also ask the children what would be the best way of organising the room to support their creative play. Using the Clarke and Moss (2001) 'mosaic approach', one can adopt a variety of ways of listening to young children's opinions about how to design their play environments.

As we have seen, books can be used with children from birth. At this age we can use books to recreate stories, giving children different characters to be. Think of the following books, stories and rhymes and discuss how you could make them into dramatic recreations:

- *Room on the Broom* – Julia Donaldson
- 'Five Little Ducks'
- 'Humpty Dumpty'
- *The Very Hungry Caterpillar* – Eric Carle

> **OVER TO YOU**
>
> Think of any children's books, stories or rhymes you know that could be made into dramatic recreations. What props and resources would be useful to accompany the drama?

Movement and dance

Encourage children of this age to choose the music they would like to dance to themselves. Ask them to pick songs they like and make up their own moves to them. How do you imagine a four- to six-year-old child might choreograph the song 'The Grand Old Duke of York'? At this age, play close attention to any feast days or holidays that the child's family may be celebrating. Movement and dance have a big part to play in one's cultural heritage. Link closely with families around any culturally significant periods in the year and think about how these could be represented through dance and movement.

Inanimate objects can be imitated through movement and dance with children of this age. Blowing bubbles with children and encouraging them to move like the bubbles opens up their world to new types of movement. Think about fireworks or waterfalls: how can these be represented through movement and dance? Riley (2007:178) states that dance has a 'unique capacity for self-expression' as it spreads past the confines of words and gives space for the pure expression of emotion.

Visual arts

At this age the child can be described as being in the 'pre-schematic stage' of artistic development. You will notice this as their circular markings with lines protruding from them begin to resemble animal or human figures. During this stage a child's drawings show what they perceive as most important about the subject. For example, if they are drawing someone speaking or singing they will draw the mouth very wide and out of proportion to the other objects in the picture. At this stage of development there is little understanding of space on the canvas or paper. You will notice that objects are placed on the paper in an apparently illogical way. The child can also use colour to express emotion at this stage.

Looking at the child's pictures you will notice that they are attempting to create representations of real-life items that they have observed in their world. Many pictures will contain people, plants, trees, houses and buildings. As the child becomes more expert at these drawings the images will become more and more realistic and recognisable. Features such as clothes and jewellery may be added. You will begin to notice the following details as the child's visual art development deepens.

- Images of people, houses and animals occur frequently.
- Details are added to categorise difference, e.g. girls have long hair.
- Children aim to use all the space on the paper to create their picture.
- They want to make a picture that tells a story and will be eager for people to hear the story.
- Before the child begins the picture they will have chosen what they want to represent on the page.

It is important at this stage of development to offer the child space and opportunity to develop their creativity. By providing resources at the child's level, drawing and painting becomes readily available, thus allowing this form of self-expression to flourish. As well as providing materials, the adult can ask questions to expand the work, for example if there is an aeroplane in the picture, ask 'Where is it going?', 'How will it get there?' or 'Are you in this picture?' You could also take the children to new places, for example going on walks in the local community, and encourage them to reflect on these new experiences through drawing, painting, sculpture, etc.

Musical arts

This is a great age to actively encourage the child to make and record their own music. Having a variety of 'real' and home-made musical instruments in your music area gives the child the opportunity to make choices about the types of sound they want to use, how they can change the sounds, how many different sounds to use and when to use them. Providing a recordable device in your music area that the child can use allows them the independence to save their own music and share it with their family and friends. Reflecting on this 'saved' music opens opportunity for music-specific vocabulary such as 'compose', 'pitch', 'duration', etc. Saving the child's self-composed music offers opportunity for positive comparisons between the music the child has made and the music they hear in their world: 'I can hear you used bells, just like in the song "Jingle Bells".'

Role of the adult

The early years practitioner has a responsibility to keep up with and encourage the child's rapidly expanding creativity. By providing opportunities for stimulating activities you are helping the child develop confidence in their own abilities. Have a look at the idea of 'attribution theory' and how a child's self-image is shaped when they see themselves becoming a master of their environment.

Give plenty of praise and encouragement: it is important to continue to make the child feel good about themselves and their achievements. This is especially important at the age of four to six as children generally begin the transition into primary school at this point. This big change can affect a child's confidence levels and a solid foundation of praise and encouragement goes a long way to build up an individual's self-esteem and resilience.

Continue to be a positive role model in the child's life, supporting the child with any challenging situations they find themselves in while giving them the opportunity to resolve these problems themselves.

CREATIVE PLAY AND DEVELOPMENTAL STAGES

OVER TO YOU

Think of a child or a small group of children aged four to six years of age and plan the following activities, taking into consideration the framework in Chapter 3.
1. dramatic play activity
2. movement and dance activity
3. visual arts activity
4. music activity.

Chapter summary

In this chapter we looked at developing creative activities for children aged from birth to six years. Looking at the different stages of development and play behaviours, we identified how the creative arts curriculum can be developed in the areas of dramatic arts, movement and dance, visual arts and musical arts; and we addressed the adult's role when supporting creative activities in the early years.

OVER TO YOU

In a pair or small group, reflect on this chapter, thinking of a group of children you know. Design a creative arts programme for one week for this group. Take into consideration the needs and preferences that individual children may have. Think about how you could find out what the children's needs and preferences are if they are non-verbal. How can you incorporate children's different abilities and needs? How can cultural difference be integrated into your creative arts programme? In the next two chapters we look at where in the early years environment creative play can happen – refer to these chapters for ideas!

5

Exploring and Creating

This chapter explores aspects of the following Learning Outcomes:
- LO 1: Examine a variety of creative media opportunities with young children.
- LO 2: Summarise the benefits of exploration and participation in creative arts for the child.
- LO 3: Explore the role of the adult in creating an environment in which children feel secure and confident enough to take risks and explore new situations.
  LO 4: Plan opportunities for consultation with children to plan and engage in creative arts experiences.
- LO 5: Test open-ended materials and natural items for creative arts, in both the indoor and outdoor environments, appropriate to different stages of children's development.
- LO 6: Explore challenges for adults in respecting choices and decisions of children.
- LO 7: Employ developmentally appropriate creative arts activities which promote the holistic development of the child.
- LO 8: Reflect on one's own role and responsibilities when engaging in creative arts activities with children, being mindful of health and safety.

In this chapter we will look at maximising the possibilities of creative arts play through carefully planned interest areas in the early years environment. An interest area, or a play area, is a space with a theme, such as a home area, construction corner, messy play area, art and craft corner, book area, music area, etc.

The design of interest areas in a preschool environment is important as these designated spaces offer a variety of different learning opportunities for young children.

Howard Gardner's 'multiple intelligence theory' sets the rationale for having structured, well-designed interest areas. In his 1983 book *Frames of Mind*, Gardner proposed that there are seven 'intelligences' or 'ways of knowing'. He states that each individual has strengths and weaknesses in each intelligence area. Mayesky (2009) looks at Gardner's original list and offers suggestions for types of activity that children will prefer, depending on their type of intelligence or 'smart':

- **Verbal/linguistic or 'word smart' children** enjoy items such as books, cutting and gluing, computers; they are interested in notices, signs and writing and enjoy stories.
- **Logical/mathematical or 'logic smart'** children enjoy table-top activities and construction toys, classifying objects by size, colour, shape and weight.
- **Visual/spatial or 'picture smart'** children like materials such as colours, crayons and paints, sculpture, collage and construction materials.
- **Bodily/kinaesthetic or 'body smart'** children are drawn to costumes, props, puppets, stories, sand play, building and tactile experiences.
- **Musical/rhythmic or 'music smart'** children enjoy listening to recorded music, playing with musical instruments, will ask to sing songs and dance and will respond positively/be sensitive towards music and sound in their environment.
- **Interpersonal or 'person-smart'** children enjoy group activities, especially meal times, circle times and co-operative home corner play; looking at pictures of people in books and in posters/pictures, etc.; they enjoy helping others and can be affectionate.
- **Intrapersonal or 'self-smart'** children prefer to play in quiet environments, enjoy time by themselves, like independent projects and didactic materials, enjoy character-based stories, table-top activities and writing materials.

Over time additional intelligences were added to Gardner's original 1983 list, including naturalistic intelligence and existential intelligence. Since an individual can have strengths in a variety of different areas, it is self-evident that room design in the early education environment should reflect these multiple intelligences.

We can also look to Colin Rose's idea of 'learning styles' when designing the early years environment. Rose and Meyer (2006) describe how individuals' learning styles can be categorised as visual, auditory or tactile. As early years educators our role is to create an environment in which we can accommodate this rainbow of difference.

Think about what types of intelligences you are drawn to. Compare your ideas with those of your colleagues and discuss the differences. Take a moment also to reflect on your individual learning style. Do you think you are a visual learner (learning through sight), an auditory learner (through hearing) or a tactile learner (through touch and doing)? Do you learn best with a combination of these styles? How could you establish which learning styles and multiple types of intelligence are present in young children?

One way of accommodating difference in the early years environment is by using designated play areas. We see this type of room design in many different early years philosophies, and especially in High/Scope settings. In this chapter we will be looking at the following areas in relation to the creative arts curriculum:

- home corner
- writing centre
- construction area
- book corner
- messy play area
- arts and crafts centre
- table-top area
- discovery centre
- small world area
- music centre.

Early Childhood Ireland has devised a comprehensive list of play/interest areas and materials, which is available at www.earlychildhoodireland.ie.

Home corner

A home corner is an area where children can imagine and play out 'real life' situations. In this space children make sense of family life and relationships through recreating scenes they have witnessed in their own homes. You will find that a lot of dinner chat, cooking, baby walking and phone conversations will happen in this area. Generally speaking children will start to play in a home corner from approximately 18–20 months old, depending on their stage of play development. The home corner is an important place to aid the development of the imagination as it allows for free expression and open-ended play.

The home corner should reflect the lives of the children in the early years room. When designing your home corner you could consult with the families of the children in the room to ensure that your home corner is authentic and relevant to the children using it. This family consultation helps in the design of a culturally accurate early years environment. Here is a list of some general suggestions for equipment in a home corner:

- child-sized oven
- sink with space for storing dishes
- fridge
- child-sized table and chairs
- bed
- dresser for dolls and child-sized clothes (for dress-up)
- full-length shatterproof mirror
- washing machine and tumble dryer/clothes line with pegs
- kitchen utensils (pots, pans, cutlery, dishes, wok, toaster, empty containers, e.g. from food products and spices)
- food (combine play food with real food such as fruit and vegetables)
- hygiene products (mops, brushes, dusters, rags, bucket, empty containers of cleaning products such as washing-up liquid)
- dolls that accurately represent different genders, ethnicities, ages and abilities
- doll furniture and accessories (cot, high chair, buggy, mobility aids, bottles, blankets, etc.)
- landline and mobile telephones, clocks, radios, cameras, laptops, tablets, desktop computers.

The home area is a great place for dress-up and for children to express themselves creatively through fashion. Think of the following examples of dress-up clothes and how both girls and boys can use them interchangeably:
- jackets, shirts, dresses, skirts, trousers
- jewellery, purses, bags, briefcases, suitcases, sunglasses
- hats and costumes (these can reflect seasons, occupations, cultures, fantasy and occasions)
- clip-on dicky-bow ties, scarves
- different-sized boots, sandals, slippers and shoes.

Occasionally in home corner play, conflict can occur if children try on a role that may be considered a 'girls' role' or a 'boys' role', for example if a boy wants to wear a dress or a girl wants to wear a 'boy outfit'. This fashion play and exploration of gender roles is all part of the child's developing sense of their identity in general and specifically their gender identity.

> **OVER TO YOU**
>
> Discuss how you can address any questions families may have about home corner play, including fashion play, in a manner which respects the child's right to choose the materials they interact with and how they wish to express themselves.

Creative arts in the home corner

Dramatic arts

The home corner offers fantastic dramatic play opportunities. This area offers a space for make believe and role play in which the child can pretend to be somebody else. The inclusion of dress-up clothes as well as other 'home props' adds to this imaginative experience. Ideally the home play area should be equipped with items such as a sturdy kitchen unit; a child-sized table and chairs; baby dolls with sleeping, feeding and dressing equipment; and kitchen equipment such as saucepans, whisks, spatulas, etc., which should ideally be 'real life' rather than reproduced plastic items. You will notice these materials being used in socio-dramatic play in the home corner. Including pictures of the children's homes, as well as newspapers, cookery books and images of community landmarks such as shops, parks and hospitals adds opportunities for discussion and can extend the play from socio-dramatic to thematic dramatic play. You may notice that children like to play by themselves or in small groups in this area. The adult can join in, but should do so carefully, following the child's lead. Asking questions such as 'Can I play?' and 'Who can I be in the game?' ensures that the child feels ownership over the play despite the adult presence in the space.

Movement and dance

The home corner should be designed to accommodate free movement. You may notice that, just as in real life, action relating to the home corner sometimes needs to happen outside the confines of the 'house'. Encourage children to move equipment out of the home corner into other areas of the room. An example of this might be when a child has a baby doll in the buggy and they move them to the book corner to 'read them a story'. In this situation the child may have imagined bringing their baby on an outing to the library.

Think about how many places a child visits outside their home, for example relatives' homes, shops, the doctor's surgery, school, the park, etc. How can the early years environment encourage children to move their socio-dramatic play beyond the home corner?

The home corner can also provide spontaneous dance opportunities. Provide a child-safe radio in the home corner which children can turn on and off as they choose. This addition offers a chance for children to experience and dance to contemporary music, which is different from the traditional nursery rhyme rhythm that is commonly heard in the early years environment.

Visual arts

The home corner can provide a space to display both the children's art work and art work from around the world. Think about your own home – is there art work displayed? Visual art can take many different forms: a picture on a wall; an illustration on a book cover; the wallpaper on a laptop or tablet. By displaying a child's art work alongside that of a famous painter such as van Gogh, Monet or Warhol, you are sending the message that their piece of art work is as valued as a masterpiece. When you get the opportunity, look around your home and identify how many pieces of art work can be seen. What types do you recognise? Surrealist? Pop art? Impressionist? Art deco? Bringing these different types of image into the home corner can open children up to many varieties of visual art, expanding both their creative vocabulary and their imagination.

Musical arts

Think of all the different types of music and sounds that are heard in a home: the beep of the alarm clock; the ring of the phone; the ding dong of the doorbell. These sounds – and thousands of others – combine to create the distinctive music of one's family life! Listen to the lyrics of Judy Garland's 'Trolley Song' and hear how beautifully they reflect this sound of daily life:

> Clang, clang, clang went the trolley,
> Ding, ding, ding went the bell,
> Zing, zing, zing went my heart strings,
> From the moment I saw him I fell.

OVER TO YOU

Think about other songs that reflect the music of daily life. Make a list of these songs in your reflective journal. How can these songs be incorporated into home corner play?

Using common household items to make music can be encouraged in the home corner. Pots and pans make a great drum set; a whisk in water makes an unusual whispery noise. Any number of everyday household utensils can be used as impromptu musical instruments. With your colleagues, organise a day when you each bring in a minimum of two household utensils. What type of music can be created with these household instruments? What can be used as percussion instruments, wind instruments, stringed instruments, electronic instruments and keyboard instruments? Can you recreate a piece of music? Can you compose a new piece of music? Think about what musical language you can use to describe the piece of music you created/recreated.

OVER TO YOU

In a home corner you might find items such as kitchen equipment and utensils, living room equipment and baby dolls that represent the unique backgrounds of the children who use them. In addition to this the home area might have a dress-up centre. Make a detailed list of items that could be in a home corner and describe how these items could be integrated into the play space. What type of creative arts opportunities could happen if you included these items in the home corner?

Writing centre

The writing area is a great way to introduce concepts such as literacy and numeracy in a fun way. This space can be changed thematically to reflect the different ways in which children witness adults using practical literacy. Think of the different places that children visit where they see people using computers or even old-fashioned handwriting! Examples might be the doctor's or dentist's surgery, a parent's or caregiver's workplace, a restaurant or a grocery shop. In the writing area it is important to follow the child's lead and reflect the places they have knowledge about and are comfortable with. Introducing customised play themes can help to alleviate anxieties a child may have about visiting 'scary' places in real life!

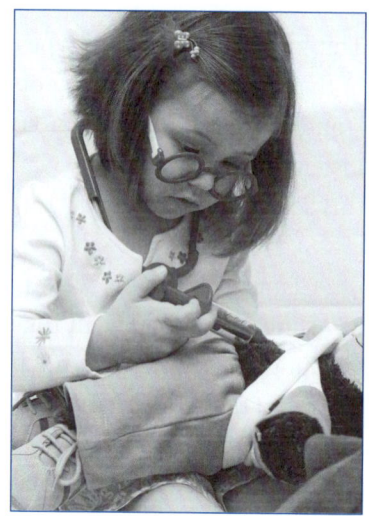

OVER TO YOU

Make a list of the different types of places where a child might witness literacy in action and discuss:
- How can the educator discover what theme the child/children want(s) to be introduced into the room?
- How can the theme(s) be introduced in a child-centred way?

Creative arts in the writing area
Dramatic arts

The writing area offers fantastic possibilities to introduce literacy and numeracy in a functional and relevant way. Morrow states that 'dramatic play activities provide an avenue for all types of talk' (2007:98). In participating in thematic play, children share their own life experiences, interact with peers and begin to gain a greater insight into their life experience. In addition to promoting literacy, the writing area introduces new vocabulary and opportunities for the young child to imagine. Have a look at the following thematic examples and think about what new words and types of play can be found in these themes:

- **Restaurant:** In a restaurant, words such as menu, order, chef, waiter/waitress, manager, cutlery, reservation, bill, etc. become very relevant. What types of conversation might young children have in their 'restaurant'? Include props such as tables and chairs, menus, play money, aprons, paper chef hats, tablecloths, empty condiment bottles and a cash register.
- **Supermarket:** In the supermarket we find trolleys, queues, shopping lists, names of foodstuffs, cleaning equipment and household items, shop assistants, a deli counter, etc. Think about what new words and numbers can be introduced in the supermarket. Include props such as a cash register, paper bags, play money, empty food containers, toy shopping carts and baskets.
- **Clothes shop:** The clothes shop involves an interesting variety of words and phrases. For example, questions such as 'How much is that?', 'What size is that?', 'Do you have it in a different colour?' can enhance the learning experience. Think about the interaction that happens between the shop assistant and the customer: 'Can I help you, sir/madam?'; 'Would you like to pay by cash or card?'; 'I'll check if I have shoes in your size'; 'I will have to order them in.'
- **Dentist:** The dentist's surgery can cause some anxiety for children. Be mindful of this and liaise closely with parents/guardians regarding any fears individual children may have. Think about the words that are used at the dentist's: check-up, mouth, tongue, toothbrush, toothpaste, X-ray, tooth fairy, molar, incisor, etc. Introducing the dentist can also offer the possibility to discuss healthy eating and hygiene habits.
- **Veterinary clinic:** If children in your care have pets they may well visit the vet from time to time. Language here might include: appointment, injection, mask, gloves, swab, form, treatment, medication, prescription, operation. Using 'pets'/stuffed toys in role play can also help reduce a child's fears about visiting the doctor. Include props such as bandages, tape, doctor's/vet's kit, stuffed animals, blankets, stethoscope and white shirts.

- **Hairdresser:** In the hairdresser a very unusual thing happens: a person comes and cuts off bits of you! That must be very scary for a young child. A hairdressing station can be a useful addition if children are cautious about going to the hairdresser. Using words such as scissors, brush, shampoo, conditioner, style as well as phrases such as 'What are you having done today, sir/madam?', 'How much do you want off?', etc. offers children the chance to feel a sense of empowerment in this environment. Think about what materials you could you use to substitute for hair when cutting and styling.
- **Post office:** With the pace of technological progress the post office does not have the prominent role in the community it once had, but it is still a very important part of our day-to-day lives. Including a post office can give children opportunities to practise their writing skills. Words such as An Post, letter, address, postcard, airmail, parcel, postman, letter box, delivery and courier can be introduced in the post office. In this area you could also bring in the concept of email by using the computer. Provide props such as used stamps, envelopes, paper, rubber stamps, a letter box and flyers.

OVER TO YOU

Choose an idea from the list above and make a writing area. Role play what it would be like to engage in dramatic play in this imaginative space.

Movement and dance

The writing area offers great opportunities for movement and dance that can evolve from the different themes in the space. The role play that occurs in this area is active and you will notice that children become the person/character they are imagining, moving and gesturing as this individual. Think about the different movements a chef makes in a restaurant in comparison to a stylist in a hairdressing salon. The opportunities for gross as well as fine motor movement in the writing area are wide-ranging: the dentist, for example, has very precise work to do with small implements such as toothbrushes and mirrors; the vet, on the other hand, may be moving large animals like sheep or horses.

Dance in the writing area takes on a non-traditional format as the dance the children carry out occurs subtly in their co-operative, intertwined movements. An example of this would be in the interaction between Sarah and Dillon, witnessed in the 'supermarket':

Dillon: 'Excuse me, shop woman, I can't reach that tin. Can you get it for me?'
Sarah: 'Which tin do you want, the tomatoes or the beans?'
Dillon: 'Tomatoes, please.'

Sarah reaches up and hands Dillon the tin.
Sarah: 'There you go. Is that all, sir?'
Dillon: 'No, I want the beans as well.'
Sarah reaches up and hands Dillon the beans.
Sarah: 'That will be two euros.'
Dillon hands Sarah play money.
Dillon: 'Here is your money.'

The back-and-forth action between Sarah and Dillon is a co-ordinated exchange in which the children act and react in relation to each other's verbal and non-verbal messages. This dance-like interaction is an important life skill for communication, social rules and independence.

OVER TO YOU

YouTube offers a fantastic insight into candid play experiences. Do a YouTube search for 'children's role play' and reflect on the clips you find. Using the Aistear Theme of Communication, look at how communication occurred between the children in the clip.

Visual arts

The writing area can include many strong visual representations. Think of the types of visual art that may be displayed in doctors' offices, hairdressers, shops, cinemas, etc. These images can transport the child into the role-play frame while offering new opportunities for creative thinking. Perhaps images of fruit by Picasso or Cézanne could be displayed in your 'supermarket'; Leonardo da Vinci's beautiful sketches of the human body could be displayed in the 'doctor's office'; and Jack B. Yeats's 'The Singing Horseman' could go in the vet's office. Rasher's 'Still Life with Melon' would work well in a 'restaurant', while photographer Annie Leibovitz's portrait art could represent the hairdresser scene. This subtle inclusion of classic and contemporary art work opens up opportunities for discussion about these great artists and their different styles of art.

OVER TO YOU

Research some other types of classic and contemporary visual art work that could be represented thematically in the writing area.

Musical arts

The sounds created in various environments combine to make beautiful life music: the ring of a cash register, the roll of a trolley, the snip of a scissors. These everyday sounds can be combined with classic songs to add a musical dimension to any writing area. Think of the following classic songs and rhymes, and match them to a theme:

- 'Polly Had a Dolly'
- 'Old McDonald had a Farm'
- 'Diddle Diddle Dumpling'
- 'Hot Cross Buns'
- 'The Teddy Bears' Picnic'
- 'Humpty Dumpty'
- 'Pat-a-Cake'
- 'Sing a Song of Sixpence'

Think about what other songs, classic and contemporary, could be used with different themes in the writing area.

OVER TO YOU

Taking the theme of a doctor's office, think about the different equipment and materials you would need for the 'waiting room/reception' and 'examination room'. Imagine what props you might include to make these areas real for a child, for example tables and chairs, magazines, eye chart, growth charts, pencils and notepads, a computer, a phone, a hand sanitiser bottle, bandages and other medical equipment.

- Make a list of the items that could be in an office/writing area.
- How could these items be integrated into the play space?
- What type of creative play opportunities could happen if you included these items in the space?
- How do you think the Aistear Themes of Wellbeing, Identity and Belonging, Exploring and Thinking, and Communication could be accommodated in this area? Think specifically of spatial awareness, gross motor movement, fine manipulative skills, and various forms of non-verbal communication that are offered.

Construction area

In the construction area children's logical and problem-solving skills can be exercised through creative active play. Children can be offered a variety of large, medium and small construction materials such as building blocks (wood/foam or cardboard), tubes, pipes, tins and tubs. You will notice that children will use these materials to build a range of models – walls, towers, castles, roads, shops, houses, etc. There is no limit to the imagination demonstrated in the construction area: great feats of architecture and engineering are designed, built, explored and – probably the most fun – knocked down! In this space children identify  shapes and their different uses in design. Space is very important in the construction area as children's designs can range from a small home to very large and impressive structures. Look at construction play in the Reggio Emilia curriculum and reflect on how it promotes creativity.

Think about what types of construction you have seen young children engage in. How did they plan and design these structures? Did they construct them alone or with the help of peers or adults? Children usually begin to display construction-type behaviour from approximately 12 months old, when they start to hold and explore toy blocks. It is not usually until roughly 24 months that the child is able to engage in symbolic representation in their play, when the building can be described as 'constructive play'. Symbolic representation can be described as when children are able to 'translate their experiences into symbolic form' (Curtis & O'Hagan 2003:42). This means that by the age of two years, possibly even 18 months in some cases, children are able to use their play materials to recreate something they have seen in life. Read the case study below and think about where Lucy might have first witnessed this scene. Reflect on the materials she is using to recreate and understand the experience.

CASE STUDY

Lucy is two years and four months old. She is sitting in the construction area by herself and being observed by her key worker.

Lucy has placed three blocks one on top of each other and has put a cotton handkerchief on top of the three blocks. She blows the handkerchief off the blocks and then knocks the blocks over with her right hand. Lucy proceeds to build the blocks up, place the handkerchief on top of the blocks, blows the handkerchief off and then knocks the blocks over. This building and knocking action happens approximately four times. Lucy's key worker approaches and states 'I can see you are building, Lucy.' Lucy looks at her key worker, points to the blocks and responds 'wolf'.

> **OVER TO YOU**
>
> Can you think of the classic children's story that Lucy was recreating in the construction corner? If you thought of the 'Three Little Pigs', you would be correct. Lucy was recreating the scene where the wolf blew the house down, using as symbolic materials the small building blocks and the handkerchief. How exactly did she do this?

The construction area is normally a very busy space and it needs to be well stocked. Provide enough blocks for between three and five children in this space and ensure that the floor area allows for a lot of movement. As children's play can be fast-paced in this space it is a good idea to limit how many people play here at one time. Accessories are very important in the construction area as they can act as an inspiration for the 'build'. Think about making the following construction accessories available on low, open shelving, in labelled containers:
- small lorries, trucks, cars, trains, farm vehicles
- traffic signs, ramps, traffic lights, etc.
- floor road map
- small toy people and small toy animals.

Creative arts in the construction area

Dramatic arts

The construction area can provide opportunities for role play. In this space the young child creates concrete images that they have designed in their mind. Imagination can be enhanced in the construction corner through the use of props such as hard hats, high-visibility vests, mobile phones/smartphones, notepads, large sheets of paper (to act as blueprints), pencils and colours (to draw designs). In addition to this, having tools in the area will help younger children develop symbolic play.

> **OVER TO YOU**
>
> In the construction corner 'woodworking' activities can happen. Think about different ages and stages of children's abilities and what opportunities could be offered to facilitate 'wood' play. With this in mind, research the Reggio Emilia approach to using tools in the construction area and have a group discussion on your findings. Look at the positives to this approach, any challenges to this approach and how the ideas of Reggio Emilia could be incorporated into an Irish early education facility.

'Junk' materials – everyday items that would otherwise be thrown out – can be a great addition for building. Cereal boxes, biscuit tins, shoe/boot boxes, old crates, cleaned milk/juice cartons, washed tins, cardboard tubes can add an extra dimension to children's constructions. Encouraging families to provide these materials can give children a sense of ownership in the play area. Think about what other 'junk' materials might promote creative play. (We discuss 'Junk' materials in more detail in Chapter 6.)

Movement and dance

The construction area offers fantastic opportunities to develop spatial awareness as well as aiding fine and gross motor skills. Including small plastic bricks (e.g. Duplo or Lego), when age appropriate, as well as large plastic bricks like Edublocks, gives children a variety in the type of movement they experience in this area. The inclusion of wooden blocks develops a different type of skill set. Wooden blocks, either closed or hollow, permit the child to explore space and dimension and have the capacity to fall down if not placed in the correct order. These wooden blocks are a self-correcting material (didactic) which means that the child does not need to seek adult assurance to check if they have succeeded in their task as the standing structure speaks for itself.

OVER TO YOU

Have a look in toyshops, early education supply shops and catalogues to identify what types of construction material are available for young children.

Visual arts

Displaying pictures of children's own homes can give a frame of reference for what a building can look like and how they can change depending on design. Including blueprints, as well as pictures of buildings that are being constructed, can indicate the process of how a building evolves over its lifetime from design to build. Having pictures of classical designs such as the Pyramids of Giza, the Parthenon in Greece, the Eiffel Tower in Paris, the Chrysler Building in New York and the Great Wall of China in the construction area exhibits how designs can change in response to culture, history and style. These images offer a chance to open conversations with young children. Think about what type of conversations might come about from looking at these pictures. What type of vocabulary could be introduced? How might viewing these pictures impact on a child's creative process?

> **OVER TO YOU**
>
> Research architecture from around the word that you find inspiring. How might you recreate this building using construction materials? Could you redesign it, adding your own individual flair?

Musical arts

As with the home corner and writing area, the noise that comes from a construction corner is quite unique. The clunking of bricks, the bang of the hammer, the knock of the wood, the click of the screw all come together to create a loud and exciting scene. How could you make these everyday noises into music? Which materials make soft sounds? Which make loud sounds? Are there any items in the construction corner that resemble or sound like traditional musical instruments? Think about matching sounds in the construction corner with sounds found in the home and in the community. Using relevant songs can entice children who are cautious about loud noises to come to the construction corner. Songs like 'London Bridge is Falling Down' or the modern classic, 'Bob the Builder', can help turn the construction area into a hive of activity! If children are cautious around sudden, loud noises such as falling 'buildings', support them with your reassuring presence in the construction area until they feel comfortable to enter it without you.

> **OVER TO YOU**
>
> In the construction area you might find items such as blocks, bricks, tools and dress-up clothes. Make a list of the types of item that could be in this area and reflect on how these items can be best integrated into the play space. What type of creative play opportunities could happen if you included these items in the space? Looking at the different types of creative arts that can be explored in the construction area, how do you think the Aistear Themes of Wellbeing, Identity and Belonging, Exploring and Thinking, and Communication can be developed in this area? Think specifically of spatial awareness, gross motor movement, fine manipulative skills, and various forms of non-verbal communication that are offered in this area.

Book corner

The book corner is sometimes referred to as the quiet or cosy corner. This area should offer a space for children to relax and ponder over stories and illustrations. The book corner should ideally be placed away from more active areas in the room such as the home play area and be surrounded by more sedentary play such as the small world or table-top area. The book corner should reflect the age, interests and development profile of the children in the environment. The books provided in this area should aim to stimulate the children's imagination and help develop their understanding of how people behave and feel. A story such as *I'm Sorry* by Sam McBratney is a lovely example of expressing remorse and empathy, accompanied with vivid illustration. Through books children develop familiarity with the written word and its symbolic role. Books have a beginning, middle and end, which helps to develop the concept of sequence and aids literacy development.

Children can also choose which book they want to look at, which contributes to the development of skills in independence, autonomy and responsibility. The early years educator can encourage this autonomy further by introducing a 'take home' library: each child chooses a book to take home for a week and enjoy with their family. When they return the book they can choose another book from the 'library'. The power of choice can be very exciting and rewarding for young children!

When choosing books for the book corner, carefully consider the following points:
- The books in the book corner should be developmentally appropriate for the children in the environment.
- Consider the durability of books. Toddlers are still in an exploratory stage of play and could possibly tear and chew soft paper cover books. For younger age groups books will need to be made of durable material.
- The content of the books should be developmentally appropriate and should not deal with themes that are 'too old' for the child. Books should also be culturally appropriate. Liaise closely with families and discuss the books that are in the book corner, and their content.
- Books should be available to children at all times. They should be at the child's level and easily accessible. Having books available for even the youngest children will get them into the habit of reading and enjoying books for pleasure.

Each key worker in the early years environment should spend time reviewing the quality of the books in the book corner. Think of the placing, range and quality of books available to children. Are they clean and hygienic (children will be picking them up in their hands)? Are they interesting? Do they capture children's imaginations? Are they the correct size for children to hold? Do they reflect the interests and experiences of children in the room?

> **OVER TO YOU**
>
> **What other criteria do you think should be implemented when reviewing books in the book corner?**

Books can be shop-bought, made by adults or children; they can include photo albums and children's magazines. You could sort them into the following categories.
- **Factual** – facts about animals and plants, real-life experiences such as going to the doctor, books about number, shape, colour, etc.
- **Nature and science** – the five senses, the human body, animal habitats and lives, etc.
- **Races and cultures** – historical and modern stories about people from various races, ethnicities and cultures, reflecting the differences in the preschool room and in society; books can be in different languages and formats.
- **People with different abilities** – who are shown in a positive manner.
- **Fantasy** – pretend stories about people and animals.

Think about the following criteria when choosing books:
- Do the stories build positive images of people who are not usually portrayed in a positive way (i.e. people who are in a minority)?
- Do the books challenge stereotypes, such as a certain type of person working in a certain profession?
- Do the books show children and families in a world context? Do they represent the life experience of children in the early years environment and that of their families?
- How do the books help to develop children's autonomy and self-esteem?
- Do they depict children of different abilities, backgrounds and cultures playing leading roles? Think about the following types of difference: gender, race, religion, age, ability, class, culture, ethnicity, sexuality, spirituality (Burnham 1993). How are these differences represented positively in the books?
- Do the books offer chances for both solitary and group play experience? Do they also offer possibilities for an adult–child experience?
- Do the books provide the opportunity to gain information about specific subjects that are of interest to children in the group?
- How do the books deal with difficult events and transitions in young children's lives (e.g. potty training, new siblings, family separation, transition to new schools)?

- Do the books give opportunities for children to acquire new ideas? Can they promote creativity?
- Are there different language and literature styles, e.g. poems, rhymes and fairy tales?
- Do the books offer children the chance to gain visual understanding skills and require them to pay close attention to details?

> **OVER TO YOU**
>
> Using these criteria, and devising your own, can help ensure that only high-quality books are permitted in the early years environment. Have a look at a book corner and assess the content using the criteria listed above.

When reading books with young children the adult should:
- Sit at the child/children's level. Reading with one or two children allows them to cuddle into you if they want.
- Show the child/children the pictures in the book. (The adult should become a master at upside-down reading!)
- The adult should know the content of book in advance and anticipate any scenes that could cause anxiety through the use of suspense. One example is the story *The Hairy Toe*. It is important to let the children know that you have read the book in advance and you know it will all be okay in the end! This reassurance will ensure that children can become involved in the story without becoming unduly worried.
- Use a tone that is pleasant on the ear – not high-pitched, dramatic but still natural.
- Practise storytelling; it is an art in itself! Can you imagine listening to an exciting story that is told from start to finish in a monochrome voice? Be exciting!
- Remember to create an atmosphere for storytelling. If you have planned to read a story to a small group of children, set the scene with an opening poem such as the 'Wiggle' rhyme:

    Wiggle your shoulders,
    Wiggle your toes,
    Wiggle your fingers,
    Wiggle your face and nose
    No more wiggles left in me,
    Now I sit,
    As quiet can be. Shhh!

- Once the children are seated and ready you can begin your story. When introducing a book, name both the author and illustrator. Introduce the book using the front

cover. Point to any pictures on it and wonder with the children, 'What might this book be about?'
- Throughout the story, use actions and gestures, and encourage the child/children to do the same. Story time should be filled with action and movement, bringing the pictures in the book alive through the children's active participation. Think of the story *We're Going on a Bear Hunt* by Michael Rosen and Helen Oxenbury and imagine what actions and gestures could be recreated with this story.
- When using books it is a good idea to use props such as puppets, pictures, and materials that are present in the story. Think ahead of what props you will need. For example, for 'There Was an Old Woman who Swallowed a Fly' you might need an old woman, a fly, a spider, a bird, a cat, a dog, a goat, a pig, a donkey and a horse! Imagine how much action and laughter can be injected into a story using these props.
- When books are in use it is important to motivate young children to listen to the story through encouragement. Young children should never be forced to engage in an activity that they do not want to do. If storytelling is happening as a planned activity it is good practice to have a second or third activity available for children who do not want to listen to the book. What types of activity could you set up that might be suitable for children to do alongside the storytelling activity?

In the book corner you could include storytelling accessories such as:
- felt board with felt people, homes, vehicles, animals
- puppets (finger, hand, string)
- puppet theatre
- posters
- listening devices, with or without headphones, with pre-recorded stories.

Creative arts in the book corner

Dramatic arts

The book corner offers a great opportunity for dramatic arts activities. You can recreate stories and bring exciting tales to life. Think about turning the book corner into scenes from favourite stories: you could create the jungle from *Where the Wild Things Are* (Maurice Sendak), the ocean from *The Snail and the Whale* (Julia Donaldson), or Old McDonald's farmyard. What resources do you think you would need to transform the book corner into a story scene?

'Story sacks' can also be used to bring stories to life. Put the following items into a

draw-string bag to create a world in which the child can become an active part of the story:
- at least one copy of the chosen book
- a recording of the chosen story on CD or DVD
- recordings and pictures of related rhymes and songs
- some small soft toys, puppets or plastic characters from the chosen story
- a non-fiction book related to the theme of the story
- activities or games related to the chosen story, colours and paper, and modelling dough.

For example, the story sack for *We're Going on a Bear Hunt* could include:
1. A copy of the book.
2. Figurines of the family (either bought in or home-made).
3. A map of the family's bear hunt (this can also be home-made).
4. A non-fiction book about bears.
5. Musical instruments, e.g. a small shaker and a drum, to recreate some of the sounds from the story.
6. Modelling clay such as Play-Doh to recreate some of the characters in the book.

When engaging the child/children with the story sack, consider the following activities and questions.
- Talk about the story and ask the child what were their favourite parts.
- Ask children questions about the characters and the plot.
- Retell the story using the models. (You will need to learn the story off by heart for this, or use a recording of the story.)
- Encourage the children to learn more about the story by looking at non-fiction books about bears/caves, etc. Ask questions such as, 'Are all bears big?', 'Do all bears live in caves?', etc.
- Encourage the children to draw or model the characters out of clay when retelling the story.
- Make your own bear hunt treasure map and take the child/children on an adventure outside! While you are on your adventure, encourage the child/children to use musical instruments to recreate the sounds from the story. Reflect on the story with the child/children by asking questions like:
  ▸ Who will we take on our bear hunt?
  ▸ What will we take on our bear hunt?
  ▸ Who might help us if we feel scared on the hunt?

> **OVER TO YOU**
>
> Think about the following stories and how you could make story sacks for them:
> - 'Goldilocks and the Three Bears'
> - 'Three Billy Goats Gruff'
> - *Guess How Much I Love You* (Sam McBratney)
> - 'The Three Little Pigs'
>
> How might the questions and activities for these stories differ from those for *We're Going on a Bear Hunt*?

Movement and dance

The book corner should encourage active play experiences. Children can be encouraged to use their bodies to recreate stories. Remember that the early years book corner is not a library – children need to be allowed to have fun and make noise when reading books. Think of Julia Donaldson's book *A Squash and a Squeeze*. This book was narrated for World Book Day 2013 by 'Mr Walton' and is available to view on YouTube. Watch this clip and reflect on the scene where the old lady is shooing a nervous cow into her house: 'The cow took one look and charged straight at the pig, then jumped on the table and tapped out a jig.' Just imagine all the movements and dance that can be recreated in the early years environment from this image alone! When encouraging movement in the book corner, focus on verbs in stories that encourage action, reflect on them with the children and invite them to bring the story alive, using their bodies as props.

Visual arts

Children's books come with built-in visual aids: the pictures. Choose books that have brightly coloured and clear illustrations. For children who are not yet literate the pictures are extremely important, as the children will understand the story through the pictures. For example, Raymond Briggs' classic children's book *The Snowman* is a fantastic example of a wordless book which conveys an emotional and powerful message to its audience through the use of pictures alone.

The book corner should have a bookshelf on which picture books are displayed with their front cover facing outwards and unobstructed. Decorating the book corner in an aesthetically pleasing style encourages participation in this area. Ensure that there are soft child- and adult-sized furnishings in this area, and that there is plenty of natural light if possible. It is a good idea to include children's tables and chairs as well as colouring pencils and paper in the book corner for children to write their own 'novels'. These books that the children 'write' can be displayed proudly in the book corner on a noticeboard that is positioned at the child's level or by placing the child's book on the bookshelf. For older school-age children, writing and illustrating their own stories can come to life in an exciting creative centre called Fighting Words, in Dublin 1. Have a look at this creative resource as a possibility for an outing if you have school-age children in your setting and are located near enough Dublin to visit.

> **OVER TO YOU**
>
> Research what types of outing could be used to facilitate children's interest in writing their own books. (Chapter 6 looks at outings in detail.)

Musical arts

High-quality stories for young children have a natural rhythm that appeals to a musical ear. Think of the following passage from the story *The Cat in the Hat* by Dr Seuss:

> The sun did not shine. It was too wet to play. So we sat in the house all that cold, cold, wet day. I sat there with Sally, we sat there we two. And I said, 'How I wish we had something to do!' Too wet to go out and too cold to play ball. So we sat in the house. We did nothing at all.

This musical-sounding passage is created through the use of word play and rhyme. *Goodnight Moon* by Margaret Wise Brown also evokes a lilting effect when it is read aloud:

Goodnight room
Goodnight moon
Goodnight cow jumping over the moon
Goodnight light
And the red balloon.

> **OVER TO YOU**
>
> Discuss the different rhythms in *The Cat in the Hat* and *Goodnight Moon*. Are there any musical similarities between the two passages? Think about the following musical concepts in relation to each story:
> - beat
> - melody
> - harmony
> - interval.

When promoting music in the book corner it is a good idea to have two sections of books on offer to young children: one section that remains consistent and unchangeable; and a second section that changes with children's interests or that reflects different themes that are relevant to the children's lives. A core set of unchangeable books not only acts as a 'familiar face' in the room but also provides a foundation for songs that can accompany them. Choose a set of stories that complement a particular age group and match a range of songs to reflect these stories. For example, up to the age of one year, children like simple words and repetitive sounds, so books with only one or two sentences per page and lots of vivid illustrations are appropriate for this age group.

The following is a list of books and songs that would be suitable for children aged roughly up to twelve months:

- *Five Little Monkeys* by Zita Newcombe – song: 'Five Little Monkeys'
- *Babies* by Ros Asquith – song: 'Pat-a-Cake'
- *Goodnight Moon* by Margaret Wise Brown – song: 'Twinkle, Twinkle, Little Star'
- *Peepo!* by Janet and Allan Ahlberg – song: 'Rock-a-Bye Baby'

Choose four books and songs that would be suitable for each of these age ranges: one to two; two to three; three to four; and four to six.

OVER TO YOU

Looking at the different creative arts that can be explored in the book corner, how do you think the Aistear Themes of Wellbeing, Identity and Belonging, Exploring and Thinking, and Communication can be developed in this area? Think specifically of spatial awareness, gross motor movement, fine manipulative skills, and various forms of non-verbal communication that are offered in this area.

Messy play area

The messy play centre offers excellent possibilities for developing the creative arts curriculum with young children. In the messy play area you might find materials such as sand, water, play dough, clay, gloop, etc.; as well as equipment that facilitates pouring, spooning, filling, emptying, building and burying. All of these experiences will engage the child's senses in a unique way. The prospect of cleaning up after messy play can occasionally concern the adult in the early years environment, but messy play does not have to be worrying. Beckerleg (2008) advises that we start small when initiating messy play activities, starting with shredded paper and dry materials before moving on to water, play dough, sand, foam, cornflour and water and foodstuffs such as condensed milk or even tinned tomatoes! When changing messy play materials, think about the transition between the textures and smells. Moving from water to foam is a smoother transition than from water to tomato juice; too great a contrast between smells, textures and colours can be too much of a jump for a cautious child.

What types of messy play materials could you start off with and progress to over a two-month period with young children? Consider the age of the group of children and what questions you will need to ask family members before introducing any foodstuffs into messy play. With messy play it is important for the adult to model fun and exploration as well as the child – so be prepared to get your hands dirty!

OVER TO YOU

In a group, choose an age range (birth to one year, one to two, two to three, three to four or four to six). Choose five different materials that you could use for messy play, decide on a date for this play, bring in the materials and prepare to get messy! There are some ideas in the arts section below on how to extend your messy play experience.

The messy play area should be designed very specifically. The floor covering must be anti-slip and waterproof; the area should be close to a sink to facilitate hand washing; and individual hand towels or a hand dryer should be available (in line with the Child Care (Pre-School Services) (No. 2) Regulations (DoHC 2006a). There should be a place to store waterproof smocks that will be used to protect the children's (and adults') clothes. Shatterproof mirrors should be available around the area so that the child can see their image while they are engaging in play.

The following is a list of equipment for a messy play area in an early years environment:
- Deep standing tray with plug – a sand/water tray. This can be used for group play. Think about getting a tray with a see-through base which allows the child to lie under the 'mess' and watch it move above them!
- Individual trays that can be used for individual messy play if children choose to play alone or are not able to reach into the standing tray. Baking trays with a raised lip can be useful for this.
- A variety of tubs and containers – tins, bowls, empty ice cream/butter tubs, plastic jugs, etc.
- Different-sized measuring spoons, shovels, scoops, etc.
- A sweeping brush and scoop to tidy away the mess.
- A bin with a lid.

- A mop and bucket to clean up any wet mess on the floor – and a 'Caution – Wet Floor' sign.

Encourage children to bring washable items from other areas in the room into the messy play area. Think about what items in the home corner could transition into the messy play area. This movement of equipment encourages children to remember and reflect on what is in the room, where it is from and where it needs to be returned to.

Creative arts in the messy play area

Dramatic arts

Messy play can bring in a variety of role play ideas. Imagine the adventures that can happen with sand: on the beach, in the castle, on the moon! Water brings a different set of dramatic play experiences, for example under the sea, in the swimming pool, in a rainstorm. If you are thinking of using foodstuffs such as tinned tomatoes in the messy play area, think about what kinds of imaginary play experiences children might envisage with them. 'Tomato play' could include squelching in mud, making dinner; even picking fruit in a faraway land!

> **OVER TO YOU**
>
> Take an opportunity to observe children above the age of two and a half years at play in the messy play area. Reflect on the variety of imaginative themes that are included in the play. Were these themes child-initiated? How could they be extended?

Movement and dance

The messy play area encourages a variety of movement such as opening and closing hands, poking, pointing, patting and pushing. In addition to these movements the pincer grip can be encouraged in the messy play area as well as the development of hand–eye co-ordination with one or both hands. Think about the types of equipment that could be in the messy area and how items such as measuring spoons offer a different movement experience from a shovel, for example. If children have the opportunity to stand and play in the messy play area, encourage this – you will notice that they will walk around the play area, stand, squat, twist and turn in line with their play. Think about different types of music to accompany the play. Listen to a piece of music such as Vivaldi's Four Seasons and reflect on how the body naturally changes its movements with the tempo of the music.

EXPLORING AND CREATING

OVER TO YOU
Think about a wide variety of musical genres and make a list in your reflective journal of examples of sounds, music and songs that could create diversity in body movement.

Visual arts

Many visual arts materials are messy by nature! Using a variety of media – painting, print, collage, photography, sculpture, video, etc. – in the messy play area creates a wealth of opportunities to make individual, child-centred work. Read the case study below and use the four Aistear Themes to think about what types of experience Luke is gaining from his play.

CASE STUDY

Luke (two years four months) is using foam in the messy play corner and is accompanied by his key worker Marie.

Luke is standing at the sand tray, which has a layer of foam on its base. The foam is a mix of colours – white, yellow and blue. Luke moves his right hand in circular motions in the foam and then looks at his right hand. He clasps his two hands together and looks at both hands. Maria says, 'You have foam on your hands.' Luke smiles at Maria and turns his head back to the tray. Luck places his right and left hand into the tray and moves the foam up and down in sweeping motions. Maria sits beside Luke with a piece of card and says, 'The foam changes colour when you mix it.' Luke looks at his hands, which have a green foam mix on them. Luke looks at the foam on his hands and the foam in the tray. Maria says, 'When you mix the colours yellow and blue it makes green.' Luke puts his index finger into the tray and picks up a dollop of foam; he brings it close to his face and looks at it.

Maria says, 'I have a piece of card here; you can use the foam on your hands to make a picture if you would like.' Luke turns to Maria and takes the card. He places it into the tray and, taking the foam on his finger, makes long vertical lines of foam on the card. As he picks up the card Maria says 'Oh look, Luke, I can see that you painted the foam with your finger on this side of the card, and on the other side of the card it made a print of what you were painting.' Luke turns the card around, looks at the printed side and smiles.

> **OVER TO YOU**
>
> If other materials were to be used in the messy play area – e.g. sand, water, lentils, play dough, gloop – discuss what other types of visual art could be created.

Musical arts

As discussed in the 'movement and dance' section, pairing the messy play materials with music can be a great way to enhance the learning experience for young children. Think about what types of music might best suit the different resources in the space. The following are a list of songs that evoke thoughts of messy play. Listen to them and think about what material would suit the song best.

- 'The Hippopotamus Song' ('Mud, Mud, Glorious Mud')
- 'The Duck Song' (Bryant Oden)
- 'If All the Raindrops' (Barney)

Play in the messy play area creates very unique sounds: the squelch of foam; the whisper and drop of water; and the swoosh of sand. Messy play allows the human hand to become an instrument with which to makes these wonderful noises! Focus on the range of sounds that the materials produce when handled in different ways. Do these sounds remind you of other environmental sounds, or of particular songs? The messy play area can create very subtle natural tones that contrast with the crashes and bangs in the home corner or construction corner. Bring these differences to the children's attention and allow them to reflect on the noise that different types of fun brings.

> **OVER TO YOU**
>
> During messy play areas of development such as spatial awareness, gross motor movement, fine manipulative skills, and verbal and non-verbal communication are highlighted. Think about these development areas in relation to the Aistear Themes of Wellbeing, Identity and Belonging, Exploring and Thinking, and Communication in the messy play area.

Arts and crafts centre

The arts and crafts centre in the early years environment is a space for young children to develop their creativity, explore, process, experience and discover. One example of exploration in the art area is the investigation of colour. In the arts and crafts area children are offered a space to name, pair and combine colours. The primary colours (red, yellow and blue) can be used to create the following shades:

- red + blue = purple
- blue + yellow = green
- yellow + red = orange

The tones white and black are used to lighten and darken the primary and secondary colours. Try it for yourself and explore how many different colours you can make using the primary colours and tones!

In the art and craft centre open-ended play experiences are developed and encouraged through a range of equipment and materials that are made available at the child's level. In this area children can gain an understanding of shapes, sizes, textures and colour, leading to deeper knowledge and understanding of the world around them. Fox and Schirrmacher (2010) describe the ideal art and crafts centre as being an artist's studio, located in a convenient and easily located place, that is well stocked, orderly and organised and has consistent rules and limits.

The art area is ideally a space to investigate 'What happens if ...' situations. What happens if ...

- ... I paint over my crayon picture?
- ... I cut where I had glued?
- ... I paint with a toy truck rather than a paintbrush?
- ... oil is added to paint? Or sugar? Or sand?

The 'What if' possibilities are endless!

The art and craft centre provides a space for young children to visually represent ideas, thoughts, feelings, fantasies and experiences in a safe, non-verbal way. Art is an important medium for communication as young children often struggle when using speech. With this in mind, the art and craft centre should be designed to facilitate independence, autonomy and freedom of expression. This form of child-centred design invites children into the area in a fun and unobtrusive manner.

Think of the following considerations when designing an art and craft centre:
- Are the shelves low and open?
- What types of container are there – clear plastic, wicker, etc.?
- Is there a child-size easel?
- Are there child-size tables, washable tablecloths and chairs?

- Are there painting shirts or smocks available to the children?
- Are there facilities for drying art work such as a 'clothes line', an air dryer or shelving?
- Are there facilities to display children's art work, e.g. a noticeboard/art wall, shelving, etc.?
- Where is ongoing and finished artwork stored?

The arts and crafts centre should be well stocked with arts and crafts materials. The arts and crafts centre is quite often one of the 'busy' areas in the early education environment. It is particularly important to keep a stock list of every item in the arts and craft area and re-stock when materials run low. One adult should be allocated this duty each week.

OVER TO YOU

Discuss the importance of 're-stocking' in the arts and crafts area and think about how a child might respond if the material they were planning to use is not available.

The following is a list of materials that could be used in an art and craft centre.
- Items to draw with and on:
  - large and small crayons (think about colours: skin tone colours, pastels, primary and secondary colours, tones, etc.)
  - pens, pencils, erasers, coloured pencils, sharpeners
  - chalk, chalk board, erasers
  - paper (various sizes and colours, lined and blank, newspaper, construction, tissue)
  - cards, paper plates, etc.
  - dry-erase boards/markers
- Items to paint with:
  - finger paints
  - water-based paints
  - paint trays
  - a range of painting utensils – brushes, rollers, squeeze and spray bottles, sponges
  - paint scrapers
- Items to complete a collage:
  - PVA glue, glue sticks, glue/paste pots
  - glue brushes/spreaders
  - paper scraps, magazines, cards, wrapping paper, ribbon
  - cardboard tubes, cardboard boxes, construction paper

- felt/fabric swatches
- wool/string
- cotton balls
- glitter, buttons, sequins, gems (remember that small materials are not recommended for children under three years of age, and all young children must be supervised)
- natural materials such as leaves, seeds, twigs, feathers, etc.
• Items for 'three-dimensional' work/sculpture:
  - play dough (handmade or purchased)
  - clay (fast-drying) or modelling clay
  - pipe cleaners

The art and craft area should also have a wide selection of tools which children can use in their creative process, for example:
- child-safe scissors (both left- and right-handed)
- paper punches and string
- sticky tape and a tape holder
- tools to use with play dough/clay/modelling clay (craft sticks, blunt knives, scissors, pipe cleaners, etc.)

It is important to note that colouring books, dot to dot images or 'worksheets' must never be used with children in an early years setting. These types of product-based activities limit a child's creative impulse and enforce a message that a drawing 'should' look a certain way. These 'should' messages impact on a child's artistic confidence. Herr (2000) highlights that colouring books only serve as a tool for hand–eye co-ordination and over time create a dependency in the child to rely on others to provide templates for their creativity.

OVER TO YOU

Think about what other tools and materials could be used in an arts and crafts area and find out how much it would cost to 'build' and stock an art area in an early years room.

Safety and wellbeing in the arts and crafts area

Safety is an important issue for every area in the preschool room, and it is a particular concern in the arts and crafts area as children are using items that could harm them if they are not used in the correct manner. Safety is discussed in detail in Chapter 9. Think about these questions that relate specifically to safety in the arts and crafts area:

1. Is the arts and crafts centre located in a place in the room that facilitates high levels of adult supervision?
2. Is there stringent supervision in the arts and crafts area? Remember, children may be tempted to put small objects in their mouth.
3. Are all paints, crayons and pencils labelled 'non-toxic'?
4. Are equipment and tools bought from reputable suppliers and labelled with a 'CE' mark?
5. If natural objects such as feathers, twigs, etc. are being used, have you ensured that they are washed and dried carefully to avoid any cross-contamination?
6. Have parents/carers been surveyed to find out if children are allergic to any substances that may be in the arts and crafts area?
7. Are all materials and art tools at the child's level so they do not need to climb or reach up high to retrieve them?
8. Are there hand washing and drying facilities available for children? Is the area close to a sink?
9. This area can get noisy: is it located away from quiet spots such as the book corner and closer to more active areas such as the home corner?
10. Are there rules and boundaries in place? Children appreciate boundaries and do their best creative work in an environment in which they feel safe. Having a few set rules in the arts and crafts area can provide a 'safety net' and allow children to explore in a happy and safe manner. Think about what rules would be appropriate in an arts and crafts centre.

Creative arts in the arts and crafts centre

Dramatic arts

The arts and crafts centre holds fantastic opportunities to visually represent dramatic play. In the previous chapter we described how a child's art work moves from the scribble stage to the pre-schematic stage. In the scribble stage, when children begin to 'name' items you will notice that they will generally 'name' their art work after people, animals or places in their lives. This is an artistic representation of socio-dramatic play. During visual art work children are projecting what they have seen rather than embodying it (role play). As children become increasingly skilled at representing memories, thoughts, feelings and ideas through visual art you may notice that the art work might start to represent 'what if' situations – otherwise known as 'imagination'. Encourage this type of complex hypothetical thinking through open-ended questions – 'What ...?', 'How ...?' 'Who ...?' and 'When ...?'

These questions open conversations and encourage dramatic storytelling in the arts and crafts area. Try it for yourself: come up with a list of open-ended questions and 'test' them on someone you know. Think about what the difference would be for the child's imagination if you were to ask closed questions (with yes/no answers) instead of open-ended questions.

The arts and crafts centre can also be used to scaffold themes and activities that are happening elsewhere in the early years environment. An example of this might be if a theme such as the colour red was in use after one of the children declared that red is their favourite colour. The book corner might be reading *The Little Red Hen*, the construction corner might be making red-brick houses, and the writing area could be transformed into a red fire engine. How could the arts and crafts centre support the theme? Think about what type of spontaneous and planned arts and crafts activities could add to theme.

Movement and dance

Movement in the arts and crafts corner is particularly expressive. You might notice that the child will make very different marks depending on whether they are sitting at a table or standing at an easel. Try it yourself and see how your body moves differently depending on whether you are standing or sitting while completing a visual art piece. You might notice that if you are standing you will turn, sway, wriggle, jiggle and tap. When you sit, however, your movements are more likely to be limited to certain parts of your body: your toes might wiggle as if independent from your legs, your fingers tap or your head nod. Test what difference this might have if you were drawing a picture or sculpting. It might be that you are more likely to use all the page if you are standing rather than sitting. When sitting you could find that the details you include in your drawings will be more precise as your concentration is focused. These different experiences when sitting, standing or moving while engaging in visual art are important for creating an active learning environment.

OVER TO YOU
Reflecting on Síolta Standard Two, Environment, note how the design of the arts and crafts centre can promote high-quality child-centred movement.

Visual arts

Visual arts are a critical part of the arts and crafts area. We have already discussed four main artistic media for young children: drawing/mark making; painting; three-dimensional art; and collage (incorporating 'junk art'). The visual arts area promotes free artistic expression and it is important to value and respect the variety of items that children will make. The saying 'beauty is in the eye of the beholder' is very apt in the art and crafts centre! As art is subjective and individuals' taste in art differs; not everybody in the early years environment may appreciate the beauty in a visual art piece that a child has completed. It is important that the adult models that all art is to be appreciated for its effort, planning and completion, regardless of its appearance.

Here are a number of suggestions recommended by Jasmine (2004) as to how to display visual art pieces in the early years environment:

- **Magnet art galleries:** Use 'child-friendly' magnets, such as the kind used on refrigerator doors, to display art work on metal surfaces.
- **Wall art galleries:** An important aspect of 'hanging art' is to preserve the integrity of the painting/picture, etc. If using sticky tape, for example, there is a chance that when removing the tape the paper will rip. Think about how to display art in your gallery in a manner that represents the child's intention when completing it. Are you going to place the art against a backdrop such as coloured card? Will you place the art in a frame? Will the art have a name plate and description beside it? Think about visiting a real life art gallery and see how they manage displays. The early years environment should be as respectful to the masterpieces that are created daily as national art galleries are to their displays.
- **Bulletin board art gallery:** Noticeboards are a great space to display visual art pieces. They should be placed at a level that is accessible to both adults and children. Bulletin boards allow the adults to use staples or thumb tacks to display heavier pieces such as collages or projects. If using bulletin boards in rooms with toddlers it is advisable to use staples rather than thumb tacks as thumb tacks are easy to remove and could be harmful to the young child. If using staples on the board, ensure that they cannot be removed from the board by inquisitive little fingers!
- **Door art gallery:** The backs of doors are a useful space to display pieces of work at different heights. These different heights encourage children to look up and down when observing their environment rather than focusing solely at eye level. Remember: only use doors which are not likely to hurt a person if opened when the gallery is in use! Think about doors that are used less often than the main room doors, such as cloakroom doors, cupboard doors, etc.
- **Low shelving:** Provide a low shelf to display 3D art work such as play dough, clay models, paper sculpture, pottery, etc. Think about how to display the child's name and story behind the sculpture when displaying it. Remember, it is important to show children that when viewing art work, eyes are used but not hands! Rules are just as important when viewing art as when making it.

- **Hanging art:** Did you know that you can exhibit art work at 'head' level through 'hanging galleries'? This can be achieved through displaying the art from string dangling from the ceiling, a clothes line, through hooks or clothes hangers, etc. If you are displaying art in this way, be mindful of safety considerations and think about the children's eye level. Can the children in the room see the art if it is displayed at adult's height?

Points for reflection when introducing an art gallery:
- How should art be chosen for display?
- How can children's names and description of art be displayed (lettering)?
- What eye level should the art be at?
- How can the art gallery attract families to observe and respect the art on show?
- What types of light could be used to offset the visual art pieces?
- How can the 'process' of the art work be displayed with the finished product?
- Would it be important to display 'classical' art work pieces in the gallery along with the children's art work?

OVER TO YOU

Design, implement and evaluate a range of visual art displays and discuss which you think are the most effective for artistic display.

Musical arts

Music is a brilliant accompaniment to visual art pieces created in the arts and crafts centre. Music can be used to support visual art media in a variety of forms, for example as a backing soundtrack to create a specific atmosphere in the area. Having a child-friendly CD/digital player in the arts and crafts centre can offer the possibility of adding a certain ambience to the area. Think of different types of music – fast music such as Rossini's William Tell overture or Flight of the Bumblebee by Rimsky-Korsakov or slow music such as Beethoven's Moonlight Sonata or Chopin's Prelude in E Minor. Try it yourself: what effect does it have on your visual art work when these pieces of music are playing in the background? You could vary the ambient sound to include noises from nature, such as 'sounds of a rainforest', 'sounds of the sea' or 'sounds of the night', for example. Imagine how these different sounds would influence a piece of art.

You can use music and songs to inspire the creation of a piece of visual art. For example, think of the song 'Heads, Shoulders, Knees and Toes'. What type of art work could you create using all these different parts of the body? The following is an example of a planned activity using this song:

- **Head:** Face painting is a great and underused resource in the early education environment. Remember to ensure that the young child is not allergic to the face paint and that you use shatterproof mirrors when the child is painting on their own face.
- **Shoulders:** We see hand prints in every child's art portfolio, but what comes after the hands? Encourage the child to continue drawing on the print – wrists, elbows, upper arms and shoulders. Where do the shoulders lead to? The neck and the head! Encouraging this extension of the simple hand print activity encourages children to think about the word 'next'.
- **Knees and Toes:** Roll a length of wallpaper/blank printing paper on the ground. Place a variety of trays with washable water-based paints at the beginning of the paper. Encourage the child/group of children to step in the paint with their bare feet and notice how the paint is darker with heavy steps, lighter with softer steps and how it fades as they move along the length of the paper. Focus on the movement of the legs and knees and how they move to allow the feet and toes to walk on the ground.

Think about the following songs that incorporate body parts and how they could be developed into a planned creative activity in the arts and crafts centre:
- 'Dingle Dangle Scarecrow'
- 'He's got the Whole World in His Hands'
- 'If You're Happy and You Know it, Clap your Hands'

We have discussed the uses of displays earlier in the chapter. One benefit of an effective display is that it encourages reflection and complex thinking about completed art work. One way to motivate this type of thinking is to ask questions of the child/group of children about the displayed pieces of art. Music can be incorporated into this process by asking questions such as: 'Does this sculpture/picture remind you of a song/piece of music?'; 'Can you make the noises that are in this picture/sculpture?' 'The picture/sculpture is silent; if it was noisy what would it sound like?' You can also ask these questions when the child is in the process of making the visual art piece. The Hanen Early Language programme method of observe, wait and listen (OWL) can be very useful here:
- **Observe** what the child is doing, looking at, moving, etc.
- **Wait:** let the child take the lead in offering conversation. A simple rule of thumb is to count to ten slowly before offering any suggestions or comments. This also applies if you have asked a question. Remember to give the child time to answer a question when it has been asked.

- **Listen:** to what sounds and words the child says and what they are trying to tell you. When the child initiates conversation or responds to your question, reply with enthusiasm and interest.

> **GROUP ACTIVITY**
>
> While completing a visual art piece to a piece of music, 'OWL' with the person next to you. Think about what it is like to be asked reflective questions about the process of your art work. What is it like to be given time to think about how to answer these questions? What is it like to be greeted warmly when you answer the questions? If you were a young child experiencing this degree of interest and patience from the adult, how would it make you feel about your visual art piece? Note these reflections in your journal.

Table-top activities

Looking at commercial table-top activities such as jigsaws, pegboards and puzzles, one wonders about integrating table-top activities with the creative arts curriculum. The table-top area can also be known as the manipulation centre or concentration corner. It is distinguished by its child-size tables and chairs, its low open shelves with containers to hold materials and puzzles and it also has a carpet area for floor puzzles, etc. As many of the materials purchased for the table-top area are didactic (self-correcting) there is a question of how children can be creative when offered materials that force an idea of 'right' or 'wrong' in play. It was noted in the *Thematic Review of Early Childhood Education and Care Policy in Ireland* (OECD 2004) that in Irish early education settings there was a reliance on 'plastic toys'. The report specifically highlighted the use of table-top games, puzzles and flash cards. This was of particular concern as research has shown that children learn best through active learning experiences that promote interactive, self-directed learning. With this in mind the creative arts can be fostered in the table-top area if the materials in it promote children's innate ability to think, explore, be curious and question. Below is a list of table-top materials categorised into building materials, puzzles, manipulative and mathematical materials.

Think about these materials and use the following questions for reflection:

1. How can these materials be used to encourage young children to be open to receiving new ideas, different types of process, new sensations and feelings?
2. How do the materials allow children to interact with them in a manner which does not send the message that how they are playing is 'wrong' or 'insufficient'?
3. Do the materials offer possibilities for open-ended play or closed play experiences?
4. Do they allow for spontaneity, imagination and 'outside the box' thinking?
5. How can young children play with these table-top materials in a manner that allows them to think, converse, and be active by themselves or with others?
6. Do the materials allow the child to reflect on what they have done?
7. Is there a possibility for collaborative play/conversation with other children and with adults while using the materials?

Table-top building materials:
- small wooden blocks
- interlocking blocks, e.g. Lego, Duplo
- bristle blocks
- waffle blocks

Table-top puzzles:
- puzzles with a variety of textures (foam, plastic, wood, etc.)
- a mixture of commercial and home-made puzzles
- puzzles of different complexities according to ability level, e.g. knobbed, without knobs, different numbers of pieces, interlocking and individual pieces, table and floor puzzles

Table-top manipulative materials:
- small and large beads with strings, bead pattern cards, bead frames, etc.
- sewing materials such as blunt needles, wool, buttons, lacing cards with laces/string
- pegs and peg boards
- zip, snap and button dressing frames
- straws/sticks with connectors
- nuts and bolts, screws
- train tracks and trains
- shape sorters
- felt pictures

Table-top mathematical materials (measuring):
- liquid/dry measuring sets, e.g. cups and spoons
- scales and weights
- tape measures, metre sticks, rulers, etc.
- thermometers
- height charts

Table-top mathematics materials (shapes):
- magnetic shapes, e.g. squares, circles, triangles, etc.
- pattern cards for any shape
- attribute blocks (different sizes, colours, shapes, thicknesses), parquetry blocks
- puzzles with different geometric shapes (commercial or home-made)

Table-top mathematical materials (counting):
- small objects to count, e.g. coloured beads, animals, vehicles, etc.
- sorting trays
- pegs/peg boards

Table-top mathematical materials (quantities):
- dominos
- playing cards
- abacus
- stacking cups
- three-dimensional graduated cylinders showing a sequence of different heights

> **OVER TO YOU**
>
> Organise groups of four to five people. Each person should aim to bring in one or two items from the lists above. Choose a day and time to experience the items, think about the questions for reflection in this chapter and discuss your thoughts. Remember, not all items in the above list can offer creative play, so be critical in your evaluations!

The table-top area is a space not only for spontaneous creative activities but also for planned activities. The table-top area can be a space in which creativity can be introduced through day-to-day care routines such as snack time. Thinking of creativity as a spark that ignites one's senses, it is important to introduce and experiment with different flavours in the early years. This exploration of taste should be implemented in a fun and relaxing manner. The table-top area promotes culinary arts activities as it's a space that encourages children to sit, try and think. Look at the following culinary arts experience, which aimed to explore different tastes at snack time, and think about how children's learning was enhanced in a creative way.

> **CASE STUDY**
>
> Emma (adult) calls the group of five children (aged between two years four months and three years six months) over to the table for snacks. She asks Tom (three years two months) to hand out plates. She asks Susan (two years eight months) to hand out the forks. Kate (two years four months) is asked to hand out the knives. Sean (three years six months) is asked to hand out napkins and Michael (three years four months) hands out water cups.
>
> Emma has placed a large plate in the centre of the table. On the plate are wholemeal crackers, cream cheese, hummus, chopped lettuce, chopped cherry tomatoes and strawberries. Emma introduces the culinary arts activity (snack time) by saying, 'We are so lucky today – we get to choose our own flavours! There is enough for everybody, so we can share. I will help.' She points to each of the different foods and says, 'The crackers are dry and crunchy, the cheese is creamy and cool, the hummus is smooth, the tomatoes are squashy, the lettuce is crisp and the strawberries are juicy. Let's start by everybody picking one taste each and then we can get more.'

Think about the activity that Emma has brought to the table-top area. How can the children be creative with these tastes? How would this type of creative activity aid in children's learning? How could you extend this activity?

Creative arts in the table-top area

Dramatic arts

The table-top area can be a space which can enhance the creative arts in other areas of the early years environment as well as supporting stand-alone creative activities. Looking at the list of materials mentioned earlier, we can see that many items can easily transfer to areas such as the construction corner, the writing area, the home corner, etc. Encourage movement from the table-top area to other parts of the room. Look at the case study below and think about how movement aided Faith's learning (use the Aistear Themes and Learning Goals as a guide) and reflect on the adults' role in table-top creativity.

CASE STUDY

Faith (three years nine months) approaches the table-top area. She takes out a tub of multi-coloured 'counting bears' and three trays, one red, one green and one yellow. Faith sits at the table with the bears and the trays and begins picking the bears out of the tub and classifying them into each of the trays depending on colour. She is placing the red bears on the red tray, the green bears on the green tray and the blue bears on the blue tray. She continues until there are no bears left in the tub and there are five bears on the trays. Faith sits and looks at the bears on the trays. She turns and looks at the children playing in different areas of the room. She picks up the red tray and walks over to the home corner. Faith, speaking in a loud tone, says, 'There's a party at the table; it's my birthday.' Holly (four years eight months) looks at Faith and says 'Where?' Faith replies 'It's a party; there's bear jellies' and points to the table-top area. Holly and Faith walk over to the table-top area and begin pretending to eat the bears.

Movement and dance

Think of all the different types of movement that are encouraged through table-top play. Flora (2006) gives us some examples of table-top movement:

- **Fine motor skills:** the movement of muscles in the fingers, hands and wrists. Jigsaws, peg boards and button frames encourage fine motor movement.
- **Hand–eye co-ordination:** occurs when the brain can integrate the message it receives from the eye to the action it wants the hand to complete. Table-top activities such as interlocking blocks, sewing and beading are examples of hand–eye co-ordination activities.
- **Visual motor integration:** you will notice this level of movement when you observe children reproducing images they have previously seen in their play materials. Visual motor integration is the skill of accurately recreating shapes. Activities could include geometric puzzles, pattern making and small building bricks.
- **Graphio-motor skills:** any movement that includes writing tools such as pens, pencils, crayons, etc. These skills are closely linked with visual motor integration.
- **Motor planning:** relates to a child's ability to carry out an instruction given by themselves, a peer or an adult in their life. For example when a child enters the table-top area, picks a puzzle off a shelf, places it on the table, pulls out a chair, sits on it, and turns themselves to face the puzzle. In these actions we can see that the child has given themselves the instruction to complete a puzzle and has carried out a series of preparation tasks in a sequential, planned manner.

- **Body awareness:** a child's ability to be mindful of where and how their body fits into a space. This is an important skill for sitting on a chair, maintaining one's own personal space and that of others, for example. Bodily awareness also helps with other table-top activities such as opening and closing activities.
- **Bilateral integration:** being able to use both sides of the body together. Think about what table-top activities encourage the use of both hands at the same time. Stringing beads is one example. Try it for yourself and reflect on the types of movement and skills that are needed to hold string in one hand and place beads on the string with the other. Pouring activities, as well as lacing and measuring, facilitate the same type of bilateral movement required for stringing.
- **Crossing mind-line:** during crossing mind-line activities we bring the top of our torso across our middle and extend to our toes. We see this during mat activities in the table-top area. Larger materials that require big body movement support this type of movement. Look at the list of table-top materials above and reflect on your own experiences of children's 'mat' play. Think of what activities would be suitable for crossing mind-line movement.

Visual arts

Including paper, pens, colouring pencils and crayons in the table-top area offers children the opportunity to explore scribbling and drawing in a focused manner. You may also want to include scissors and glue in this area to facilitate cutting and pasting. Deiner (2011) believes that children should be offered the chance to participate in a visual arts piece each day. The table-top area can provide a different type of atmosphere for completing process-based visual arts creations as it is generally a quieter space than the arts and crafts centre. In addition to this the table-top area can provide an opportunity for children to complete visual art pieces in pairs or small groups.

Templates or 'workbooks' should not be used in an early years environment. These encourage children to 'cut along a line' or 'colour in', and are often advertised in bookshops, toy stores, etc. This type of product-based material is inappropriate for the table-top area or indeed anywhere else in the early years environment as they send the message to the child that they can only complete a piece of artwork if they have something to copy. The following experiment demonstrates the impact of product-based visual arts versus process-based visual arts.

Set up an experiment with two groups of adults.

Get Group A to sit in a circle, give each person a piece of play dough and tell them, 'Mould anything you want.'

Now get Group B to sit in a circle, give each person a piece of play dough and a picture of a play dough bunny and say 'Mould anything you want'.

The aim of this experiment is to witness how creativity can be stifled when prescribed templates are added to young children's play.

How did introducing the template of the bunny impact on the process of:

- Planning what to sculpt – how did the bunny template impact on individuals using their imagination? You may notice that some people in Group B began to mould the play dough into the image of the bunny in the picture. How many people in Group A made a bunny like the one in the picture?
- Conversation at the table – how did people talk when there was the bunny template at the table and when there was no bunny? Did anyone in Group B use phrases like 'I'm awful at this' or 'It looks nothing like the picture'?
- People's reaction to what they made – how did the individuals measure whether they were happy with their sculpture? Did they feel the need to compare their work with that of the other people at the table?
- How long people spent sculpting – this can indicate the level of an individual's interest in the work.

Were there any other findings from the 'experiment' that could give an insight into how introducing templates can impact on people's creativity? Why did we suggest using adults rather than children for this 'experiment'?

Musical arts

You might choose to include percussion instruments in the table-top area. Think of the following instruments and how they could complement learning in the table-top area:

- xylophone
- wood block
- triangle
- tambourine
- jingle bell
- table-top piano
- maracas
- castanets
- bongo drum.

These instruments can be a great addition to the table-top area as they promote open-ended play while encouraging fine motor movement. Remember, if these instruments are available in the table-top area children should be enabled to move around the room with them. Think of a marching band or a traditional New Orleans jazz band, which would be very boring without the addition of free movement! The purpose of adding musical instruments to a table-top area is to develop children's muscles and also to offer opportunities for fun and creativity, using improvisation skills. Theses instruments can also be used to explore sound in a safe and meaningful way.

> **OVER TO YOU**
>
> Looking at the different types of creative arts that can be explored in the table-top area, how do you think the Aistear Themes of Wellbeing, Identity and Belonging, Exploring and Thinking, and Communication can be developed in this area? Think specifically of spatial awareness, gross motor movement, fine manipulative skills, and various forms of non-verbal communication that are offered in this area.

Small world area

In this area there will be items such as a garage with small vehicles, a dolls' house and accessories, a barn with small toy animals and farm machinery. This area will promote many of the same socio-dramatic play opportunities as the home corner and construction corner; but it is distinct from the other areas in the room as it offers the child the opportunity to project play on to  characters they are interacting with rather than embodying characters through role play. Dodds and Jarvis (2008) describe the small world area as being an important tool to facilitate children in recreating experiences they have witnessed in their lives as well as allowing them the opportunity to imagine and create new experiences through fantasy play. This area also promotes co-operative play, empathy and negotiation skills, while extending vocabulary, exploratory play and knowledge.

Think about the following themes that could be included in the small world area and how they could enhance a child's creative abilities:
- In the Jungle
- On the Farm
- At the Zoo

- Under the Sea
- The Arctic Circle
- My Home
- Land of the Dinosaurs
- In the Builder's Yard

You may have noticed that soldiers and action figures are not included in these themes. Whether or not to include 'battle' type materials is a decision for each setting and should be introduced with careful consideration and in partnership with families. Holland, in her book *We Don't Play with Guns Here*, has suggested that in cases where young children, often boys, continually engage in 'gun play', it can be useful to integrate this type of play in the small world corner. She states that research has shown that banning this type of play is not supportive to the child's needs and she ascertains that no link between war/superhero play and aggressive behaviour has been definitively proved (Holland 2003).

In this area one might include small animals/people, places where the animals/people could live, food for the animals to eat, backdrops for these scenes, and pictures and photos of animals/people in their natural environments. When you are providing miniature people, remember to include diverse ethnic characteristics, ages, abilities and genders. If including animals, be mindful of what belongs where in terms of classification (zoo, farm, domestic, native, dinosaurs, etc.). Animals should be represented accurately in terms of size; for example the dog should be smaller than the sheep, the sheep should be smaller than the cow, the cow should be smaller than the horse and so on. You could also bring 'real life' materials such as hay, grass, pebbles and sand into the area to make it feel more authentic.

OVER TO YOU

How might you identify what themes could be integrated in to the small world area to reflect the children's interests? How could challenges be introduced in the small world area to encourage problem-solving skills?

Creative arts in the small world area

Dramatic arts

The small world area provides multiple opportunities for thematic socio-dramatic play. Tactile materials such as sand, clay, grass, etc. add a new dimension and can spark fresh play ideas. One of the adults' roles in the small world area is to closely observe the types of play that are being carried out and extend these themes through questions, books and stories. With children's and families' permission, take photos of the children while they are engaged in a dramatic play sequence, print the photos and make a story line that can be displayed in the small world area.

Movement and dance

In the small world area children's movement takes place in the actions of the figures and equipment they are manipulating. Look at the range of motions needed when moving these miniature figures:
- hunching, sitting or lying on the ground
- propping oneself up to support body weight
- holding a figure with one hand and manipulating its limbs with the other
- twisting one's wrists to makes the miniatures move
- lifting dolls' houses, garages, etc. using gross motor movements.

These types of action, along with thousands of others, combine to give the child the scope of movement they require to be able to dance with ease and fluidity. Looking at the thematic nature of the small world area, perhaps dance and movement could be included in this space. For example, think about the theme of the Jungle and how the animals in the jungle might dance. How would an elephant dance? Would they do anything distinctive with their trunk and tail? How about a giraffe? What would a giraffe's neck and long legs do when dancing? A hippopotamus would dance very differently, as would a lion! The possibilities are endless when promoting dance in the small world area. Try it for yourself: design a small world area and think about what types of dancing could happen depending on the theme that you choose.

Visual arts

The small world area is a fantastic space to use visual arts in a practical way. Making home-made backdrops that relate to the play theme demonstrates to young children that visual arts can be used for more than 'looking at'. As the theme changes, so too should the visual scene. This scene will ideally be made in partnership with the children in your care. Sit and plan with the children what could go into the backdrop. Use a variety of colours, textures (rough, bumpy, slick, scratchy, smooth, silky, soft, prickly, etc.) and media (collage, photographs, paint, drawing, etc.).

In addition to backdrops a 'playscape' can be used to add a three-dimensional aspect to the small world area. Use papier mâché, textiles, craft trays, linoleum, etc. to make amazing sculptures that enhance creative play in the small world area.

EXPLORING AND CREATING 105

OVER TO YOU

Create your own playscape using Theme 1: Space or Theme 2: Under the Sea.

- Theme 1: Space. Using a large cardboard backdrop, think about how you could incorporate some or all of the following elements using different visual artistic elements: the planets: Mercury, Venus, Earth, Mars, Jupiter, Saturn, Uranus, Neptune, Pluto; the sun; moons; stars; satellites; dark matter; astronauts; meteors.
- Theme 2: Under the Sea. You can use the following materials to create a 'beach' playscape: blue cotton/felt textile or large blue sheet or paper or plastic tray to hold water; PVA glue; natural sea shells and pasta shells; play sand or a large roll of sandpaper; pictures of fish (children's drawings or photos); small twigs and pebbles; seaweed; plastic miniatures of whales, dolphins, etc.; small plastic boats.

When the playscape is completed, think about how this activity could develop young children's visual arts skills. Think also about how the presence of this playscape in the small world area could impact on young children's play and imagination. Would there be any materials you would add or take away from the playscape?

Think about what materials you could use if you were to incorporate alternative themes in this space.

Musical arts

The small world area is a great place to observe children and gain an insight into their interests and imaginations. Griffiths (2012) suggests looking for 'provocations' where you can enhance learning that may have begun in the small world area but can then be extended elsewhere in the environment. During small world play, think of songs that reflect the type of play the child is engaging in. When reflecting with children about what they were playing with, introduce these songs. The adult in this role will ideally learn a number of songs in advance and be able to recall them in response to the child's creativity. When you are deciding on the theme of the small world area with the children, ensure that you have a variety of songs and music that can accompany this theme. Here are some suggestions:

- At the Circus: 'Nellie the Elephant', circus-type theme music
- On the Farm: 'Old McDonald', 'The Farmer in the Dell'
- Under the Sea: 'Once I Caught a Fish Alive', 'Slippery Fish'

> **OVER TO YOU**
>
> Looking at the different types of creative arts that can be explored in the small world area, how do you think the Aistear Themes of Wellbeing, Identity and Belonging, Exploring and Thinking, and Communication can be developed in this area? Think specifically of spatial awareness, gross motor movement, fine manipulative skills, and various forms of non-verbal communication that are offered in this space.

Discovery area

The discovery area can also be referred to as the science area, the nature table or the discovery centre. The aim is to bring a piece of the outside world into the indoor environment and open the young child's mind to view nature as a muse for their creativity. Think about Barnes's (1987) exploration of 'trees' and all of the creative arts ideas that can grow from this one natural concept:

- **Language activities:** stories, rhymes, questions and vocabulary, e.g. forest, wood, oak, pine, etc.
- **Outings:** to parks, forests, green areas, etc. and bringing home samples such as twigs and leaves.
- **Woodworking:** in the construction area – carving, etc.
- **Visual arts activities:** paintings, rubbings, collage, sculpture of trees, looking at the different shades of colours in bark and leaves.
- **Musical activities:** songs about trees, the sound of wind through leaves, etc.
- **Drama and movement activities:** swaying like branches, standing firm with roots in the ground.

The discovery area should have low shelves at the children's level so that they can touch, feel and experience the items included in it. It is important to ask children and families to find items for themselves and include them in the discovery area. This family partnership in the discovery area will empower children and encourage a sense of ownership of the area. Think about the following materials and what age groups they would be suitable for:
- flowers, moss and leaves (be mindful of allergies such as hay fever)

- seashells and rocks (small enough to hold but too large to pose a risk of choking)
- acorns and pine cones
- abandoned birds' nests and feathers
- fossils, bones, etc. (small enough to hold but too large to pose a risk of choking)
- wood, twigs, branches, driftwood.

A discovery area can also include living things such as a plant or even a classroom pet. Classroom animals can be a fantastic inspiration for creative play as children are drawn to their difference. You may have noticed that many early years environments include aquariums/fish bowls, snails, tadpoles, small birds, hamsters, etc.

If including a pet in the nature area the following points must be considered.

- What type of pet is acceptable under the Child Casre (Pre-School Services) (No. 2) Regulations (DoHC 2006a)?
- What are the views of parents/caregivers about having a pet in the setting?
- Do any of the children or adults suffer from any allergies?
- Are there other safety issues to consider?
- Do any of the children or adults have fears or phobias?
- Who will be responsible for the pet (feeding, finances, vet visits, hygiene, looking after during evenings/weekends/holiday breaks)?
- How will a discussion happen if the pet gets ill or dies?
- How can/will the animal be handled in a respectful way?
- What level of supervision is needed to keep the animal and children safe?

If it is unfeasible to have pets in the early years environment it is a good idea to put up a bird house or feeder that is visible from a window in the nature area to allow children to view animals in their natural state.

Aim also to provide materials such as nature and science books, posters, games and puzzles in the discovery area. Think about the following items and how they might provoke creativity in the young child:

- factual books/posters on animals, plants, birds, fish, the human body, seasons, weather, planets and the environment
- maps, a globe, atlas, real-life X-rays
- puzzles about nature or natural sequences, such as the life cycle of a frog, butterfly, chicken or plant, or about the human body
- smelling cans (filled with spices and herbs), feeling boxes with different natural textures.

> **OVER TO YOU**
>
> Set up a discovery area with a group of adults and spend some time exploring and playing with it. After you have finished experiencing the different objects on the table, engage in a creative arts activity. Reflect on how this exploration of nature has influenced your creativity and note your findings in your reflective journal.

Creative arts in the discovery area

Dramatic arts

Wilson (2012) encourages the early years educator to design the discovery area as a 'nature themed environment'. The following case study has used this idea to redesign the interest area:

> **CASE STUDY**
>
> Oisín (aged three years two months) comes into the preschool holding a photograph. The photograph shows Oisín and his dad building a sandcastle. Oisín's key worker (Michelle) sits with him and suggests putting the picture in the discovery area. As Oisín and Michelle go over to the area a second child, Fiona (two years eleven months), joins them. Michelle shows Fiona Oisín's photo. Fiona points at the messy play area before going over and retrieving a bucket. Michelle says, 'That's a great idea, Fiona, will we make the discovery area into a beach today? What else will we find in the room that could go on a beach?' Oisín walks to the book area and gets the book *Under the Sea* and Fiona goes to the messy play area and gets a spade. Michelle lays a large piece of plastic on the ground in the discovery area and pours sand on the plastic. Fiona, Oisín and Michelle continue to find items in the environment to make the discovery area into a 'beach'.

What type of dramatic play could happen when the discovery area becomes a beach? Think about Michelle's role as key worker; what did she do to introduce this dramatic element into the area?

Movement and dance

The discovery area aims to ignite the young child's curiosity. This area should provoke the questions: What is this for? How does it work? Where does it come from? How can it move and how does it stop? This inquisitiveness can be promoted through adult support and gentle prompting. Depending on the time of year, different materials can be included to induce different types of movement. Take for example a dandelion seed head, which becomes very prominent in summer. Think about the movement that occurs when the dandelion seed head is in contact with wind – hundreds of tiny white parachutes flutter and disperse into the air. How are children's creative instincts ignited when they are encouraged to embody this movement rather than simply observe the phenomenon?

Think about the following items that might be found in a discovery area and the movements that they make:
- feather
- earthworm
- cress seeds
- waves/water
- wind.

OVER TO YOU

Looking at the flora and fauna we see in spring, summer, winter and autumn, make a chart of all the different types of natural material that can be sourced at different times of the year and discuss how these materials 'move'.

Visual arts

In the discovery area it is a good idea to display bright images such as posters and vividly illustrated factual books on nature. These posters and books may be bought or home-made. Think about bringing a camera on nature walks and encouraging children to take pictures of items that they find interesting. Printing these pictures and displaying them in the discovery area can be a fantastic way to integrate the children's personal interests and creativity. Carry colouring materials and paper on nature walks, encouraging children to draw or sketch what they see and display these images in your discovery area too. Remember to pay particular attention to how visual art pieces are displayed in the interest area – children's work should be presented in a respectful and clear manner.

Think about having paper, pencils and crayons in the interest area so that children can draw any items that interest them. You can extend this further by providing sculpting material such as modelling clay or dough so that children can make 3D images of the natural materials they are viewing. Imagine the types of sculpture that can be created using natural materials such as twigs, stones, shells and leaves.

> **OVER TO YOU**
>
> Have a look at some Reggio Emilia-inspired nature tables on Google or Pinterest and think about how they incorporate nature as part of visual arts and stimulate creativity in young children.

Musical arts

Harris (2009) describes children as 'natural observers' and encourages the early years educator to use the discovery area as a place to promote musical development. Through observing and discussing the sounds and silences in nature one is asking the child to think about how noise is created using natural variations in tones and tempos.

In addition to this the adult and child can identify where nature is depicted in everyday songs. Ask children to reflect on what the composer was thinking and feeling when they wrote these pieces of music:

- 'Rupert and the Frog' (Paul McCartney)
- 'Baa Baa Black Sheep'
- 'Colours of the Wind' (from Disney's *Pocahontas*)
- 'Incey Wincey Spider'
- 'Under the Sea' (from Disney's *The Little Mermaid*)

> **OVER TO YOU**
>
> What other pieces of music can you think of that are inspired by nature? Do you think any sounds from nature could inspire the child to write their own songs?

Musical instruments can be made to enhance or recreate the sounds of nature, for example a rain stick or a wind chime. Try making nature-inspired instruments for yourself and think about how they could be used to promote process-based creative play. What other musical instruments could recreate sounds found in nature?

Music centre

Síolta Standard 2.6.3 (Environment) states that the 'sound and music area' should hold a wide variety of musical instruments that reflect the variety of cultures in the early years classroom as well as society as a whole. Ideally the music centre should have low open shelves to hold music materials, with a table and chairs as well as space to dance and move.

There are many philosophies that aim to 'teach' young children music, for example Eurhythmics, Education through Music, Kodaly, Kindermusik, Gordon's music learning theory and the Suzuki method. These methods share a common understanding that young children learn best through action. With this active learning approach in mind we can focus on early years music as a play activity rather than one that requires 'instruction'. Take a moment to reflect on the differences between music as a 'play activity' rather than an 'instructed activity'. Who generally has ownership in play verses instruction?

In Chapter 1, we identified that music in the early years consists of three main strands: listening and responding; performing; and composing (DES 1999). With these strands in mind we can identify types of material and equipment that can be accommodated in an early years music centre:

- **Musical instruments** (home-made and/or commercial):
    - bells
    - table piano/keyboard
    - triangles
    - xylophones
    - rhythm sticks
    - guitar
    - tambourines
    - drums
    - maracas
    - cymbals
- **Audio equipment:**
    - CD player, Mp3 player, radio/ digital music player
    - playable recordings of different types of music (e.g. folk, classical, popular children's songs, jazz, rock, reggae, rhythm and blues, music from various cultures and in various languages)
    - music from children's homes (ask families to supply a recording of favourite music played in the home)
    - headphones
    - song books, microphones and device to record own music
    - paper and pencils to 'compose' own music.

> **OVER TO YOU**
>
> Using the above list, discuss how the materials and equipment could be used when children are listening and responding, performing and composing. Think about these three strands: do you feel that any of them is sometimes neglected in the early years curriculum?
>
> On entering most early years settings you will notice that there is often music playing in the environment. Children are frequently invited to sing and play musical instruments. But how often are young children encouraged to write and record their own music? Discuss how doing this can help children's linguistic development with regard to vocabulary, rhyming words, memory and recall.

Creative arts in the music centre

Dramatic arts

Songs and other pieces of music enjoyed in the music centre can be used to inspire play scenes. Have a look at the following case study and think about how music was used to enrich the play experience.

> **CASE STUDY**
>
> Zachary (aged four years two months) is sitting on the floor beside the shelves in the music centre. He is shaking bells and singing 'The Wheels on the Bus'. Amy (three years five months) approaches and asks, 'What are you doing?' Zachary points to the instruments and says, 'The bus song'. Amy picks the maracas off the shelf, sits beside Zachary and starts to shake the maracas. Rebecca (key worker) approaches and joins in with a drum. When the song is finished Rebecca asks, 'Will we make a bus to sing our song on?' Zachary and Amy say 'Yes' and stand up. Rebecca, Zachary and Amy begin to gather chairs and place them in pairs in a row. Rebecca says, 'Who is the bus driver?' Zachary sits on the top chair and says 'I am'. Rebecca says to the rest of the group, 'Zach is driving the Wheels on the Bus today – does anybody want to come along?' Amy sits beside Zachary, Rebecca sits behind her, and two other children join in. Rebecca hands the additional children a box with musical instruments in it. Susan chooses castanets and Henry picks the triangle. The group sit on the chair 'bus' and sing 'The Wheels on the Bus' to the accompaniment of the musical instruments. Rebecca asks Zachary, 'Where is the bus going, driver?' Zachary responds, 'To the zoo'. Rebecca asks, 'Will we sing our zoo song?', and the children play their musical instruments and sing, 'We're Going to the Zoo'. When this song is finished Zachary says loudly, 'We're going to a farm, Old McDonald.'

In this case study we can see how the music activity can be extended through the use of dramatic props and play scenes. Think of the following songs and how they could be extended through dramatic arts activities:
- 'I'm a Little Teapot'
- 'My Bonnie Lies Over the Ocean'
- 'The Teddy Bears' Picnic'
- 'How much is that Doggie in the Window?'

Music and stories are an integral part of an individual's culture and heritage and can be used in the early years environment in a fun and interactive manner. Asking families what music is played in their homes and in the homes of extended family members such as grandparents, aunts, uncles and cousins provides an opportunity to integrate music into children's socio-dramatic play as well.

Music also offers a way of exploring one's emotions in a safe and secure environment. Think of the following examples of emotive music and discuss how engaging with this type of music can give the listener an insight into their emotional fields. (Note: since music is subjective, you may have a different emotional reaction to the pieces of music below.)
- Anger: 'Hound Dog' (Elvis Presley: rock and roll)
- Fear: Requiem (Verdi: classical music)
- Loneliness: 'Five Little Ducks went Swimming One Day' (traditional children's song)
- Happiness: 'Better Git It in Your Soul' (Charles Mingus: jazz)
- Sadness: 'It's My Party' (Lesley Gore: rhythm and blues)
- Surprise: 'It's Oh So Quiet' (Björk: pop)
- Love: 'Me and You' (Barry Louis Polisar: contemporary children's song)
- Curious: 'I'll Tell Me Ma' (traditional Irish folk song)

OVER TO YOU

Put together a compilation of music from some or all of the following genres: folk, classical, popular children's songs, jazz, rock, reggae, rhythm and blues; and match them to these classic children's stories, taking into consideration the emotions and tones in the stories. (Note: if using contemporary music, ensure that the editions used with children are 'child friendly'/radio edits.)
- **The Three Little Pigs**
- **Cinderella**
- **Little Red Riding Hood**
- **Goldilocks and the Three Bears**

Movement and dance

The music centre lends itself to dancing and movement as bodies naturally move to the rhythm and beats of music. Provide dancing aids such as scarves, streamers, hula hoops and ribbons. Encourage dance by modelling movement with the children and ensure that there is enough space for children to move safely. Musical instruments can also be used to provoke dance. The 'Mozart and the Young Mind' programme promoted by Harris (2009) discusses how playing musical instruments can be viewed as an extension of body movements. Think about what happens when a person plays the tambourine, for example. You hold the tambourine in one hand and shake it so that the zils make the distinctive jingle. The second hand then adds another layer to the sound with a rhythmic thump. These actions generally happen in a fluid motion, without conscious thought or inhibition.

The human body can be used as its own musical instrument. By clapping, finger snapping, stamping, pounding, whistling, singing, clicking and thumping we can make fantastic noises just by utilising our body movements. Try it for yourself; explore from your head to your toes what types of movement sounds the human body can make. Younger children and babies with limited movement can sit on their key worker's knee, or be held in their arms, swaying to the rhythm of music, experiencing the body movements of the adult.

In the early years environment it is useful to include songs that actively promote movement. Think of the following songs and explore for yourself what types of movement and dance they inspire:
- 'Teddy Bear, Teddy Bear'
- 'Ring a Ring a Rosie'
- 'Incey Wincey Spider'
- 'If You're Happy and You Know it'

Visual arts

The music centre is a great space to display pictures of musical instruments in a variety of different styles. Degas' 'Dancer with Tambourine', Herpfer's 'Family Concert' or some of Braque's cubist takes on musical instruments can be a welcome addition to this space. Take photos of children interacting in the music centre and position these pictures beside the children's favourite singers and bands. Displaying the children's images with those of people they admire sends a strong message that they can be as musically creative as their favourite stars!

In addition to this it can be useful to display sheet music to introduce the concept of musical literacy. Position the sheet music at children's level, with images of the words placed above the musical notes. Combine this sheet music with music that children have 'composed' themselves. Think about the following case study and discuss how you think Thomas's music could be displayed.

> **CASE STUDY**
>
> Before lunch Áine (key worker) is sitting with four children. She turns to Thomas (three years and ten months) and asks him, 'Where did you play today, Thomas?' Thomas points to the music centre and says, 'I sang a song.' Áine replies, 'A song? Can you sing it for me?' Thomas sings 'la, la, la'. Áine claps and says, 'That sounds like a beautiful song. Can you sing it again?' Thomas sings 'la, la, la'. Áine responds, 'Beautiful! Does your song have a name yet?' Thomas replies 'No.' Áine says, 'It really is a lovely song; I don't want us to forget it. Will we write it down so we don't forget it?' Thomas says 'Yes.' Áine and Thomas go to the music centre and pick up some blank music paper and a pencil. They return to the lunch table and Thomas puts a line on the page and says 'la' followed by a second line 'la' and a third line 'la'.

Musical arts

Children are born with a musical ear; from a very young age they can distinguish different voices, tones and tempos. It makes sense, therefore, to use this innate interest to facilitate learning in the early years. Singing is a great way to get children actively involved in the music they are listening to. Encourage singing through modelling singing in the environment and through positive encouragement (smiling, clapping along and focused praise). Respond to children's musical interests by extending their activities using song. Children learn to recreate music best through listening, repeating and doing. The adults' role is to introduce a limited number of songs into the environment and as children get to know and sing along with these songs, only then begin to introduce additional music. Too many new songs at one time could confuse the learning. The adult should know the words of any songs they bring into the curriculum and how to mirror the music dramatically through movement and gestures.

The adult has an additional role in the music centre – to introduce musical vocabulary into the young child's world. Harris (2009) identifies a number of creative concepts that can be discussed through musical play:

- **beat:** beat vs. rhythm (a beat is a consistent pulse that runs throughout a piece of music; rhythm is the difference between the duration of notes)
- **tempo:** fast vs. slow, simple vs. duple (referring to how many beats in a bar)
- **dynamics:** loud vs. soft

- **rhythm:** rhythm vs. beat
- **pitch:** high vs. low
- **harmony:** monophonic singing ('one sound' singing, e.g. the song 'Happy Birthday'), ostinato singing (a musical phrase repeated over and over, e.g. ABBA's 'Take a Chance on Me')
- **form:** phrase, phrase and mapping (grouping consecutive notes, e.g. in the 'Alphabet Song')
- **timbre:** voice, body percussion, pitched percussion, orchestral families
- **expressive elements:** staccato (detached notes), legato (no definition between notes).

OVER TO YOU

Looking at the different types of creative arts that can be explored in the music centre, how do you think the Aistear Themes of Wellbeing, Identity and Belonging, Exploring and Thinking, and Communication can be developed in this area? Think specifically of spatial awareness, gross motor movement, fine manipulative skills, and various forms of non-verbal communication that are offered in this area.

Chapter summary

This chapter explored the music centre, the small world area, the discovery area, the table-top area, the arts and crafts centre, the messy play area, the book corner, the construction area, the writing centre and the home corner. We explored the how these spaces can be used to develop creative play and children's imaginations. Looking at the types of equipment and different materials in these designated areas we identified different creative arts experiences that could be uncovered in the early years environment: dramatic arts; movement and dance; visual arts; and musical arts.

OVER TO YOU

Choose an age group (birth to one year, one to two, two to three, three to four or four to six) and design a creative 'curriculum' for one day that incorporates all the different interest areas in an early years environment. Think about what resources would be needed for both planned and spontaneous creative play in these areas. Think about how you might assess what types of creative learning occurred during play.

Exploring and Creating: The Outdoor Play Space

This chapter explores aspects of the following Learning Outcomes:
- LO 1: Examine a variety of creative media opportunities with young children.
- LO 2: Summarise the benefits of exploration and participation in creative arts for the child.
- LO 3: Explore the role of the adult in creating an environment in which children feel secure and confident enough to take risks and explore new situations.
- LO 4: Plan opportunities for consultation with children to plan and engage in creative arts experiences.
- LO 5: Test open-ended materials and natural items for creative arts, in both the indoor and outdoor environments, appropriate to different stages of children's development.
- LO 6: Explore challenges for adults in respecting choices and decisions of children.
- LO 7: Employ developmentally appropriate creative arts activities which promote the holistic development of the child.
- LO 8: Reflect on one's own role and responsibilities when engaging in creative arts activities with children, being mindful of health and safety.

In Chapter 5 we discovered different ways of incorporating the creative arts curriculum into the early years indoor environment. This chapter focuses on bringing creativity outside and using the 'unroofed classroom' as a medium to explore creative arts, looking specifically at the benefits for young children of bringing creative play outside. We will discuss these benefits, identify outdoor play interest areas and use the Aistear framework to inspire creative play ideas.

Research commissioned by the Irish Heritage Council in 2011 found that the amount of time children spend playing outdoors has fallen in recent years, partially due to the ever-increasing role that television and video games appear to play in many young lives, and to families' concerns over supervision. These findings increase our responsibility as early years professionals to plan for daily outside play, regardless of the cold and the rain. Alana Kirk Gillham wrote an interesting article in the *Irish Times Health Supplement* (Gillham 2011) entitled 'Let those angels get dirty faces', which highlighted that Ireland holds two significant records in Europe: we have one of the highest birth rates; and we are also one of the highest (or heaviest) countries for obesity rates. The sedentary lifestyle that many Irish children are experiencing impacts not only on their physical and mental health but also on their creativity. As technology progresses and virtual play becomes an ever-increasing reality in children's lives it can take away the need for original thought and spontaneity in one's behaviours.

> **OVER TO YOU**
>
> Discuss what would be the difference between online games such as 'Farmville' which is popular among young children and experiencing play on a real life farm?

Margaret McMillan said, 'The best classroom and the richest cupboard are roofed only by the sky.' As early years educators we have many roles in the lives of young children, and one of these roles is to promote outdoor play by planning fun and creatively stimulating activities. We can expand on the learning opportunities from the inside environment out to our outside space. The Child Care (Pre-School Services) (No. 2) Regulations (DoHC 2006a: Section V) state that children should have access to adequate outdoor play facilities 'weather permitting'. Using these guidelines and the precept that 'there's no such thing as bad weather – just the wrong clothing' we can plan for outside play that is enriching and beneficial to a child's overall growth and development.

> **OVER TO YOU: GROUP TASK**
>
> Research our European neighbours, specifically Denmark and Sweden, and their use of the 'Forest School' philosophy. Discuss this type of early years education and how the outside play space is viewed. Include in this discussion a comparative view on Irish early education culture and how we use the outdoor environment.

For a child the outdoor play area is a place for physical and emotional release. It forms such an important part of a child's life that it warrants the same degree of thought and design as the indoor play areas. A well-thought-out playground will ensure that

children's physical and social needs are supported and that they have an opportunity to experience fresh air and explore different ways to play. *The We like This Place* document (DoHC 2005) highlights the outdoor space as being especially important for young children's development and as providing great opportunities for:
- jumping and climbing
- playing with water and mud
- collecting 'outdoor' objects, such as pebbles, sticks, etc.
- hiding and making camps
- rolling down slopes and stepping on stones or lines
- pushing and pulling vehicles
- growing things and harvesting them
- observing flora and fauna
- watching wildlife, sky and the effect of ever-changing weather on the landscape.

Looking at this list, think about the different types of play a child experiences and reflect on how an outside play space can encourage the following types of play:
- exploratory/practice play
- construction play
- socio-dramatic/pretend play
- game and activity play
- sports and recreational play
- media play (producing arts and crafts)
- academic play (books, technological equipment/smart equipment).

Planning for the creative arts in the outside space

Outside play provides space and freedom for children to engage in spontaneous activities. These elements specifically encourage physical development, the use of one's imagination, the opportunity to use one's initiative, and provide opportunities for an individual to express their creativity. Educational pioneers such as Rousseau, Pestalozzi, Froebel, Smith Hill and the McMillian sisters, to name a few, highlight the need for outdoor play in early education. Best practice would advise that each child spends a portion of their day outside engaged in both structured and unstructured play.

When planning play outdoors, consider the following points:
1. **Sunlight:** Outside areas should be designed to receive the maximum amount of sunlight. Areas which are south facing receive the most sunlight. Be mindful in

the outdoor space about which areas are exposed to direct or indirect sunlight. Think about creating shade through the use of trees, awnings, parasols, etc. It is important to remember sun safety when playing outside. Sensitive skins can get sunburnt even on an overcast day. Think about sun hats, sunglasses, sun cream and proper hydration when playing on warm days. These safety considerations need to be applied to any adults who are outside as well as children.

2. **Wind:** If wind is very severe it can affect children's play. Is the outside area sheltered so that children can play with the wind rather than against it?
3. **Rain:** Ireland is renowned for its beautiful green pastures and to maintain this Emerald Isle we need rain! Ensure that appropriate clothing is available to children and adults on rainy days. Raincoats, rain hats, wellington boots, umbrellas, overalls, etc. are great additions to an early years facility. Playing in the rain is a fantastic learning opportunity and great fun!
4. **Ice and snow:** We have had an increase in snowfall in Ireland in the last few years, but comparatively speaking we still experience relatively few 'snow' days. On days where there is snow, ensure that you are prepared by providing lovely warm clothing – hats, scarves, gloves, coats, etc. – and get outside to enjoy it! It is such a delight to watch little faces light up as they play in snow, discovering new ways to move and imagine in a white landscape!

Outdoor play is essential for all age groups in early childhood, including infants and toddlers. When planning outdoor environments for 'pre walkers', include in your design areas for lying, sitting, crawling and unsteady walking.

Outdoor play time is as successful as the planning that goes into it! The design of the outside space should incorporate the concepts of free exploration as well as maintaining a high level of child supervision. It is essential to plan outdoor activities, just as with indoor play.

These are some of the duties of the early years educator when planning for high-quality outdoor play:

- **Develop an outdoor play policy:** An outdoor play policy is a written document which details an early years service's philosophy on outdoor play. This document describes, in detail, how one aims to implement outdoor play in the service, how one aims to record the provision of outdoor play and how one assesses the success of the outdoor play space in the service. This policy can be referred to as a 'working document' as it changes with the development of the practice in the service.
- **Plan for individualised outdoor learning** in the short, medium and long term. These personal learning plans incorporate outdoor play as an integral part of

children's development rather than seeing the outside space as 'break time', 'free play time' or a 'transition area'.
- **Ensure that there is a friendly, relaxed atmosphere** in the outside space. In this space children are encouraged to play in a way that respects individual choice. The adult in the outside space should take on the role of playmate, supporter and cheerleader.
- **Assessment** should happen in the outside play space in the same manner that it occurs in the inside play space. A continuity of practice should flow between inside and outside assessments.
- The early years practitioner needs to be committed to a high quality of education and care through maintaining **adequate child/staff ratios** as well as all other aspects of the Child Care (Pre-School Services) (No. 2) Regulations (DoHC 2006a).

OVER TO YOU

The following sections in this chapter outline different types of outdoor play which promote creativity in young children. Before we continue, reflect for a moment on outdoor play practice you may have observed in an early years setting. Think about these questions as signposts for reflection:

- How long do children in the service spend outdoors?
- Do children of all different age groups get time outdoors every day?
- What extra resources are available in a service specifically for outdoor use?
- What types of play opportunities are offered in the outdoor space?
- How are 'outdoor' times decided? Who decides it is time for outdoor play?
- Where can you find the access point to the outdoor environment? Is there a route to the outdoor area directly from the indoor environment?
- What is the adult's role during outdoor play?
- What type of activities occur outdoors – planned, spontaneous, a mix of both?
- How is children's learning assessed in the outdoor space?
- Rate your own quality as an outdoor play facilitator on a scale from 0 to 10, with 10 being the highest score. How can you improve your own outdoor play practice?

Outdoor interest areas

The outside area should have designated areas of interest, much like the indoor environment. In Chapter 5 we looked at the music centre, the small world area, the discovery area, the table-top area, the arts and crafts centre, the messy play area, the book corner, the construction area, the writing centre and the home corner in the indoor environment. The outdoor environment should reflect many of these areas. We will now look at specific outdoor interest areas and discuss how to promote the creative arts curriculum when playing outside.

Music and movement area

The music and movement area is generally the largest space in the outside play area. In a high-quality music and movement area there will be designated areas for wheeled toys, with markings indicating roundabouts, crossings and one-way arrows. This space will also accommodate large apparatus such as swing sets, slides, climbing frames, tunnels, etc. This degree of space and freedom lends itself well to expression with musical instruments. These activities, when undertaken indoors, generally need to be somewhat constrained due to space restrictions or the need to keep the noise level controlled; outside, however, the sky is literally the limit! It is helpful to identify an area within this space in which to accentuate environmental sounds, for example by including wind chimes, whistles, etc. On stormy days the noise from the chimes can create a very dramatic backdrop. Think about including instruments such as outdoor metal drums, xylophones and mounted bells in the music and movement area. How do you think children might be creatively different in an outside space with musical instruments in comparison to an inside space?

Creative arts and Aistear in the outdoor movement and music area

Wellbeing

One of the fundamental elements of the Aistear Theme of Wellbeing looks specifically at physical play to promote healthy exercise habits in young children. Outdoor physical play can provide opportunities for climbing, running, jumping, walking, rolling, sitting down, balancing, hanging, sliding, pulling, catching, hopping, throwing, bending, kicking, skipping and sitting up. If we break down basic body movements we can identify that there are ten main components involved:

1. **Space and direction:** the position of one's body in relation to one's surroundings.
2. **Balance:** controlling our body movements by transfer of weight.
3. **Rhythm:** developing movement flows and co-ordination to a beat, sound or pulse.
4. **Fine muscle development:** particularly in the fingers and toes.

5. **Large muscle development:** particularly around the pelvic and shoulder areas, arms and legs.
6. **Basic body movement:** moving skilfully and freely.
7. **Symmetrical activity:** the ability to co-ordinate right and left side and to develop movement in both sides.
8. **Hand–eye co-ordination:** linking movement between hands, eyes and arms, all working in unison.
9. **Eye–foot co-ordination:** linking movement between eyes, legs and feet, all working in unison.
10. **Manipulative development:** muscle development in hands to complete dexterous tasks.

OVER TO YOU

The outdoor play space is a fantastic area to develop the movements described above. Think about the following planned activities. How could they be implemented in a manner that promotes child-centred play and allows children to express themselves creatively?

- obstacle course
- outdoor yoga
- children's zumba
- flying kites

The second element of the Wellbeing Theme looks at children's psychological wellbeing. How do you think the above activities can promote young children's emotional health? (We will discuss this topic in detail in Chapter 7.)

Exploring and Thinking

The outdoor music and movement area is a perfect space for children to discover and reflect on how their body moves. Herr (2000) explains that movement is an important non-verbal tool for children to express themselves creatively. Children's movements reflect their age and stage of development. It is an exciting and surprising time for young children; as they develop and grow their body changes and moves in different ways. Activities that challenge children to try new movements are great in an outdoor space. Remember when introducing new learning opportunities to do so using a 'small step' approach. It is positive to challenge children, but if the task is too difficult they can become uninterested and even distressed. Reflect on Vygotsky's 'zone of proximal development' theory when planning for new learning.

> **OVER TO YOU**
>
> Read the case study below and think about what exploring and thinking opportunities Casey gained through this outdoor scene. Use the Exploring and Thinking aims and learning goals from Aistear as reflection points. Also consider:
> - In what way was this activity creative?
> - How was Casey supported to be creative?
> - How was this spontaneous activity child-centred?
> - How can learning be assessed from this activity?
> - How could Casey's learning be extended from this activity?

> **CASE STUDY**
>
> Casey (aged 13 months) is walking along the perimeter of the outdoor play area, grasping the fence with one hand as she walks. As she comes to the gate she places both hands flat on the gate and walks against the gate. Casey has now reached the window sill of the playroom. She bends down, places one hand against the window and walks along the window sill. As Casey approaches the end of the window sill she stops and looks at the fence. There is a space between where the window sill ends and where the fence begins. Casey is about to get on her hands and knees and crawl over to the fence when her key worker (Olive) stands at Casey's side and says in an enthusiastic tone 'You are walking, Casey! Yeah! Take a step to the fence.' Olive holds out her hand and Casey looks at her and smiles. Olive's hand is just out of Casey's reach. Casey, still at the window sill, takes both of her hands away from the support, reaches for Olive and takes an unsupported step.

Communication

The outside music and movement area is a great space for children to develop their verbal and non-verbal communication skills. Think about the types of message that are communicated if a child makes the following movements:
- standing with their arms folded, head down, pursed lips
- jumping up and down, waving arms, smiling mouth
- sitting on a tricycle and pushing the person in front of them.

Although no words are spoken, non-verbal communication is very effective in transmitting one's views! The music and movement area is a busy space, full with active movements. This level of activity lends itself well to non-verbal commands as

individuals are moving quickly and may not hear oral instruction when in a play frame. Think about encouraging the development of non-verbal understanding by introducing some of the following materials and activities into the music and movement area:
- traffic lights: red for stop, green for go, orange to slow down
- sounds to indicate transitions, e.g. a bell/alarm as a five-minute warning to finish the game and a second bell/alarm to indicate tidy-up time
- visual signposts in the outside play space to indicate different interest areas.

OVER TO YOU

Think of different materials, games and activities that you can introduce into the outside play space to promote non-verbal language skills.

Identity and Belonging

Children thrive in an environment where they feel included, loved and respected. The music and movement area can promote these feelings in some very simple but effective ways. We shall now look at four strategies to promote Identity and Belonging.

1 **Encouragement:** The music and movement area is a space in which a child takes many risks: both physical – the risk of falling and hurting themselves – and also emotional – they might try and fail. It is important that in this large space that there is a high level of supervision and support for a child who has fallen – physically or emotionally – to help them get back up again. In this space you will observe many successful feats. Some will be tiny achievements; others will be major milestones; but each one is important to the individual accomplishing it.

OVER TO YOU

Think about the following types of praise, discuss the importance of each and note how they can be developed in the music and movement area:
- adult to child praise
- adult to adult praise
- child to child praise
- self-praise.

2 **Ownership:** An important aspect of identity and belonging is feeling that you are welcome in the space you are in. This is especially relevant in the music and movement area as it is generally a large space and children can feel 'lost' in it. Invite children to use equipment through modelling actions and giving them support until they feel comfortable in the space. Remember to use each child's name when speaking with

them. This simple act reassures the child that your attention is focused on them. Think about including items in the music and movement area that have special significance for each child; perhaps a special colour, a piece of equipment they like, such as a bike or swing, or even a specific themed toy such as a dinosaur, dog, fish, etc. A child can also feel ownership in an area when they are given the opportunity for free choice in play. Ensure that there are enough materials and equipment in the music and movement area for all children in the space.

3 **Positive messages:** The music and movement area is a brilliant space to develop one's physical movements. This space also highlights differences in individuals' physical abilities. From a very early age children begin to compare their own accomplishments with those of their peers. We see these comparisons occurring as early as the parallel stage of play, when children begin to copy each other's movements. The adult has an important duty to send positive messages about differences and to reinforce messages about children's strengths rather than focusing on what a child 'can't' do. When sending positive messages about the 'cans' you are using a 'strengths-based approach' rather than a 'deficit-based approach'.

4 **Peer relationships:** As we mentioned previously the music and movement area is a large and busy place. It is important to observe who the children are playing with. Do they have friends? Are they interacting with peers in a way that indicates that there is equality in the relationships? Are they being told what to do by a dominant play partner? Can you see sharing happening? Is the child continually playing alone? When children reach the co-operative/collaborative stage of play development it is especially important to watch for relational patterns in play. The adult's role here is to model positive interactions, to intervene if negative patterns are emerging and to put in place activities which promote friendship and empathy in the large movement areas. Positive relationships can be fostered early in a child's development. Including equipment in the movement area such as tunnels and hiding spots where young children can play 'peek-a-boo' games fosters the idea that interacting with others is fun and exciting!

The discovery area/gardening centre

When thinking of an outside space one of the first things that comes to mind is nature – plants, grass, trees and wildlife. It is a good idea to include these features into an early years outdoor environment. If the outside space is made from an artificial material and cannot facilitate digging and sowing, add planting pots, troughs, trellises, a greenhouse and growbags, for example. Adding this type of equipment to the discovery area allows children the opportunity to test out their green fingers.

Creative arts and Aistear in the outdoor discovery/garden area

Wellbeing

The garden area can be a great starting point for introducing the concept of healthy eating to young children. Growing vegetables, herbs and fruit in the garden can get children actively involved in their own nutrition. The Teagasc *Guide to Growing Vegetables* (Alexander 2013) advises that vegetables can be grown on most soils as long as they are well drained. The growing space should be open and receive sunlight but be sheltered from the elements. Growing edible materials provides children with a fantastic sense of achievement and develops muscles through movement and activity. Giving children a choice of what they grow, how they choose to plant their vegetables and how they use them in cooking offers a creative insight into gardening activities. Think about the experience of growing herbs such as basil, lavender and mint. These different sights, smells, tastes and touches are a great way to stimulate children's senses!

Exploring and Thinking

The garden/discovery area injects scientific and mathematical concepts into children's play. In the garden/discovery area you may notice the following activities.

- Objects, equipment and resources are sorted and categorised.
- Number skills are developed through real-life experiences such as counting seeds, handing out planting equipment, identifying numbers on measuring jugs, etc.
- Patterns, shapes and colours are created and explored using natural materials such as flower petals, leaves, pebbles and rocks.
- Objects are matched according to similarities: 'The cloud looks like ...', 'The bird sounds like ...', 'The flower smells like ...', etc.
- Size, length, capacity and weight are compared in an active manner. One example of this is comparing two different flowers: 'The sunflower has bigger petals than the daisy.'
- Discussions occur about the passing of time during the day, months and seasons.
- Spatial awareness is explored through different types of body movement.
- Positional and directional words are used, e.g. in, out, forwards, backwards, in front of, behind, above and below.
- Mathematical language (e.g. heavy, light, full, empty, long, short) is used.

> **OVER TO YOU**
>
> Think about spontaneous play activities in the garden/discovery area for children of different age groups. Discuss how their exploring and thinking skills, dispositions and interests can be developed in this space. Use the Aistear Exploring and Thinking learning goals as a guide.

Communication

The garden and discovery area brings a variety of language into the world of young children. In the section above we looked at some scientific and mathematic concepts. The garden/discovery area also offers possibilities for communicating about empathy and social awareness. Tending to plants and growing vegetables, etc. opens opportunities for discussions around feelings, which expands children's emotional literacy skills. Looking after plants and animals gives children a sense of responsibility over their environment as well as offering the opportunity to care for it and to see situations from different perspectives. Including items such as a wormery, feeding tables for birds, nest boxes, a fish pond (covered), as well as simply observing the movement of insects and spiders, gives children the opportunity to feel compassion and warmth towards fellow creatures.

Identity and Belonging

Wilson (2012) discusses a theory that when children are actively introduced to nature at a young age they are predisposed to a number of positive life skills, including environmental awareness and a positive attitude towards community involvement. White supports this view, adding that when young children engage with nature they 'become aware of their community and locality, thus developing a sense of connection to the physical natural and human world' (2011:68).

> **OVER TO YOU**
>
> Think about the following example of creative activities in the garden area and discuss how they promote environmental awareness and develop one's connection in their community.
>
> - Name of activity: Planting
> - Age group: Children aged two years six months and above.
> - Resources needed: Packets of different flower seeds, individual planters, compost, colouring pencils, paper labels, shallow water trays
> - Outline of activity:
>   - Introduce the activity, explaining to the children they can each pick three seeds from the different packs.

- Children are encouraged to fill the flowerpots/planters with compost.
- Children are encouraged to water the compost.
- Adult places seeds, one at a time, into her/his own planter; children are supported to model this action with their individual planters.
- Adult takes out colours and pencils and begins to draw what they imagine their flowers will look like; children are asked if they would like to do the same.
- Adult goes to each child and writes the child's name on their own planter.
- Children are asked to place their pot on a large tray.
- Adult tells children that flowers 'eat' sunlight and wonders with the group which part of the garden gets the most sun – this is where we will place the flower pots.
- When flowers bloom, children and adults think about the difference the colours from the flowers have made to the garden.

Table-top area

This area can be used for a variety of purposes: for circle time, to rest, for meals and snacks, and for children to engage in puzzles that need concentration, such as shape sorters, bead frames, etc. Including resources such as safety scissors in the table-top area is a great way to give children opportunities to cut natural materials such as grass, leaves and flowers for floristry displays.

Outdoor furniture should ideally be made from natural materials such as wood and can include traditional tables and chairs, benches and stools, etc.

Much like the indoor space, the outdoor table-top area is not limited to tables! This space can also be used for activities such as baseball, hurling, cricket, bowling and games with different-sized balls.

OVER TO YOU

Make a list of the different types of material you think could be useful in an outside table-top area.

Creative arts and Aistear in the table-top area

Wellbeing

One feature of the theme of Wellbeing identifies how young children interact with others. Síolta Standard 5: Interactions also highlights developing strong relationships as key to a person's health. Outside play is a great opportunity for planned pair and small group activities as well as spontaneous child-led activities which promote young children's decision-making skills and independence. Look at the following interaction between Emily (three years two months) and Dermot (three years eight months) in the outdoor table-top area and discuss how individual well-being is enhanced in this scene.

CASE STUDY

Emily and Dermot are sitting on a bench in the outdoor table-top area and are individually playing with clear plastic screw-top jars filled with acorns, large stones, pine cones, leaves and twigs. Emily has started to separate her items into different piles according to type. Dermot is feeling the natural items in the jar and laying them on the table.

Emily: I only have stick, I need one.

Emily attempts to reach and pick up the stick that Dermot is holding.

Dermot: This one is mine Emily, you have one.

Emily: I need another one, like stick men.

Dermot: You can have it when it's finished.

Emily looks at Dermot and picks up a pine cone.

Emily: Do you want to swap?

Dermot looks at the pine cone and shakes his head.

Dermot: When I'm finished.

Emily picks up a large stone and places it in front of Dermot. She also puts the pine cone in front of Dermot.

Emily: Here you go, you're finished?

Dermot smiles at Emily and hands her the stick.

Dermot: Finished.

Emily picks up the two sticks, one in each hand, and begins to project voices on them pretending they are characters from the book *The Stickman* (Julia Donaldson). Dermot looks at Emily, walks over to the garden area and picks up a twig. He sits back beside Emily, holding the twig in his hand, pretending it is also a 'stick man'.

Dermot: Can I come too?

- We can see that at the beginning of this case study the children had a minor conflict over materials. How did Emily and Dermot resolve this conflict? Reflect on Síolta component 5.1 in relation to the above case study.
- We can also see that the table-top materials in the case study were open-ended and reflected the natural surroundings. Discuss how this spontaneous activity promoted creativity in play.
- The latter part of the case study evolves as the activity extended naturally into a creative role play activity. Think about the early years educator's role when supporting children's outdoor table-top play.

Exploring and Thinking

In the case study above, Emily and Dermot were exploring jars filled with naturally sourced materials. The outdoor table-top area is a fantastic space for heuristic and sensorial play. A treasure box filled with natural materials is a great addition to this space. This simple yet sophisticated activity (Gascoyne 2012), devised by Elinor Goldschmied, is enhanced when the materials the children are seeing, listening to, touching, feeling and tasting belong in the outside space. Although treasure baskets were initially envisioned for play with babies, they can be adapted for use with older age groups also.

OVER TO YOU

Devise a list of natural outdoor items that one could put in a treasure basket. Think about including a lot of variety in terms of sight, smell, touch, taste and sound. Remember, the aim of the treasure basket is to spark children's imaginations through active engagement with the materials.

The following list provides suggestions of how the outdoor treasure basket can be adapted to enhance young children's play as they grow.
- **0–1 years:** Classic treasure basket for sensorial play.
- **1–2 years:** Treasure basket focuses on heuristic play for exploration and functional play: 'What does this do?'
- **2–3 years:** Treasure basket includes items that can be sorted and categorised as children become interested in where items belong. Include containers to categorise by type, size, smell, colour, etc.
- **3–4 years:** Treasure basket play can develop into role play situations. Think about including items such as story books with links to items in the basket, as well as foodstuffs which can be used in socio-dramatic play. You might even include a

treasure map in the basket (fantasy play) which leads children to find the places in the garden where the materials in the basket were sourced!

- **4–6 years:** As the play becomes more focused on games with rules, include this interest in the treasure basket. One game could be for the children to find materials for their own baskets. Provide a 'shopping list' with pictures of natural materials on a piece of paper. Have this list and an empty basket in the outside area and let children source their own materials. You can extend this by encouraging the child to choose what they want on the list or encouraging them to design their own list.

OVER TO YOU

Looking at the above variations in treasure basket play, think about how these different variations on the original activity might enhance a child's creative development.

Communication

The table-top area is great place to have meals and snacks. Communication during sharing food is a fantastic way to hold natural conversations with young children. This social activity promotes a relaxed atmosphere and the novelty of an outdoor meal brings with it the 'picnic' feeling. When sharing a meal with young children the adult must always remember that they set the tone for the mealtime behaviour. The process of preparing the table is an important time. Children should be involved in carrying out responsibilities such as laying the tablecloth, handing out cutlery and utensils, giving out napkins and even 'reading' the menu! This period of transforming the table-top area for mealtime prepares children for the transition between movement in play and sitting during a meal.

The table should be aesthetically appealing to young children and should encourage them to want to sit at it. Imagine if you went to a restaurant that had a dirty, ill-prepared table – you would walk out! It is important to give young children's meals the same level of respect that you would find in a high-class restaurant. The adult/key worker should sit and eat at the table with the children. When the adult shares a meal with children they model how to eat and how to use utensils such as plates, bowls and cutlery. The adult also has an important role in leading conversations at the meal table and supporting children to hold their own 'chats'. There are so many topics of discussion during meals: the taste of the food; how it was prepared; where the meat, vegetables, fruit came from; the colour of the food; how to share it; what to drink – the possibilities for group conversations are endless!

Encourage children to serve themselves from a shared central platter of food and focus on positive eating behaviours. If children choose not to eat the meal, encourage them gently though positive reinforcement techniques. Never force a child to try a food they don't want to. When the meal is finished encourage children to help tidy up by giving them small, easily achieved tasks to complete. This shared tidy-up aids 'community development' within the group.

> **OVER TO YOU**
>
> Observe a mealtime with young children and record the conversation flow during the meal. Reflect on this conversation and think about how children's communication skills were facilitated during the activity. Was creativity fostered during this time? How could conversations be extended to aid with planning for the creative arts curriculum in the outdoor environment?

Identity and Belonging

The outdoor table-top space comes with many challenges for young children. Dexterity skills, sharing space and materials, concentrating with so much activity around them; it can be a daunting environment. The adult has a very important role in sending positive messages to the child about who they are and the contributions the child makes to the space.

A fantastic way to show young children that you respect and value their views is to include them in the design of the outdoor table-top space. Ask young children what materials they would like in the space. Where in the outdoor area do they think the table-top equipment should be housed? Ask them to imagine what types of play should happen at the table-top area. In Chapter 4 we mentioned at using the Clarke and Moss (2001) 'mosaic approach' when finding out young children's views, and this approach can also be used when designing or changing the outdoor table-top area. Children can describe their ideal outdoor table-top area using speech, drawings, paintings, collage, construction, sculpture or any other means of communicating their views. This method of communicating promotes Síolta Standard 4: Consultation and shows children in a real way that they belong to and are a part of the early years service they attend.

The arts and crafts centre

Visual art opportunities in the outside area are enhanced by the natural surroundings. The changing colours in the sky, the dramatic nature of clouds, the ever-evolving flora and fauna all inspire children's art in a very unique way. The additional freedom when outside promotes creativity, allowing children extra space to breathe and develop their artistic talents. The outside art area can include experiences for children to explore a variety of materials and to work at either a vertical or horizontal level. Imagine the following outdoor art activities and think about the sense of freedom, flexibility and fun they evoke:

- spraying water-based paint on the outside wall and observing how the paint changes in relation to the elements such as rain
- chalking the ground with different colours
- on wintry days, fill balloons with water and food colouring. Leave these filled balloons outside overnight to freeze. Burst the balloons in the morning to find ice marbles in the garden!
- making sculptures using clay and natural materials found in the garden
- creating large outdoor weaves by encouraging children to use scarves, crêpe paper, pieces of ribbon to wrap around, over and under equipment in the outdoor area to create an exotic and colourful maze to navigate

- painting with natural materials; use feathers, rocks, sticks, leaves, roots of plants instead of paintbrushes
- with gloved hands, use ice for mark making on a warm day and watch the images evaporate on the concrete surface. You can use a bucket, water and paint brushes to create a similar effect
- on sunny days, get large pieces of brightly coloured construction paper and encourage children to place distinctively shaped items on the paper, e.g. leaves, seashells, pieces of ribbon, etc. Leave for a few days in the sun and when the items are removed the paper will be left bleached with the outlines of the materials.

It is important to plan the location of the arts and crafts area away from the music and movement space. In the arts and crafts area children may be crouching or lying on the ground to create their visual art work. If the arts and crafts space is in close proximity to more physically active areas accidents can happen.

Creative arts and Aistear in the outside arts and crafts centre

Wellbeing

In the outdoor arts and crafts area young children can have exciting experiences, as in this space they are given a wealth of freedom to express themselves creatively. This freedom of expression provides a solid foundation for children's overall mental and physical wellbeing. During outside arts and crafts one is not concerned with what a piece of art work looks like; focus is put on the effort, thought and emotion that went into the piece. This outside area can give children the mental space to express wonder about life in a visual and concrete manner. The early years practitioner has an important role to provide a variety of materials, both natural and commercial, to promote painting, drawing, sculpture, photography, collage and so forth. It is important that this area provides some cover from the elements as children may be stationary in the space for periods of time. Ideally this corner of the garden should be close to quieter activities, allowing for moments of thought and reflection. An easel as well as child-sized table and chairs would be useful, as well as individual cushions or comfortable mats for children to sit on if they are completing their art work on the ground.

OVER TO YOU

Think about the equipment and materials that would be useful in an outside art area; compile a list; and devise an art activity for children of a variety of age groups using the materials form your list.

Exploring and Thinking

The outdoor space provides plenty of natural materials for children to explore and create with. Think of the humble leaf and all of the different types of art activity that can be created using this material:
- freehand drawing and painting of leaves, focusing on the changes in shape and colour during the seasons
- leaf-rubbing activities with crayons, charcoal and chalk; these rubbings give children an added insight into the texture and individuality of leaves
- leaf sculptures using clay, dough, mud or sand with water
- collages, using leaves of different types, sizes and colours chosen by the children themselves
- photography of leaves; far away, up close, on trees, on the ground, etc.
- mosaics using torn leaves to create a unique tiled effect
- painting with leaves instead of paintbrushes.

The outdoor art area is a fantastic space for children to be curious, flexible and to implement 'outside the box' thinking.

> **OVER TO YOU**
>
> Think about how the following materials can be adapted to mark making, painting, sculpting and collage activities:
> - feathers
> - sticks
> - seashells
> - clay
> - flowers.

Communication

The outside area in the early years setting is often shared by a number of children in the facility. This occasionally means that time outside can be limited. If this is the case, make the very most of the time you have in the resource through active play and interactions between adults and children. The outside arts and crafts area can sometimes be neglected as a space for conversation. When children are quietly concentrating on activities they are sometimes left to 'work away' by themselves. It is important for the adult to reflect with the child during the artistic process to gain a level of insight about the art work. Observing a child creating their art work and gently commenting on what you see opens conversations and provides an opportunity to hear about the child's thoughts and feelings about the art.

> **CASE STUDY**
>
> Jake (two years and two months) is sitting on a mat on the ground in the outside arts and crafts area. He is holding a paint brush and a small pot of water that he retrieved from the low shelves. He is alternating between dipping the paintbrush into the water and making marks on the concrete and dipping his hands in the water and then slapping them on the concrete. Molly (adult) is sitting close to Jake observing him.
>
> *Molly:* I see you are using the water to make marks on the ground.
>
> Jake looks at Molly and hands her the paint brush.
>
> *Molly:* Do you want me to paint too? What can I paint?
>
> *Jake:* Woof, woof!
>
> *Molly:* Woof, woof – a dog. Are there any dogs in your painting?
>
> Jake points to the water on the ground and slaps it.
>
> *Molly:* That looks like a dog jumping in water; I will put water here too.
>
> Molly pours some water on the ground and slaps it; Jake and Molly smile at each other.

In this case study a number of non-verbal messages are communicated between Jake and Molly:
- Molly observing Jake shows Jake that she is interested in his work.
- Jake handing Molly the brush indicates that he wants her to join in.
- Jake makes the noise of a dog, communicating the theme in the art.
- Molly mimics Jake's actions, showing that she appreciates what he is doing.
- Jake and Molly smile at each other, showing mutual respect for the interaction.

Can you see any other non-verbal messages in the case study? How could Jake's art work be recorded? How would Molly be able to assess whether Jake is learning from his spontaneous activity? Can Molly extend this activity for Jake in any way?

Identity and Belonging

The outdoor arts and crafts centre is a very personal space for each child. In this place children reveal parts of their imagination that no other person could recreate. Displaying art pieces in a manner that respects individuality is very important. Respectful galleries of work show children that their efforts are welcomed, valuable and heard in the early years environment. Outdoor galleries can be challenging as they are exposed to the elements – rain, sun, wind and dew. Think about having an outdoor display case to protect children's art from these environmental factors. You could choose to display children's work on the inside of classroom windows facing outwards onto the garden area. You could even choose to house any art work in a well-lit garden shed to which children have free access! Remember that children may want to bring some of their art work home. Take photos of any pieces that you want to display. Large immovable sculptures, weaves and art pieces that are not durable, such as water painting, ice marbles, etc., are also best displayed through photography. Use the same techniques for display outside that you use in the inside space, creating a consistency in the value placed on visual art created both inside and outside.

Messy play area

The outdoor environment lends itself to messy play: the rustling and crunching of leaves, the squelch of mud, the splash of water, the flow of sand! The only restriction on messy play outside comes from the cautious nature of the adult! Being outside gives children additional freedom to be energetic, be noisy and get dirty. White (2008:90) describes a successful creative outdoor area as being more of a 'work site than a workshop' and its sometimes messy appearance should reflect this. Children should have access to 'messy wear' to protect their day-to-day clothing: waterproof gloves, wellington boots, rain jackets, smocks and aprons should be available for outside messy play. Soap, water and hand-drying facilities are also an important aspect of any messy play activity.

Young children like routine in play and familiar activities should be offered daily with variety injected into the play depending on children's choices. Take, for example, the typical sand and water trays. These are great messy play pieces of equipment and the materials in the trays can be varied depending on children's ever-changing abilities and interests. Adding new materials such as buckets and spades, as well as natural resources such as seashells, rocks and even seaweed, can add a new experience to the familiarity of the sand and water tray.

Creative arts and Aistear in the outdoor messy play area

Wellbeing

In the outdoor messy area children can engage in sustained free flow play (Bruce 1991). It is important that when in the midst of free-flow play children are allowed to be messy and to leave a trail of resources in their wake! You might often observe an overly cautious adult following the play, putting away the materials or requesting the child to 'tidy up'. This level of intrusion on the child's messy play time can interrupt the activity, disturb the creative process and even undermine the child's play choices. The Aistear principles and themes booklet states that 'being flexible and having a positive outlook on learning and on life is crucial. All these experiences help children to become resilient and resourceful and to learn to cope with change and situations in which things go wrong' (NCCA 2009:16). During messy play the adult educator should model this flexibility, respecting the child's right to be messy! Observing a calm and relaxed adult will provide the child with a concrete example of how to be composed in a situation where others have control, thus promoting a 'go with the [messy] flow' attitude!

Exploring and Thinking

The outside messy area is a fantastic aid for exploring scientific and mathematical concepts. Think about using resources that belong naturally to the outside area to reflect the seasons in a messy way. The following water activities promote the exploration of the scientific concept of cause and effect.

- **Activity 1:** On a winter day, leave an inch of water outside to see how thick the ice is the following morning and time how long it takes to defrost in the wintry sunshine. Give each child the opportunity to break the ice and discuss its properties.
- **Activity 2:** The texture of sand becomes very different when water is added. How much water is too little to create a difference? How much water is too much for playing with the sand? What is the ideal amount of water needed to make the sand stick together?
- **Activity 3:** What happens when paper saturated in water is hung in the warm sunshine? What effect does the warmth of the sun have on water?
- **Activity 4:** Adding different substances to water changes its composition and its sensorial effects. What happens when the following items are added: blue food colouring, flour, sugar-free cordial, lemon essence, a sieve?

OVER TO YOU

Think about the following scientific concepts and how creative arts in the messy play area can be used to explore these: change, diversity, organisation, variation.

Communication

The outdoor messy play area should be designed with the aim of holding children's interest and curiosity. The area should be exciting and challenging, inviting children to discover new experiences and to lose themselves in play. This level of engagement will motivate young children to share their learning with others, as they will want the people they love to experience the joy they felt. With this idea of sharing experiences in mind, we can see that the outdoor messy play space is a very important environment for young children's communication. Use the outside space to inject subtle variety into messy play experiences. Observe changes in the environment and let the seasons inspire you to implement amazing messy play opportunities for children.

Think about the following messy play experiences and how they inspire communication between child and adult, and between children:
- adding ice to a water tray on a warm day
- jumping in mud and puddles
- running through a water sprinkler and a paddling pool
- dancing in the rain
- building a snowman
- throwing water balloons
- walking on dewy grass with bare feet.

> **OVER TO YOU**
>
> These types of messy play activity ignite children's emotions, grab their imaginations and inspire them to extend the experience and make it their own. Think about the seasons – spring, summer, autumn and winter – and devise a list of messy play activities that reflect the changes in nature.

Identity and Belonging

Aim 4 in the Aistear Theme of Identity and Belonging asks the early years educator to maintain environments in which children 'see themselves as capable learners'. The outdoor messy play area is a fantastic space for children to recognise their potential as investigators, creators and philosophers. The outdoor messy play area promotes open-ended activities in which the child decides if they have been successful in their learning or if they need to continue in their endeavours. This space promotes play that is personal to the child as the activities offered will ideally be based on children's interests and reflect their homes, life experiences and cultures. If we think about Síolta Standard 14: Identity and Belonging, we can see the importance of adults' roles when promoting positive discourse in the environment regarding each person's individuality and right to be different. Look at the following creative messy play ideas and reflect on how self-esteem, difference and diversity can be promoted during these activities. Think specifically of the right to be different in terms of one's: race, ethnicity, culture, appearance, religion, language, family background, gender, age and ability:

- building sand castles
- making mud pies
- collecting leaves
- moving through shrubbery/gravel, etc.
- pouring water.

Quiet area

In the outside area it is good practice to include a space where children can sit, reflect, be still and relax. Using the ideas of 'mindfulness' we can think of the outside quiet area as a space to be present, to breathe deeply and to experience life in the 'here and now'. This atmosphere can be created by designing the quiet area away from the hustle and bustle of active play, adding a

EXPLORING AND CREATING: THE OUTDOOR PLAY SPACE

method of seclusion such as a low fence or hedge and providing materials such as comfortable seating and shade from the elements. You may even want to add features such as a child-friendly water feature (be mindful of safety concerns) and/or a mural of a calming scene to add a sense of serenity to this space.

> **OVER TO YOU**
>
> Take a moment for yourself. Close your eyes and take a breath. While breathing in and out, reflect on your heartbeat, the position of your body and how you are feeling today. These reflective moments give us space to regulate our own feelings and become aware of our emotions. Think about how this space would be useful in the life of a young child.

The quiet area can also be used for children to take some time to look at books, leaf through photo albums, observe the wind in the trees, the clouds in the sky, or simply watch their friends at play. Mark-making materials such as crayons and paper can be added to encourage children to express their feelings and views visually as well as verbally. The quiet area offers fantastic opportunities for thought and repose. Greenland (2010) noted that when a child is offered the chance of quiet reflection they have greater capability to develop their individual creative talents and imagination. In this quiet space one can label emotions, use metaphors to make sense of life experiences and use visualisation techniques to understand any challenging circumstances that may be occurring.

> **OVER TO YOU**
>
> Look at the following scene and think about how the quiet space could help Frank (three years eleven months) express his feelings creatively.
>
> Outdoor Scene: Patricia (key worker) is kneeling on the ground in front of Frank. Frank is crying. He had planned to play with the blue bike today. Chloe is playing with the blue bike and Frank does not want to wait for Chloe's turn to be over. Patricia says to Frank in a gentle tone of voice, 'I can see from your tears that you are upset. I understand that. It's hard to wait. Would you like to choose another activity to play with, do you want to sit on the bench and wait for Chloe to be finished or would you like to go to the quiet corner to think about your tears?' Frank points to the quiet corner. Patricia responds; 'I see you want to go and have some quiet time. Would you like to go alone, do you want me to go with you or do you want to bring a friend with you?' Frank holds his hand out to Patricia and they walk to the quiet corner. Frank climbs on Patricia's knee and snuggles into her body. Patricia says, 'This seems like a strong feeling you are having, Frank. You really wanted to play with

the blue bike today. Would you like to tell me where you were going to go with the bike with your words or would you like to draw them with the colours?' Frank steps off Patricia's knee and picks up the colours. He makes marks on the page using the crayons and shows his image to Patricia.

> **QUESTIONS FOR REFLECTION**
> 1. What difference did having the quiet space make to Frank?
> 2. How did Patricia motivate Frank to express his emotions in a positive manner?
> 3. If Patricia were to explain 'waiting' to Frank using a metaphor, what could she say?
> 4. Frank expressed his thoughts using mark-making tools. What other creative resources could be added to the quiet area to promote expression of emotions?
> 5. Did Frank have to go into the quiet area? What could Patricia have done if he had refused?

Creative play and Aistear in the quiet area

Wellbeing

The outdoor quiet area is a great space to promote the Aistear Theme of Wellbeing, specifically Aim 3; 'to be creative and spiritual; become reflective and think flexibly'. In the outdoor quiet area young children get a chance to recharge and relax. Greenman (2005) uses the phrase 'places to pause' when describing outdoor quiet areas and reminds us that spaces can speak to a person and load one's body with sensorial information. The messages that a space conveys affects our emotions in a very profound manner. Greenman (2005) describes the ideal outdoor quiet area as being a 'low-load environment'. In here moods are modulated, there is a feeling of safety and familiarity and the area has a simple design. A contrast to this would be a 'high-load environment', which promotes high-intensity reactions through new experiences. High-load spaces, such as an amusement park, a busy shopping centre or a circus, trigger intense emotions such as excitement, anticipation and anxiety.

Have a look at the following resources found in a 'low-load' outdoor quiet area and discuss how they would promote reflection and flexible thinking skills:
- overhanging trellis/hedgerow to create supervised privacy
- cushions to sit on
- child-sized recliner/chairs suitable for outdoor use
- blankets/throws to rest on or under
- plants of different sizes and types

- child-friendly water feature for ambience
- books sourced from children's homes
- photo albums with pictures of children's play and home photographs
- paper and colouring utensils
- play dough in an airtight container
- full-length shatterproof mirror.

> **OVER TO YOU**
>
> Look at the resource list above and add your own ideas of materials and equipment. Design a quiet area which promotes reflective thought and space for silence for young children. Think of the different age groups up to six years of age and how the space can be adapted to reflect the development of the child.

Exploring and Thinking

In the outdoor quiet area one can silently ponder while watching the world go by. Sit with young children in the quiet space and encourage them to use their senses in the area. Wonder with the young child how their senses are stimulated by nature and that feelings can remind us of other life experiences. Look at the list of conversation starters/reflections below and think about how these metaphors and similes can ignite a child's creative process.

- **Sound:** 'The wind is strong today; I can hear it whooshing through the trees. It is the same type of sound as when the tap pours the water quickly into the bath. I wonder is the wind as fast as tap water? If I hold out my hand I might feel how fast it is.'
- **Touch:** 'The cushion is so soft and the blanket is so fluffy. It feels like I am sitting on the couch at home in my sitting room with my puppy and we are about to cuddle in and watch a movie. When I remember nice times with my puppy it makes me happy.'
- **Smell:** 'There is a new smell in here today. It smells like it has rained and made the grass and trees wet. I wonder do I smell like rain when my hair gets wet!'
- **Taste:** (eating a snack in the quiet area) 'Let's close our eyes and think about what this orange tastes like. I wonder how many words we can find for the orange! Juicy, tangy, sweet, fruity, yummy; does the orange taste like anything else you have eaten?'

> **OVER TO YOU**
>
> Spend a few minutes sitting outside in a quiet outdoor space; reflect on how it makes you feel, how it impacts on your senses and how it has affected your pattern of thinking. Note these thoughts in your reflective journal.

Communication

As we can see from the reflections above, the quiet area provides vast opportunities for focused conversation. One specific personal development field the quiet area promotes is emotional literacy/emotional intelligence.

Christine Bruce (2010) highlights five main aspects of emotional intelligence for young children:

1 **Self-awareness:** being able to recognise feelings as they happen.
2 **Emotional control:** the ability to regulate one's own emotions.
3 **Self-motivation:** overcoming challenges through persistence and determination.
4 **Empathy:** being able to understand situations from other people's perspectives.
5 **Handling relationships:** being able to work collaboratively with and also lead in groups of people.

We can see the importance of emotional literacy in many early years frameworks, such as Aistear, Steiner, High/Scope and Reggio Emilia among others. The quiet area is an ideal space for children to converse with their key worker, sharing feelings, thoughts and ideas. Developing one's emotional intelligence is a lifelong journey and it can be a very difficult one. It is important that children receive strong adult support during this personal process. The adult's role here is to support the young child, observing their words and behaviours, introducing new vocabulary that may help them describe any perturbing feelings and providing learning opportunities that help make sense of feelings. Think about including child-friendly mirrors in the outside quiet corner as well as books containing pictures of people experiencing different types of emotion. Remember to be available in the quiet area to provide both verbal and non-verbal messages about the child's inherent goodness and worth. A cuddle, a smile and a hug can go a long way in making a person feel supported!

The quiet area is also a fantastic space to support a small group circle time. During this planned activity children can listen to each other and the adult, hear a story, recite poems and songs and be together in a relaxed, happy manner.

OVER TO YOU

Plan a circle time activity designed for the outdoor quiet area for a small group of children. How will your 'circle time' complement the reflective nature of the quiet area?

Identity and Belonging

As we can see from the ideas above, the outdoor quiet area is a superb place for chats and discussions. It is also ideal for the individual to sit and think alone. One important learning goal in the Aistear Theme Identity and Belonging is for children to 'be able to share personal experiences about their own families and cultures, and come to know that there is a diversity of family structures, cultures and backgrounds'. Think about including the following resources in the quiet area to provoke explorations about families, cultures and each person's right to be different:

- photos of individuals' families, both immediate and extended
- photos of family occasions that reflect one's culture: festivals, mealtimes, weddings, holidays, homes, social events, recreational events, sporting activities, etc.
- pictures of different types of family: two-parent/nuclear family, single-parent family, blended family, extended family, single-sex-parent family, dual-sex-parent family, adopted family, foster family, child-free family, etc.
- pictures of different types of cultural occasions in Irish society and further afield
- multi-ethnic illustrated cookery books.

The early education experience can be a confusing time for young children as people with different home values, cultures and boundaries mix in the one space. The quiet area gives children an opportunity to observe differences they might see in their friends and key workers from an 'outside' participant's perspective. It is a good idea to encourage families to bring in items from home for the outside quiet area, for example comfort toys, books, a security item, etc. Think back to your own childhood: did you have a toy or comfort item such as a blanket that made you feel safe? These are very important artefacts in a young child's life and it is important that the bond between the child and their comfort toy is respected in the early years environment.

OVER TO YOU: SELF-REFLECTION

Take a moment and close your eyes. Imagine that you are on a train leaving for the day. Visualise yourself sitting in the train, feeling excited that you are going to meet a friend in the next city. As the train pulls away you realise that you have left your mobile phone at home. How do you react? Do you feel uneasy? Do you want to go back home and get your phone? Do you worry that you won't be able to contact your friend?

Think about these insecure, unsettled feelings in the context of a young child who has been removed from their security toy. The sense of unease and anxiety when we do not have contact with an item that makes us feel safe is quite distressing. How would you ensure that a young child does not experience these feelings in the early years environment?

Outside role play area

The role play area in the outside space offers a variety of play experiences. It can be used for socio-dramatic play, using items such as pots, pans, dress-up and home corner experiences. It also facilitates construction play, with woodworking, wooden blocks and building equipment; and it provides space for small world role play with miniature figures, homes and play scenes. This type of outside role play aids young children in becoming aware of and respecting the needs and feelings of others (empathy) and this is in turn reflected in children's own behaviour and development. The outside role play area also helps young children to learn about following rules, developing skills such as acceptance and perseverance, exploring, experimenting, being adventurous and experiencing what it is like to take risks.

This space is active and is best placed near busy areas such as the music and movement area and discovery area. Resources for socio-dramatic play in the outdoor role play area could include:

- child-size house/Wendy house
- real-life home materials such as pots, pans, cutlery, plates, bowls, cups, phones
- baby dolls with accessories
- dress-up clothes
- picnic basket
- blankets and cushions.

Outside construction play resources could also include large, medium and small wooden blocks, child-sized high-visibility jackets and hard hats. In addition to this equipment one could add resources such as spirit levels, measuring tapes, child-friendly hammers and screwdrivers, which are useful for construction role play outside. Construction play, like socio-dramatic play, will migrate throughout the outdoor play area. This whole-space movement ignites young children's imagination, supports creativity and promotes overall holistic development.

Small world materials will generally reflect the play that occurs in the indoor space. You may choose to have separate small world toys for outside play, or you could transport materials from inside to the outside environment. If there are specific small world toys for outdoor play, ensure that they are well maintained and well stocked.

Keep an inventory of the outdoor small world toys and regularly replace any broken or lost materials. Small world toys will be used for play that includes sinking them in water, burying them in sand and mud, hiding them in bushes, etc., so ensure that the resources sourced for play are good quality and durable. The small world materials should reflect the interests of the children in your care. Closely observe what types of small world play children prefer and be open to changing the materials if you notice that children are no longer playing with them or have got bored with them.

Creative arts and Aistear in the outdoor role play area
Wellbeing

It is important to give young children opportunities to act out socio-dramatic play in an outside space. The freedom in the outdoor environment encourages voices to soar and imaginations to flourish! You will observe children acting out scenes from their life and this is an important communication tool for young children. The adult's role is to play with the child in the role play area, being careful not to force their influence on the play. The following case study looks at the story of Casey and the 'babysitter'. Notice how this imaginative socio-dramatic scene enhanced Casey's understanding of her parents going on a 'date night'.

> **CASE STUDY**
>
> Casey (four years two months) and her key worker Maria are in the outside play area. Casey is pushing a buggy with a baby doll sitting in it and Maria is walking beside her.
> *Casey:* Maria, I am the mammy and you are the auntie.
> *Maria:* Okay, Mammy, what does the auntie do?
> *Casey:* The auntie babysits.
> *Maria:* Who will I babysit, Mammy?
> *Casey:* Daddy and me are going out and the baby stays here (points to baby doll).
> *Maria:* Where are you and Daddy going?
> *Casey:* It's a date and it's only for mammies and daddies because mammies get tired and need time with daddies alone.
> *Maria:* What will I do with Baby when you go on your date with Daddy?
> *Casey:* Baby will cry, because she misses Mammy, and you say, 'Poor Baby, it's okay, they'll be home soon' and then she sleeps.
> *Maria:* And when Baby is asleep, what do Mammy and Daddy do on the date?
> *Casey:* Em, they get a taximan and go to the cinema and get popcorn. [She picks the baby doll out of the buggy and rocks her.] It's okay, Baby, shh shh, I'll be home later. [Hands Maria the doll.] I have to go, I have my phone.

> Casey walks away from Maria.
> *Maria:* Okay, Baby, Mammy and Daddy are at the cinema and when you wake up they will be home.
> Casey walks back to Maria.
> *Casey:* I'm home! [Takes the baby from Maria.] I told you I'd be home, shh shh shh don't cry Baby.

OVER TO YOU
Spend some time observing and recording a role play scene in an outside play area. In the scene you observed, what life experience were the children 'making sense' of?

Exploring and Thinking

The outside role play area is a great space for creative and intricate construction tasks. Children are able to intertwine traditional construction materials such as blocks and bricks with natural materials such as leaves, stones, rocks, sticks, etc. Ensure that small world figures such as toy people, cars, animals, etc. are available to extend the activities. Think about the following creative construction ideas and how you could inspire young children to design and build their own:

- fairy fort
- bear cave
- tree house
- pyramid
- water slide
- castle with moat
- Olympic stadium (obstacle course).

OVER TO YOU
Choose one of the constructions above and discuss what types of natural and commercially bought resources could be used to design and implement the structure.
- **How could you introduce this activity to an individual child, pair of children or a small group of children?**
- **What would the adult's role in the activity be?**
- **How could the activity be supported so that each child's voice is represented in the process of designing and building?**
- **How could you assess a child's learning from this activity?**

- How could you record the process of completing this activity to use as a reflection-based discussion with an individual or the group in the future?

Communication

The outside role play area is a place where communication happens in a natural and ongoing way. This type of play provokes dialogue, observation, co-operation and occasionally conflict. During role play children talk, listen, think, understand and learn to communicate in a two-way manner. Some children will rely more than others on non-verbal communication, as communication is dependant on individual ability. The role play area allows for difference and respects individual strengths and weaknesses. Much of the communication in role play occurs in the 'unsaid' rules of social patterns.

Think about the following types of communication and how you might observe children using them to express imaginative messages in the outdoor role play area:
- talking
- listening
- utterances
- gestures
- body language
- mirroring.

Identity and Belonging

The outdoor role play area is a special place. In this space children can pretend to be themselves! Role play for young children often reflects home life, values and family cultures. Support young children sharing their home life experiences through 'catching' differences in the outdoor play area. If you notice a value or custom specific to a child and their family, celebrate it through highlighting its importance. The following scene shows how Ben's cultural differences were 'caught' in the role play area and celebrated by the children and adults in the space.

CASE STUDY

Ben (two years eight months), Sophie (two years one month) and Richard (three years one month) are in the outside home area. They are playing alongside each other. Katherine (key worker) is observing the play from a few metres away. Ben is filling a pot with water from the tap and pouring it down the drain, Sophie is pushing the buggy and Richard is sitting at the table talking on the phone. Katherine hears Ben, who speaks Spanish at home, use the word 'agua' to describe the water. Katherine goes into the role play area and says, 'I see you are getting some agua Ben. Agua is water in Ben's house, isn't that a great way to say water? It's Spanish.' Ben hands Katherine the pan and says 'Quieres agua?', Katherine smiles and says to Richard, 'Would you like some agua, Richard?' Richard says, 'Agua please, Ben.' Ben hands Richard the pan and says, 'Aquí tienes, Richard.' Katherine calls a second key worker over and says, 'Fiona, we are speaking Spanish today like in Ben's house. Hola, Fiona', Fiona responds, 'Hola, Katherine, hola Ben, hola Richard, hola Sophie. Hasta luego; see you later.'

OVER TO YOU

Think about what other types of cultural variation you might 'catch' in the outside role play area. How can you celebrate these differences in a respectful and fun manner?

Bringing creativity in from the outside world

We have looked at how we can bring the creative arts curriculum to an outside space using a variety of methods. We will now look at how to use the outside world to bring creative arts into the early years environment. Sourcing alternative materials is a great way to inject variety into play. Have a look at a toy catalogue or visit a toy shop and you will find that the majority of commercial equipment and materials are made of plastic and that there is very little choice in texture. Alternative play materials are known by a variety of names – junk, recycled, reusable, throwaway or scrap. Walter F. Drew and Baji Rankin's (2004) article 'Promoting creativity for life using open-ended materials' encourages the use of reusable materials and highlights their function in open-ended creative play.

Items such as fabrics, wool, cork, leather, foam, plastic, old furniture and home utensils, paper and card products, pieces of wood, wire, etc. can be used in the early years environment. Educational philosophies such as Reggio Emilia, Montessori, Steiner and High/Scope demonstrate that real-life materials have been promoted as active play for generations. Using recycled materials not only saves the educational setting money, it also increases learning opportunities for the young child. In the following scene Molly, aged thirteen months, is playing with a treasure basket that has been made using alternative materials. Read through the case study and answer the reflective questions that follow it.

EXPLORING AND CREATING: THE OUTDOOR PLAY SPACE

CASE STUDY

Molly is sitting on the ground and is exploring a treasure basket that has been put together by her key worker. In the basket there is a range of materials that have been sourced from families, items the key worker brought from home and pieces that have been donated by local businesses. Molly has tipped the basket onto the ground in front of her and she is sitting among the materials. Her key worker Kevin is sitting close to her. Molly picks up a piece of tin foil and tears it, she looks at Kevin and smiles, Kevin smiles back and says, 'The silver rips up in your hands.' Molly continues to tear the foil, throwing the pieces in the air; Kevin sings, 'It's raining.' Molly begins to sway and turns her attention to a set of keys. She shakes the keys, mouths them and rotates them from one hand to the next. Molly's attention now turns to a mobile phone, which she puts to her ear and then hands to Kevin. Kevin mimics Molly, putting the phone to his ear, and says 'Hello'. Molly smiles. Molly now picks up a large heavy chain and rattles it on the ground.

This exploration continues with a variety of items including a sachet of pot pourri, a metal whisk, a wooden spoon and a pestle. Molly explores the treasure basket for approximately twelve minutes. She holds a set of measuring spoons and crawls over to the soft play area.

QUESTIONS FOR REFLECTION

1. What considerations might the key worker have taken account of when designing the treasure basket?
2. What creative learning opportunities did Molly experience?
3. What learning goals (in terms of the Aistear framework) did Molly experience?
4. How could Molly's learning be recorded and assessed to help Kevin plan for future play experiences?
5. How could the alternative materials used in the treasure basket improve the family–service relationship?
6. How could sourcing the treasure basket materials improve links with the local community?

OVER TO YOU

Think about where an early education setting could be able to source alternative materials for the creative arts curriculum. How could you as an early years educator contact the following people and community members with the aim to generate creative resources in your centre?

- Parents and guardians.
- Extended family members.
- Local businesses.

Draft a letter to the above stakeholders outlining the value of alternative materials for young children's creativity. You can use the sample below as a guide to start you off!

Dear Families

Here in …………………………, we believe in recycling, and our motto is 'Don't bin it – Play with it!' With this in mind we would like you to take a few moments to read our reasons for why using recycled materials is so important. If you feel inspired by our words, please have a look at the list attached. If you have any of the items at home which are not in use/are ready for the bin, please bring them in!

Recycled materials are important to us because: . . .

Sincerely,

The Early Years Team

Using alternative materials to promote creativity

One main benefit of alternative materials is their use in open-ended play. When reused materials are brought into the early years environment they bring with them a 'newness', a possibility and a freedom, as a material that once had a particular purpose has now taken on an undefined purpose. Odegard (2012) introduces Foucault's concept of 'heterotopia' when discussing junk materials. This concept proposes that when objects meet that are typically incompatible, they can join together to create something new. This joining together of materials promotes innovative thought and a sense of 'I can make anything' during the play frame. What an amazing feeling young children experience when they see materials in front of them and are not constrained by rules, boundaries or a fear of failure. Imagine for a moment how freeing that feeling must be. Think about when that sense of wonder and attitude of 'anything goes' begins to fade in people.

OVER TO YOU

Research the Remida – the creative recycling centre in Reggio Emilia – ReCreate Dublin and the Play Resource Centre in Belfast. Discuss the role of the early years educator in providing junk materials for young children. Take a few moments to make a list of junk materials that could be useful in an early years setting.

Open-ended play with alternative materials

Drew and Rankin (2004) highlight seven main guidelines or 'principles' for using open-ended alternative materials with young children:

1. **Children's spontaneous, creative self-expression increases their sense of competence:** During play, ideas of reason and 'cause and effect' can be suspended to hold a space for curiosity, the unexpected, uncertainty and original thought. Encourage the child to imagine and explore with materials.

2. **Children extend and deepen their understandings through multiple, hands-on experiences with diverse materials:** As the young brain rapidly develops it yearns for active learning experiences. These active learning opportunities are best supported through high-quality education in which the educators plan for diversity and individuality in play. Use a key worker system in conjunction with personal learning plans to support an individualised curriculum.

3. **Children's play with peers supports learning and a growing sense of competence:** When children play together they experience what it is like to succeed, to have their play behaviour reinforced through positive attention and to have one's ideas and opinions respected and supported. Observing each other's open-ended play also gives children the space to appreciate not only their own achievements but also those of their peers. When using alternative materials, children are encouraged to play together in an open-ended manner. In this play frame children do not need external motivation as the reward comes in the form of the play relationship.

4. **Children can learn literacy, science and mathematics joyfully through active play with diverse, open-ended materials:** The open-ended nature of alternative materials promotes a holistic learning experience for young children. These limitless items encourage children to poke, prod, carry, throw and investigate all their possible uses. This important skill of wonder and learning can stay with children throughout their life if fostered and developed from an early age.

5. **Children learn best in open-ended explorations when adults help them make connections:** 'When children have the chance to notice, collect, and sort materials, and when teachers respond to their ideas, the children become artists, designers, and engineers' (Drew & Rankin 2004:6). Using the ideas of social learning (Bandura) and scaffolding (Vygotsky) we can see that children's explorations with alternative materials are best supported through high-quality interactions with adults whom they love and trust.

6. **Teachers are nourished by observing children's joy when learning:** This principle reflects a central theme in the Reggio Emilia philosophy. When we see young children respond and laugh with the materials and activities we have

provided it inspires us, the educator, to experience this joy again. Think now of a child that you know and visualise their joyful face smiling – it is an energising memory! The adult in the early years environment becomes the student in response to an inquisitive child. You begin to ask the questions, 'What shall I introduce next to see that smile again?' 'What other types of material will bring about this level of learning?' This level of curiosity in the adult is a revitalising and exciting experience!

7 **Ongoing self-reflection among educators is needed to support best practice:** To ensure that high-quality, open-ended learning occurs with alternative materials, the adult in the early years environment has the role of reflecting on the types of play that are happening, what is proving successful in the environment, what is proving challenging, what is not working, what needs to change and how that change can happen. Using an 'active research' approach (discussed in Chapter 3), the educator can assess open-ended learning opportunities in the environment to ensure that children are receiving high-quality education experiences.

OVER TO YOU

Note how alternative materials promote learning in young children. Use the Aistear themes of Identity and Belonging, Communication, Exploring and Thinking, and Wellbeing as guides for reflection.

The creative arts curriculum and 'throwaway' materials

Dramatic arts

Alternative materials can be used during role play activities and can provide inspiration for young children as they engage in imaginative sequences. In the home corner, think about providing old clothes such as hats, scarves, dresses and suits for use in socio-dramatic play. General household utensils such as used and cleaned food containers, colanders, pots, pans, old hairdryers, phones, laptops, desktops, cameras, etc. can all be used as props. Think about using recycled fabrics to create new costumes reflecting the individual preferences of the children in the setting. Commercial 'dress-up' clothes found in general toy shops can be expensive and can also limit children's play choices based on gender.

OVER TO YOU

In small groups, design a superhero who promotes a positive self-image for young children. Have a look through old clothes, fabrics and other 'junk' material in your homes and create this costume. Assess what learning could be achieved if this activity were carried out by young children with their key worker.

Using recycled materials in the construction corner also holds multiple opportunities for creative play. Cardboard boxes, blueprints, real-life tools (decommissioned to be child-friendly), pieces of plastic and wood can offer children variety in their architectural feats. Over the next few days spend some time observing all of the different textures, materials, shapes and sizes that go into creating a piece of engineering. The same level of choice should be available to young children when they build their innovative structures!

Movement and dance

Adding recycled fabrics to movement and dance activities can ignite children's imaginations and loosen their bodies. These colourful props can bring with them a new freedom, and a relaxation of inhibitions! Including ribbons, scarves, long pieces of string and yarn, as well as old pieces of material cut into strips, creates a fantastic resource which young children can use in a spontaneous fashion or through planned activities.

Think about the following activity and how it could be used to promote creative movements with children of different age groups:

Activity: Scarf Dance
- Age group: From sitting ability upwards
- Resources needed:
    - a variety of scarves/long strips of materials of various colours and textures
    - music for background tone and rhythm
    - floor space (inside or outside).
- Implementing the activity:
    - Leave the selection of scarves/pieces of material beside the child/group of children and encourage each child to choose one or more pieces.
    - Play a piece of music. Move with your scarf in time with the rhythm/beat, encouraging the children to move in their own unique ways.
    - After the children have settled into the activity, introduce a theme for the movement based on the group's interest, e.g. a fish.
    - Suggest to the group that they can move like a fish. What would a fish's head do? How about its mouth? The fish has a tail – does it wiggle? Its fins can flap, etc.

- When 'fish' movements are completed, suggest to the children that they can use their scarf to be anything they want with movement! Can they be a kite? A firework? A frog? How about a jack in the box?
- Conclude the activity by inviting children to continue to move with the scarves if they want to do so.

QUESTIONS FOR REFLECTION

1. How would this type of activity promote creativity and original thought in young children?
2. How could learning be assessed from this type of activity?
3. How could you record this activity to reflect on it with the child/group of children in the future?
4. How could this activity be extended?

Visual arts

In Chapter 5 we looked at the resources that are needed to maintain a well-stocked arts and crafts centre. Make a list of items that can be used in the arts and crafts centre for use in mark-making activities, collage, photography, sculpture and painting. Divide this list into what needs to be commercially purchased and what can be sourced through recycled goods. You will find that the list of recycled goods is quite significant. Circulate this list among stakeholders in your service. You might find that families and friends of the service are very generous when giving away their 'junk' rather than simply binning it!

OVER TO YOU

Design a three-dimensional junk art sculpture. Be as innovative as you can be; there are no limits in this sculpture! If you are stuck for a starting point, you could use some of the ideas below for inspiration.

- A new fish that has just emerged from the bottom of the sea.
- An animal that has never been seen before – it has been asleep in a cave since the Ice Age, but it has just woken up and wants to play.
- A rocket that can fly to the moon using potato skins as fuel.
- A street lamp that gives out sweets instead of light.
- A house for the 'Old woman who swallowed a fly' – she decided not to swallow all of the animals but to build extensions so that they could live with her!

In the early years environment remember that you have a role in recycling, too! Look at what would normally be put in the bin; can it be used to create visual art pieces? The following resources and activities highlight the role of the early years educator in saving 'rubbish':

- **Crayon stubs:** Create fantastic melted crayon activities using crayons, glue and a warm hairdryer.
- **Plastic bottles:** Put some water-based paint and a dash of water into a plastic bottle with a squeeze top. Squirt the mixture onto paper or card from a short distance.
- **Tin cans:** Clean and use to make plant holders, stationery pots, to paint on, etc.
- **Broken toys:** Use in collages and mosaics.
- **Play sand:** Once it has fallen on the floor sweep it up into a container with a holed top, such as a flour shaker, and use it in textured prints.
- **Paper:** Use old newspaper, discarded photocopies, etc. in cutting and pasting activities, etc.

OVER TO YOU

Have a look at what materials are thrown away in the course of a day and think about what could have been created with these items. Visualise any item that is put in the bin as a lost learning opportunity! If you are getting stuck in your creative ideas, use a website such as Pinterest as inspiration.

Musical arts

Using recycled materials with music opens a child's mind to a world where reinvention is possible and 'wrong' is not in the vocabulary! Think about including disused pots and pans to make impromptu percussion instruments. Wooden and metal spoons make great drum sticks, as do spatulas, whisks, combs and hairbrushes. Use recycled tin cans, adding rice, pasta and sand to create home-made musical instruments. Tissue boxes covered with elastic bands make a fantastic sound, as do cardboard/paper tubes when they are sung into! How could these traditional musical instruments be made using alternative materials? Accordion, rondador, harp, xylophone, banjo, bongo.

OVER TO YOU

Think of a variety of musical instruments that are specific to a certain culture(s) and plan how these could be recreated in the early years environment using 'junk' materials.

Planning creative arts outings

Síolta Standard 16, Community Involvement, highlights the importance of connecting children with the resources in their community and society. Outings are a great way to introduce young children to a world outside the early years environment. They also offer a range of opportunities for young children to explore new places, give them a chance to experience play in a new place, and provide new and exciting opportunities. Outings also bring with them new learning challenges as children are asked to try out activities they may not have experienced before. Outings can range from a simple walk to a local park or grassed area to more complicated outings that require detailed planning. Outings are an important part of every child's education experience and are promoted by a number of early years curricula, including Aistear.

When planning outings the following considerations are important.

1 Ages and stages of development

What are the ages and stages of development of the children? The child/children's developmental stage should be the first consideration when planning an outing as it sets a solid platform for decision making. Outings can happen from a very young age, when young babies can be transported by buggies/prams. It is important to note that young children will generally value their care routine over any outing you may provide. For very young children, make sure that any trips outside the setting do not clash with mealtimes and sleep routines if these cannot be facilitated when outside the setting. The developmental stage of the children will provide you with valuable information such as:
- length of time the outing can be
- type of place you might visit
- what resources you need to provide
- how many children and adults can go on the outing.

OVER TO YOU

What different needs would a six-month-old baby and a four-year-old child have on an outing?

2 Aim of the outing

Planning an outing should not happen in a vacuum. An outing is just like any other early years activity, albeit more complicated to implement! When planning an outing think about:
- What is the purpose of this trip?

- Has this trip been organised in consultation with the group of children, families and other relevant parties?
- Would the children be interested in visiting this place?
- How can this trip facilitate children's learning?
- How might this outing fit with the Aistear Themes of Exploring and Thinking, Wellbeing, Communicating, and Identity and Belonging?

When planning any outing, visit a place which the child/group of children will like, where they will have an opportunity to be actively involved in the new environment and have their imaginations ignited by the experience!

3 Where are you going?

Think about the place you are planning on visiting. Have you been there before? As the adult in charge it is important to visit the venue before the outing to ensure that you are comfortable that the children will be happy and safe while on their visit. Completing a 'recon' visit will aid the leader's confidence levels and ensure that planning can happen in a safe manner. During your pre-trip visit, carry out a 'risk assessment' (see Chapter 9). During this assessment you can decide whether or not you are happy to choose this venue for the outing. Think about toilet and nappy changing facilities. Are the facilities hygienic and child-friendly? Where can children eat and drink on the trip if they get hungry or thirsty? Is there a place to have a rest if they get tired? It is important to remember that poorly organised outings can lead to tragic outcomes. It is your responsibility to ensure you minimise any risks to the children's safety.

Once you have chosen the venue, ensure that you know who is responsible for booking and paying for the venue. Imagine arriving at your destination with a full coach of children, only to find that you are not booked in!

OVER TO YOU

Group research: look at archived newspaper articles online about early years outings that resulted in a safety risk to children. Discuss how a 'recon' visit could have prevented these accidents/incidents.

4 When are you going?

Think about the time of day, week, month and season of your outing in relation to children's care routines. On outings, young children still need to eat and drink, go to the toilet/have their nappy changed, nap or sleep. Are you leaving the service early in the morning? How might this impact on a child's mood? A child who is upset at having their morning care routine disturbed will not enjoy their trip. Think about where you are going: are there any pre-scheduled events in the venue on the day you wish to go? Might this clash with/impact on your outing? Think about the month and time of year – will the weather determine what resources you need to bring? Think about the following scenario and the considerations you may need to be mindful of regarding timing.

> **Outing Scenario**
>
> You are working in the baby room. It is 18 July. Next Tuesday you will have three babies, Holly (eight months), Fiona (six months) and Billy (eleven months), in your care. You will be accompanied by your co-worker Martin. You are hoping to bring the group to the local park, approximately ten minutes' walk away. You want the group to be at the local park at 9 a.m. as the birds will be singing in the trees at this time and Billy recently got a new bird at home. Holly does not usually come into your care until after 10 a.m., so you have asked her Dad to bring her in early on that day. Billy is usually the first to arrive each morning at 7.30 a.m. Fiona has no 'regular' drop-off time as her Mum works different shifts. You saw on a community noticeboard that a local 'boot-camp' fitness group meets in the park at 9.15 a.m. each Tuesday.
>
> Think about what time of day (care routine), week (community and family scheduling), month and year (weather) considerations you need to apply to this scenario.

5 Insurance

When planning to bring children outside the service you must first check if the facility's insurance covers this type of activity. Check that the policy is fully paid and up to date. It is important to read any stipulations in the insurance policy regarding child/adult ratios allowed while outside your service, the minimum number of adults on the trip and whether there are any restrictions on where to visit/what types of equipment the children can and cannot use while on the outing. If in doubt, contact the insurance company directly at the number provided on the insurance policy.

6 Child/adult ratio

Under the Child Care (Pre-School Services) (No. 2) Regulations (DoHC 2006a) strict rules apply to adult/child ratios in a preschool service. When children are on outings these ratios are generally tighter, under the insurance terms we mentioned above. Refer to your service's insurance policy for specific ratio allowances. As adult/child ratios generally increase during outings, this can sometimes leave early years services with a human resources dilemma: on the one hand you want to plan an outing; on the other you do not have enough staff in the service to facilitate the increased ratios. To overcome this barrier, think about planning family days where parents/guardians/extended family members accompany their child on the outing with you. Remember that if going on an outing, volunteers and students are not included in the adult/child ratios and cannot be responsible for the welfare of children. While on the outing, think about which staff members are responsible for which child/children. Best practice would advise that this list is written down and shared with the adults attending in advance of the outing. A master copy should be retained by the person leading the outing.

7 Transport

When you have planned where the outing will be and how many children and adults will be attending, the next thing to consider is how you will get there. Can you walk, or take public transport such as a bus or a train? Do you need to hire a taxi, a mini bus or a coach? Each method of transport brings with it some questions for consideration:

Walking
- How far is it?
- Are there safe paths all the way to the outing site?
- Will you need walking aids, such as push chairs, for children?
- Are there safe places to cross roads?
- How will you protect children from walking on any roads which are used by vehicles?

Public transport
- How regular is the bus or train?
- Do you need to book it in advance?
- How much will it cost?
- How will you pay for it?
- How many people can travel by this method?
- How safe is boarding the method of transport?
- Where will the outing participants sit on the vehicle? Can they all sit together?
- How safe is alighting from the method of transport?
- Are there any hazards in terms of risk from other passengers on the bus/train?
- How flexible is this method of transport in facilitating any specific needs children may have, e.g. travel sickness, toileting, eating, sleeping?

- If this type of transport is required to have seatbelts, are they provided?
- Do the children need booster seats? If so, are they provided by the transport authority or by families?

Private transport

The questions above apply, and in addition you should ask:
- Is the private service provider reputable and fully insured?
- Have the drivers been Garda vetted?
- Will the children be accompanied by a staff member/family member at all times?

8 Time frame

When planning an outing one should consider what length of time you will be out of the service. How long will it take to get to the venue, how long will you be there, and how long will it take to return to the service? Outings need to be meticulously planned to ensure that children get the maximum amount of pleasure from their trip.

> **OVER TO YOU**
>
> Think about the journey to and from the outing. How can you make the route fun and interesting for the group? Can you introduce play into the journey?

When you are in the venue, assess what types of activity are on offer and how long each activity will take. Be mindful of each child's concentration span when planning the outing and organise activities to match individual children's abilities. It is a good idea to carry materials that children will engage with if they have completed or choose not to participate with the planned activity. As we previously mentioned, children's daily care routines will continue to happen while out of the service. Incorporate periods for toileting/hygiene, refreshments and rest while on outings.

> **OVER TO YOU**
>
> Reflect on the routine of a child you know who is aged approximately two years of age. How might you reflect their daily needs while on an outing?

9 Equipment

What will you need to bring with you? Look at the list below and think about the importance of these items while on an outing:
- mobile phones – which are fully charged and have no limit on making or receiving

calls. Relevant contact numbers should be stored on the phone(s), including emergency contact details
- name labels for children and adults
- refreshments (food and drinks)
- feeding equipment (bottles, beakers, etc.)
- sun creams (where relevant)
- appropriate clothing/materials for weather
- nappies, wipes, etc. (where relevant)
- change of clothes for children
- cleansing wipes in case faces/hands get sticky
- walking aids (where relevant)
- first aid kit
- camera/digital recorder
- equipment and materials for specific planned activities during journey, in venue, etc.

OVER TO YOU
What other types of equipment might be needed during an outing?

10 General outing care

Every outing will be a unique experience and each experience will be different depending on the children going, the adults involved, where and when the outing will be. With so many variations it is difficult to discuss all considerations when planning an outing, but here are some additional general points to consider.

Adults' roles

What are the adults' roles during the outing? Before leaving the centre the adults attending the outing should be very clear on their role:
- Which children will each adult be responsible for?
- How will head counts be recorded?
- Who is responsible for administering first aid, if required?
- Are all adults aware of any allergies children have, medication they need, differences in their ability levels, etc.?
- When a child is being accompanied to the toilet, etc., who is responsible for the remaining children?
- What activities will each adult facilitate?
- What equipment will each adult bring?

- Do adults have a way of contacting other members of the group, e.g. mobile phone?
- Are adults fully aware of the service's polices on child protection, behaviour management, curriculum, etc.?
- If an adult observes a co-worker/volunteer/student/family member on the outing not complying with their role, what should they do?

Service policies and procedures

While on an outing, the early years service policies and procedures still apply. This is particularly relevant for child protection and behaviour management policies. It is important to emphasise to any family members who attend the outing that any discipline that needs to be administered should be done so by a staff member rather than by themselves. If they need to discipline their own child for any reason it should be in line with the service's behaviour policy. Other policies also apply, such as curriculum, toilet hygiene, nappy changing and nutrition policies.

OVER TO YOU

Discuss how you could ensure that all adults attending the outing are aware of and will observe the service's policies before the outing takes place.

11 Family considerations

When taking children out of the service, written parental consent must be obtained from parent(s)/legal guardian(s) and a copy should be kept in the child's file in the service. Parents/guardians should be given advance notice of where the outing will be so that they have time to make an informed decision about whether or not they want their child to attend. Provide parents/guardians with a contact number if they need to speak with a person during the outing. If parents/guardians have to provide any money for an outing, be mindful that a family may not be able to afford the cost of the trip. In your budget ensure that you take this into consideration and allow the family to pay in instalments/pay a portion of the fee, etc. If family days are organised, ensure that parents are given plenty of advance notice to organise time off work, etc.

OVER TO YOU

Think about what other family considerations should be thought about when planning an outing.

12 Possible dangers on an outing

Children wandering off

When children begin to walk it brings with it a newfound freedom and also the risk that while on an outing they may wander off. The fear that a child could get lost while on the outing is very real to the early years practitioner. Think about the following points in reducing the risk of 'wanderers':

- Does the service have a policy in place for this eventuality?
- Is there a key worker system in place while on the outing?
- How often do head counts happen?
- Will the child be wearing a name label/indicator that they belong to your group?
- Have the adults on the outing carried out a role play in advance to prepare for this possibility?

If a child does separate from the group it is important that each adult on the outing is aware of the outing policy and follows the procedure exactly.

> **OVER TO YOU**
>
> Look at the following 'lost child' procedure and critique its proposed effectiveness.
>
> Scenario: Child is unaccounted for.
>
> 1. The leader in the group gathers the children together and takes a head count.
> 2. The leader assigns staff members to stay with the remaining children.
> 3. The leader phones the service, asking for the manager/person in charge and informs them of the situation.
> 4. The manager contacts the child's parents/guardians and informs them fully of the situation.
> 5. If possible, the leader asks members of the public to help look for the child, being especially mindful of spaces that should be searched immediately such as car parks, roads and areas with water.
> 6. The Gardaí must be contacted by the leader if the child cannot be located within the first five minutes.
> 7. The leader contacts the manager in the service at this point and informs him/her of the progress.
> 8. In the service, the manager makes arrangements for the return of the remaining outing participants.
> 9. The manager goes to the place where the child was last seen and takes charge of the incident.

Looking at this procedure, how could the adults in charge promote an atmosphere of calm to help the search effort?

Human hazards

On an outing there is also a risk of human hazards, or 'stranger danger'. The vast majority of the public are caring, compassionate human beings, but there is a risk, however slight, that you might encounter a dangerous human on the outing. Children should get the opportunity to learn about outing safety before the outing happens, and they should be informed about 'strangers' in an age-appropriate manner. Where appropriate, use a 'buddy' system in which children are paired with their friends. If children are too young or impulsive for the buddy system, ensure they are safe by making sure that they hold an adult's hand. Make sure that during the outing children are always in sight and at a distance where they are easily accessible. Children should never go to a toilet or any other area in the venue unattended. Remember that even when a key worker system is in place, each adult has a duty of care to every child in the group. Keep your eyes open for any suspicious behaviour you may notice and act on anything that makes you feel uncomfortable.

Injuries

As children's physical abilities are still developing, there is a definite possibility that they may trip up or bump themselves while on an outing. Ensure that a staff member on the outing has a registered and up-to-date first aid certificate. You should also have with you a stocked first aid kit.

The early years service should be aware that more serious injuries can occur during the outing. Policies and procedures should be in place for this eventuality.

OVER TO YOU

Look at the following sample procedure, similar to the procedure for the missing child, and think about how the following steps might be useful in an emergency.
Scenario: Seriously injured child

1. The leader gathers the children together and takes a head count.
2. The leader assigns a staff member to stay with the remaining children.
3. The leader calls 999/112 for assistance.
4. The leader phones the service and informs the manager of the situation.
5. The manager contacts the parents and explains what has happened and which doctor's office/emergency room their child will be attending.

6   The manager makes arrangements for the return of the remaining outing participants to the service.
7   The manager goes to the outing venue where the child was injured and takes charge of the situation or goes directly to the doctor's office/emergency room, depending on the situation. (In the latter scenario the group leader will have accompanied the child to the doctor's office/emergency room.)

Assessing the outing

When the outing is over, it is important to record any significant events that occurred with the aim of either recreating anything you found positive or preventing any challenging situations happening in the future. For more information on assessment, refer to the assessment techniques outlined in Aistear (described in Chapter 3).

A well-planned outing should aim to actively engage young children's hearts, bodies and minds. Outings open children's eyes to the layers of structures in their community as well as giving them a better understanding about their world. When on an outing, remember to go at the child's pace. It's not often, for example, that while out walking a child gets the opportunity to watch the world around them in a slow and reflective manner. Use the outing experience to promote communication through discussion and play. When children are very young, keep the outings simple and manageable; a walk to the local park or even a trip to post a letter at a post box is sufficient to ignite the young child's imagination. As children get older and are about to make the transition to primary school, outings can become more complex. In the section below we will look at some examples of how the creative arts can be used to provide a solid play foundation during outings.

Examples of creative arts outings

Dramatic arts

Linking the Reggio Emilia approach with Síolta Standard 16: Community Involvement, we can see that strong links with one's community are beneficial for young children's development. Have a look at the services that are in your local community and think about how you could link with these resources to plan outings that are respectful of both the outing venue and the child's need to explore. Think about how these local resources could help expand a child's dramatic play:

- greengrocer
- farm
- butcher
- supermarket

- post office
- hairdresser
- newsagent
- garage.

When planning to bring children on a visit to a local resource, first contact the manager of the facility to seek permission for the visit, and to discuss with them the possibility for exploration and active play in the service. Find out how many children they would recommend visit at one time. When visiting local resources, children do not have to go in a large group. If you are visiting a place where space is limited (e.g. a post office) or where there might be a lot of people (e.g. a supermarket), it is more effective to go in a few small groups rather than one large group. Look at the following case study and discuss how the small group experience may have enhanced learning in this circumstance.

CASE STUDY

It is coming up to Mother's Day and Sarah (room leader) and Rachael (early years assistant) have made cards with each of the children. Sarah and Rachael plan to bring the children to the post office to post the cards to each child's home. In Sarah and Rachael's room there are twenty children aged between three years eight months and three years eleven months. Sarah meets the manager in the post office and he is happy for the children to visit. He says that he will make a staff member available to sell the stamps to each child individually and then help them put the stamps on the envelopes. He reminds Sarah that the post office is quite small and not all the twenty children will fit into the post office at the same time. Sarah shares this information with Rachael and they decide to take the children in groups of five. Sarah asks her line manager (Thomas) for two staff members to help out on the outing day, one person to go on the outing and the second to stay behind with the remaining staff member and children. Thomas says that he will go on the outing with the children and asks Anne Marie (early years assistant) to stay in the room. The outing is planned after lunch time to accommodate staff lunches and the trips to the post office are organised as follows:

- 2.00–2.30: Rachael, Thomas and five children
- 2.30–3.00: Rachael, Thomas and five children
- 3.00–3.30: Sarah, Thomas and five children
- 3.30–4.00: Sarah, Thomas and five children.

In addition to visiting facilities where children can watch the real-life alternative to socio-dramatic play, think about the value of visiting the local library with young children. Linking closely with the head librarian you can organise dramatic readings of favourite books, including props, puppets and costumes.

One major benefit of outings in the local community is the value of the journey going to and from the destination. Use this time to reflect with children about local structures, using questions such as:
- I wonder how that was built?
- Who might have built it?
- What was used to build it?
- What might have happened if the builder had decided to build the house with marshmallows instead of concrete?
- I wonder why they decided to put the road on the ground instead of in the sky.
- If there were no cars on the road, what could it be used for instead?

Remember, the outing does not start at the destination; the adult's role is to identify every possible learning opportunity and use these times to promote thought and reflection with the young child.

Dance and movement

Young children love movement. They have an abundance of energy and it can be restrictive to spend every day in the same play spaces. Identify places locally where children can engage in full body movements in a fun and free manner. Look to local enclosed green areas such as parks or fields where children can run, jump, roll, skip and hop without the restriction of adults' hands holding them back. Local parks may also have jungle gyms, swings, climbing frames, see-saws and slides to promote active movement. Other local resources such as swimming pools or play centres can also be great spaces for movement. Have a look in your local telephone directory to see whether there are any local dance studios that you can visit and explore. These dance spaces are specifically designed to encourage movement. Link closely with the instructor from the studio and devise activities for the children to engage in while in this creative space.

Visual arts

While walking around your community, take the opportunity to look at environmental art. Graffiti, advertisements, billboards, posters in shop windows can all be used to inspire a child's creative process. Use photography while on the outings to show children that beauty can be found in everyday objects. Bring a supply of paper and pens for children to sketch any interesting shapes they see. Remember to bring a bag to carry any items back to the service that children may want to use in art work, such as leaves, pebbles, flowers, etc. As children get older – between the ages of five and six – you might want to consider visiting any local art galleries or museums. If planning this outing remember that it is not possible for children to spend an extended length of time speaking in hushed tones. If visiting gallery or museum spaces, focus on one or two exhibitions, link closely with the manager in the space and plan how to make the gallery experience into an active learning opportunity.

Musical arts

Plan outings where children can hear natural music 'playing'. Think about sounds that are created naturally, for example in a forest, field/green area, farm, zoo/wildlife park, aquarium or on the beach. There are a huge number of musical concepts (discussed in Chapter 5) that children can learn from nature.

In addition to natural sounds, look at local musical societies or local choirs and ask if you can visit them during a rehearsal to hear how songs are practised. Are there any local recording studios that you can visit? How about local theatres that produce musicals? The practitioner's role is to explore the local community, hunting for creative arts experiences.

OVER TO YOU

Choose an age group up to six years of age and plan a creative arts outing for this group. Use the following questions as a guide.
- **Planning the outing:**
  - What are the child's interests and where is the best venue to nurture these interests?
  - What is the aim of the outing?
  - What are the objectives of the outing (the step-by-step plan of how the aim will be reached)?
  - How will this outing facilitate learning? (Use the Aistear Themes and Learning Goals as signposts.)
  - Resources: what do I need for the outing?
  - What policies and procedures are in place?
  - What equipment and materials are required?
  - What personnel are needed?
  - What are the safety considerations?
  - How will the outing be financed?
  - How will time be best managed?
- **Going on the outing:**
  - Travelling to the venue: How will this be managed and transformed into a fun time?
  - At the venue: What types of activity are on offer to enhance the experience?
  - Travelling from the venue: How will children's needs be met on the way home?

- Reviewing the outing:
  - When will you give yourself time after the outing to reflect on its highlights and challenges?
  - Where will you organise space to write up an 'outing report'?
  - What will you reflect on/what questions about the outing do you want to answer?
  - How do you want to reflect/what type of assessment method will you be using?
  - Who will you reflect with?
  - How might you plan for future learning opportunities?

Visits from members of the local community

We have discussed that outings are a great way to introduce children to their local community in a fun and creative way. In addition to regular outings it is a great idea to bring members of the local community into the early years environment to visit the children. Look at the following list of service personnel and think about what types of question young children might have for them.

- firefighter
- garda
- hairdresser
- lifeguard
- butcher
- farmer
- teacher
- nurse
- soldier
- waste collector
- shopkeeper
- bus driver.

As well as inspiring original questions, these visits can be used to encourage a child to look at the professional as a role model for their own future career. It sounds strange to describe young children looking for career advice, but recent research, such as that described by Bryce and Humes (2003) highlight that career guidance can begin in the early years. Scotland, for example, recommends career education from the age of three years old.

Inviting people into the environment encourages partnership with the local community and provides strong roots for children growing up in the neighbourhood. Here are some ideas for creative arts visits to the service.

Dramatic arts

In the home corner, construction area and writing areas, observe what and who children role play – home makers, shopkeepers, restaurant workers, hairdressers, doctors, firefighters, builders, taxi drivers, policemen, etc. – and invite people whom the children have an interest in. Before approaching members of the community you may be unfamiliar with, look first towards the families in the service. Mothers, fathers, carers, grandparents, aunts, uncles, family friends can have a range of roles and occupations that would ignite children's imaginations. Forge close partnerships with parents/carers and invite them in to talk and play with children about their role in society.

> **OVER TO YOU**
>
> In a group, discuss how you can be respectful of family's different occupations. Think about how people value some professions over others. Should this perception of a profession be passed on to children? How can children be encouraged to choose what they feel is a meaningful profession for them? Alan Watts' lecture 'What If Money Didn't Matter?' (available online) offers an interesting viewpoint that might inform your discussion.

Music and movement

Looking first among families and friends of the service, invite people who specialise in dance to spend some time moving with the children. Does anybody have an interest in gymnastics, yoga, pilates, boxing, martial arts, t'ai chi, etc.? Ask parents, carers and family members if they are involved in sports or know somebody who is. This form of partnership with parents is fantastic for building relationships as the family member can feel empowered and respected by being given the responsibility of organising a 'visitor'.

Visual arts

Are there any local artists in your community, not only traditional artists, such as sculptors, painters, photographers, but also everyday visual artists – people who work with colour, such as a house painter or interior designer? You can also define people who work with sculpture, such as carpenters or architects, as artists.

> **OVER TO YOU**
>
> Identify some everyday professions and think whether they have a visual arts element in them. How could this be represented if these professionals visited an early years environment?

Musical arts

Local communities are filled with music and generally we don't even notice it! Identify local musicians in a variety of different genres; soul, rock, classical, traditional, etc. Invite these musicians into the service to show the children what they do and demonstrate a live gig. Find out if any family members play a musical instrument and if they are willing to come in and play it with the children. Are there any local DJs who would play music for the group? Think about where you could find out about these local resources and what would be the best way to invite people into the service, respecting that they have busy lives.

Chapter summary

In this chapter we noted that research has found that outdoor play opportunities for young children are on the decline. Increased supervision as well as technology have brought children's play indoors. It is the early years educator's role to move learning experiences outside the confines of an inside space. An outside play policy is an important element to any early years setting. We described how a well-designed play space can open up creative arts opportunities. Dividing the outside area into specific interest areas ensures that children's play is focused and purposeful. Open areas, quiet areas and active areas can be further divided into the music and movement area, the outdoor discovery/garden area, the table-top area, the arts and crafts centre, the messy area, the quiet corner and the role play area. These spaces provide children with a place to be free with their imaginations, use innovative skills and try something new.

This chapter also looked at how to bring the outside world into the early years setting through the use of alternative materials. These 'junk' materials are used to promote open-ended play as well as being a useful resource when working within a budget. Sourcing alternative materials is also a great way to partner with families and members of the local community while promoting a message of sustainability to young children.

This chapter discussed how to plan creative arts outings. We identified how the creative arts can be used to inspire destinations for outings, focusing on the local community as a valuable resource for young children's learning.

We finally looked at how we can bring members of the local community into the early years service to ignite imaginations, provide new experiences and show community role models, as well as giving children a wider perspective on careers they might choose in the future.

OVER TO YOU – RESEARCH PROJECT

Visit an early years service that you are familiar with and in co-ordination with the management, staff, children and families investigate one aspect of their 'outside world' policy, identifying how it could be improved.

7

Creative Play and Positive Mental Health

This chapter explores aspects of the following Learning Outcomes:
- LO 1: Examine a variety of creative media opportunities with young children.
- LO 2: Summarise the benefits of exploration and participation in creative arts for the child.
- LO 3: Explore the role of the adult in creating an environment in which children feel secure and confident enough to take risks and explore new situations.
- LO 4: Plan opportunities for consultation with children to plan and engage in creative arts experiences.
- LO 5: Test open-ended materials and natural items for creative arts, in both the indoor and outdoor environments, appropriate to different stages of children's development.
- LO 6: Explore challenges for adults in respecting choices and decisions of children.
- LO 7: Employ developmentally appropriate creative arts activities which promote the holistic development of the child.
- LO 8: Reflect on one's own role and responsibilities when engaging in creative arts activities with children, being mindful of health and safety.

Historically in Irish culture mental health has taken a back seat to physical health. It is easier for people to talk about a physical ailment than disclose that they are having emotional problems or 'feeling down'.

In early education we focus on working with the 'whole child'. In past years the 'whole child' approach focused on a child's physical wellbeing than their mental wellbeing. The introduction of the Aistear curriculum framework in 2009 saw a national shift in thinking about young children's mental health. This Aistear framework, in co-ordination with Síolta and the pre-school regulations, promotes play as the main context for learning in Irish early education settings. Using research from Cannella and Viruru (1997), Aistear highlighted that when play is used as an instrument of learning children are more likely to be happy and mentally well.

Discussing the topic of mental health often brings with it thoughts of mental illness and disorders. A report in the *Irish Times* entitled 'A little more talk about mental health. Please' by Dr Jacky Jones highlights that mental health relates to a person's 'resilience, ability to think, dealing with feelings, behaving assertively and problem-solve' (Jones 2012). This article puts forward the view of the World Health Organization (WHO) that a solid foundation for positive mental health begins in early childhood, particularly between birth and two years of age.

Young children and mental health

Babies are remarkable creatures! Even before they are born, messages sent between the mother and foetus prepare them for their life outside the comforts of the womb. Annie Murphy Paul gave a very interesting TED talk on this topic called 'What we Learn Before We're Born' (available on YouTube). Research highlights that the most important indicator of mental wellness is the young child's attachment with their primary caregivers. John Bowlby and Mary Ainsworth are the two foremost attachment theorists in child development, assert that the manner in which the primary caregivers respond to the infant is the critical element influencing the development of a secure attachment. This attachment with the caregiver has a physical impact on the structure of the newborn baby's brain. With each passing moment of the baby's life, synapses in the brain are formed at the rate of one million per second. Dr Jones (2012) says that these 'loving and interesting experiences create pathways to mental health'. It is sobering to reflect that by the age of two years the majority of the human's brain formation has taken place. It is crucial therefore that the earliest life experiences should be filled with love, laughter, positive challenges and opportunities to grow into a happy and healthy human being. With this information in mind, what can we do in the early years setting to promote infant and toddler mental health?

Using Maslow's 'hierarchy of needs' from his 1943 paper 'A theory of human motivation' as a theoretical framework we can identify some areas where positive mental health can be promoted in young children. Maslow used a pyramid to describe all the different 'needs' a person encounters in their lives. He called the bottom four levels of the pyramid the 'deficiency needs'. When these lower-level needs are met a person is contented and happy, but if they are not met that same individual becomes anxious and preoccupied. The deficiency needs are:

- **physiological needs**: eating, drinking, sleeping
- **safety needs**: feeling physically and emotionally secure
- **social needs**: having friends and receiving affection from people you love
- **ego needs**: self-esteem and recognition for achievements.

When all a person's deficit needs are met they can turn their attention to the fifth level of the pyramid, which Maslow described as the 'growth need'. This level enables an individual to reach their fullest potential, which he called 'self-actualisation'.

Although Maslow's theory has received criticism over the years for being overly simplistic in its view of human motivation, it can act as a useful guide when putting in place positive mental health interventions in the early years. Linking Maslow's idea with the child-centred philosophy of the Reggio Emilia approach, in this chapter we shall rename Maslow's 'hierarchy of needs' as a 'hierarchy of rights'.

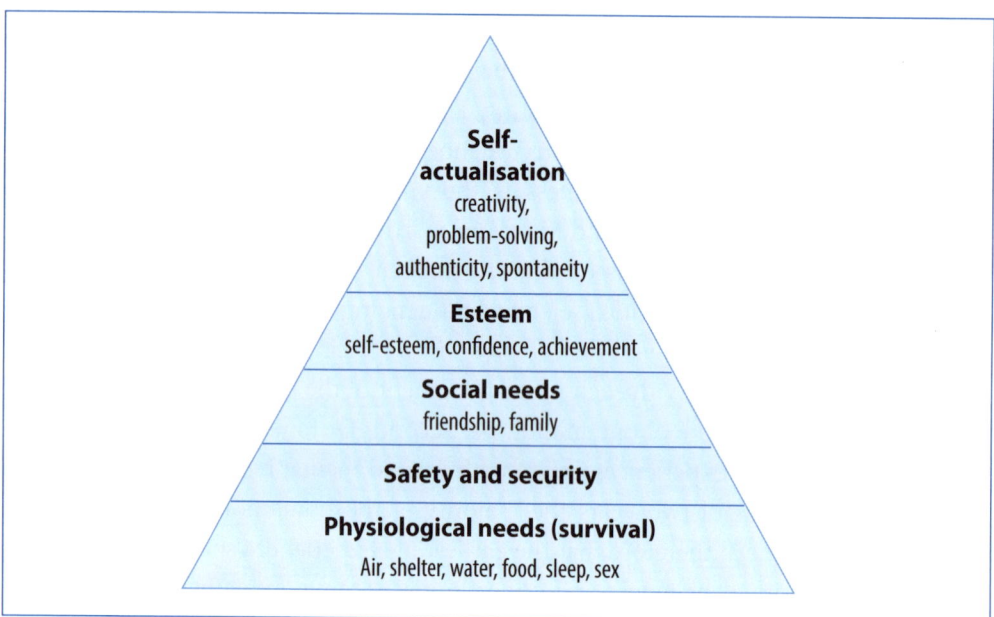

OVER TO YOU

What is the difference between using the word 'rights' rather than 'needs' when implementing daily routines for young children? When reflecting on these terms, have a look at the articles of the United Nations Convention on the Rights of the Child (UN 1989) and Síolta Standard 1: Rights of the Child.

Implementing children's rights to promote positive mental health

Physiological rights

The body's physical survival requires water, air, food and sleep. It is important that when working with young children a solid and consistent care routine is in place. The Child Care (Pre-School Services) (No. 2) Regulations (DoHC 2006a) give early years providers clear instructions on facilities for rest and sleep as well as other care-based needs of the young child. In addition, the *Food and Nutrition Guidelines for Pre-School Services* (DoHC 2006b) advises services about appropriate nutrition for young children.

OVER TO YOU

Think about what would happen if you tried to engage a young child in a creative arts activity if they were tired or hungry.

Safety rights

Young children have a right to feel safe in their environment. We saw in Chapter 2 that a feeling of security is essential in developing creativity. We can ensure that children feel safe in a number of ways:

- Promote the secure bond between the child and their primary caregivers such as their parents, for example by providing a designated breast feeding space in the service. Have an open door policy and encourage a strong partnership with parents/families.
- Form consistent and loving relationships between adults and children in the early years environment through interventions such as a key worker system.
- Put in place a consistent daily routine where the child can predict what will happen in the day.
- Ensure that the early years environment is physically safe through ongoing and meticulous safety checks and a high-quality hygiene routine. (Remember that if the adult cannot feel sure about the children's physical safety they will not be able to relax and play with them.)
- Maintain an emotionally safe environment through providing positive reinforcement, high-quality supervision and modelling 'friendship' behaviours between peers (see Chapter 2 for more details). In this emotionally safe space the child should feel welcomed into the environment, feel a sense of belonging and have a range of stimulating play experiences freely available to them throughout the day.

Social rights

Social rights are incredibly important for promoting the creative arts curriculum. Every child has a right to feel loved. In an environment where there might be many children and just one or two adults, this 'love' feeling can be lost. Look at the following case study and discuss how Darragh's right to feel loved could have been better accommodated.

> **CASE STUDY**
>
> Nap time is just ending. The five children in the toddler room are walking up at their own pace. Siobhán (key worker) is attending to Cormac (sixteen months), by putting on his shoes and giving him his beaker of water. Darragh (eighteen months) has just woken up. He reaches for his blanket but cannot find it. His mouth turns into a frown. He walks over to Siobhán, who is kneeling on the floor, and attempts to sit on her knee. Siobhán says, 'I'm putting on Cormac's shoes, Darragh.' Darragh begins to cry.

In this case study we can see that at a vulnerable moment Darragh's right to social interaction was not met. How might this impact on Darragh and Siobhán's relationship?

> **OVER TO YOU**
>
> **Being open and loving with the children in your care is the cornerstone of the early years educator's role. Close your eyes and imagine that you are in a room with a group of people who love you and whom you love. Feel what impact that sense of love has on your heart, body and mind. Now imagine you have left that room and entered a place full of people you have never met before. How do you feel now? Nervous? Lonely? Perhaps even scared? These tense feelings create a physical reaction in the body that can cause stress and anxiety. Imagine what it might be like for the young child entering a preschool environment. How can you as the early years educator ensure that the infant, toddler and young child know that they are welcome, they belong and that you love them?**

Ego rights

The importance of high self-esteem cannot be underestimated in a person's life. Self-esteem gives an individual the ability to believe in their personal worth and helps them disregard any harmful thoughts they might have about themselves. Self-esteem builds resilience and motivates us to aim high in life. As children try, fail, try and succeed they begin to build an image about themselves and their capabilities.

There are a number of ways in which self-esteem can be fostered in the young child.

- **Give the young child opportunities to try new things:** Ensure that new experiences are supported in co-ordination with the key worker and that the child knows that trying, not winning, is the definition of success.
- **Offer the child achievable challenges:** Using Vygotsky's 'zone of proximal development' model, assess what level or stage a child is at and introduce challenges that are slightly above this baseline level. These individually tailored challenges give opportunities for children to problem solve and overcome adversity in a safe and supported environment. Mini-successes send a message to the child that they are capable of overcoming difficult situations in their lives.
- **Provide open-ended play activities:** Open-ended play gives children the sense that possibilities are endless and that the sky, and sometimes beyond, is the limit! This limitless play evokes the idea that the child is the master of their own destiny. Open-ended play is empowering and gives children the concept of responsibility over their life.
- **Ensure that the environment encourages peer interaction:** Playing, talking and laughing with others lifts a child's spirits and brings them a sense of joy. Watch for any children who often play alone and encourage them into group games. Peer interaction in the early years environment should be supported by adults to ensure that play partnerships are equal and fair.
- **Watch your words!** Be mindful of the verbal and non-verbal messages that are sent to young children. If the adult is hurried or tense a slip of the tongue or stern tone can knock a child's confidence. Children hold on to these harsh words and messages and they can become a part of a child's self-image. The adult's role is to exclude these negative attitudes from the early years environment and have a 'grouch-free zone' when it comes to interacting with young children.

OVER TO YOU

Can you recall anybody in your life who sent you a negative message about yourself? Did you believe them? What impact did this negative message have on your self-esteem? If that individual had never sent you that negative message, how might you be different today?

- **Be a positive role model:** The early years educator has a varied job, as they hold multiple roles in one body. One of these roles is to be the young child's advocate, their personal cheerleader! You were asked above to reflect on a person who sent you a negative message. Now think about a person who sent you a positive message about yourself. What was it about this person that made you believe them? Was it their persistence in the message? Was it their relationship with you? What impact did this positive message have on your self-esteem? If that individual had never sent you that positive message, how might you be different today?

- **Provide a high level of supervision for the children in your care:** Through observation and having a close relationship with each child you might be able to identify any negative self-image the child has picked up. Counteract these thoughts through activities, experiences and reinforcement that highlight a positive view of the child. Phrases such as 'I can't do it' and behaviours such as handing you their coat to put on them rather than trying to put it on themselves are examples of negative self-image. When you are in the process of reversing any negative self-thoughts, it is the adult's role to catch the child being 'good'! Be affectionate through your words and actions and actively show the child that you are proud of them.

Growth rights

Support young children to feel confidence in themselves through positive reinforcement. Encourage children to speak up for themselves when they have done something they are proud of. Model this through praising yourself and others and motivate children to applaud the achievements of their peers. Personal growth values include wanting to learn and develop for oneself rather than to please others. Personal growth also highlights the ability to be self-aware and to be motivated to do 'good' for reasons other than personal recognition.

> **OVER TO YOU**
>
> Choose an interest area (discussed in Chapters 5 and 6) in an early education environment and discuss how the idea of personal growth could be promoted through creative arts activities in this area.

Therapeutic benefits of creative arts

We have seen that the creative arts curriculum aids children's development in many ways, but did you know that offering a solid creative arts schedule in the early years environment also has therapeutic benefits for the young child? Schmid describes how the creative arts give individuals a temporary respite from anxiety, releasing blocked feelings and building self-confidence; high-quality creative arts opportunities 'break down barriers within the mind' (Schmid 2006:87).

A longitudinal study on Irish children's lives, entitled *The State of the Nation's Children*, has to date published two reports, the first in 2006 and the second in 2012 (DoHC

2006c; DCYA 2012). The 2006 report highlights that an individual's self-esteem and self-perception are intertwined with mental health. It is interesting to note the findings from the 2006 report, which asserts that young females are more likely to have lower levels of self-esteem and self-worth than young males. For both genders it was found that self-esteem decreases with age. The 2006 report cites the view expressed in the *National Health Promotion Strategy 2000–2005* (DoHC 2000b) that mental health is as important as physical health to a child's overall wellbeing. For school-age children the SPHE (Social, Personal and Health Education) curricular component represents one aspect of how the state is promoting positive mental health among children. In the early years sector we have the Aistear framework, which uses a four-pronged thematic approach to address children's holistic development. Children's mental wellness is promoted in all four themes (Wellbeing, Identity and Belonging, Communicating, and Exploring and Thinking), but is seen especially in the theme of Wellbeing, which aims for children:

- to be strong psychologically and socially
- to be as healthy and fit as they can be
- to be creative and spiritual
- to have positive outlooks on learning and on life.

OVER TO YOU

Looking at the Aistear theme of Wellbeing, discuss how its aims and learning goals could promote positive mental health in an individual. How do the additional three Aistear themes also promote mental wellness?

The 2012 *State of the Nation's Children* report also refers to children's mental health. This report places children's mental health in the context of mental illness and referrals to psychiatric care. There is a contrast between how young people's mental health is perceived in this 2012 report and the WHO definition, in which 'mental health' is seen as an part of the person rather than as a 'condition' to be remedied. The High/Scope philosophy describes how high-quality play environments can promote mental wellness in young children without the use of labels such as 'illness' or 'condition'. Look at the project detailed below and reflect on how this approach yielded such dramatic results in the lives of young children.

CASE STUDY: THE PERRY PRESCHOOL PROJECT

History
The High/Scope Perry programme ran between 1962 and 1967 in Ypsilanti, Michigan. The programme included weekly home visits to aid families support the Perry educational process at home.

Philosophy
The High/Scope Perry preschool curriculum aimed to enhance children's cognitive, socio-emotional and physical development. In this model children were encouraged to plan their own open-ended play activities, carry them out and reflect on them (Plan, Do, Review). The adults' role was to arrange the early years environment to support learning in various areas, to play alongside children as they planned activities, support children to solve their own problems, and motivate children to think through their own ideas. The adult in the High/Scope curriculum completed ongoing 'child observation records' based on a number of learning objectives which aided in designing an individualised plan for each child in the group.

Creative arts philosophy and High/Scope
High/Scope divides the creative arts curriculum into five different components:
1. **Art:** Children were given space and opportunity to communicate what they observed, thought, imagined, and felt using two- and three-dimensional artistic media.
2. **Music:** Children were free to express themselves through music, representing what they observed, thought, imagined, and felt.
3. **Movement:** Children were given space and time to move and dance in the environment, expressing their observations, thoughts, fantasies, and feelings.
4. **Pretend play:** Children were offered real-life materials and equipment which allowed them to express and represent what they observed, thought, imagined, and felt through role play.
5. **Appreciating the arts:** The creative arts were appreciated through visual displays, reinforcement and praise. Children were encouraged to freely express their views on the aesthetics and messages the arts represented to them.

Long-term results
Students were followed from preschool through to the age of forty. The results showed:
- improved educational outcomes for the participants
- less need for special needs provision

- fewer pregnancies in teenage years
- increased employment and earning potential among the participants
- increased retention and high school graduation among participants
- decreased crime among the cohort of students
- participants were more likely to have health insurance
- they were less likely to join criminal gangs/engage in gang-related activity.

OVER TO YOU

Looking at the summary of the High/Scope philosophy and the Perry Preschool Program, reflect on the list of long-term outcomes that resulted from this intervention. Why, do you think, were the children in the programme more successful in life than peers who did not attend the programme? Look at Irish early years interventions, such as the Tallaght West Childhood Development Initiative or the Young Ballymun programme, which also used the High/Scope approach. Research these initiatives' aims for children's mental wellness. Can you find any other Irish early years programmes in place around the county which focus on mental wellbeing?

Using creative arts to promote mental wellness

The creative arts curriculum in the early childhood environment can be a great space for young children to relax and play in a manner that reflects their individuality. When children are given opportunities for spontaneous and planned arts activities they engage their innate creativity, connecting their minds and bodies with an inner freedom that can sometimes be lost if not properly nurtured. Creativity can be fostered and given a space to develop when one employs a high-quality play ethos in the early years service. The Framework for Early Learning (NCCA 2004) outlined that in an early years environment young children's learning should be an active process. This active learning occurs when the child is offered a variety of tasks that encourage curiosity, risk taking, concentration, resilience, creativity and fairness, in an environment that challenges the child to be motivated and to seek knowledge. This type of 'pure' play allows the child to immerse themselves in the play frame and become engrossed in the feelings, actions and thoughts the activity brings.

The creative arts curriculum supports children's learning at a fantastic rate, and it can also be used outside the early years environment as a specialised therapeutic tool. Drama, art, music and play therapy are just some interventions that can be used with young children who are undergoing or have lived through trauma in their lives. Parental separation, death, the emigration of family members, as well as more everyday life transitions, such as the birth of a sibling, moving house or even the change from nappies to toileting, can have a significant impact on a child's mental wellness. Creative arts therapies can be useful in helping the young child communicate their feelings and thoughts without the use of lengthy discussions. You can find more information on creative arts-based therapies in Ireland from the Irish Play Therapy Association (www.ipta.ie) and the Irish Association of Creative Arts Therapists (www.iacat.ie).

CASE STUDY

Michael is three years two months old. Over the last two weeks he has displayed feelings of sadness and he is refusing to play with his peers or with you, his key worker. He cries often and is anxious when his mum drops him into the service in the morning. Michael is easily irritated by the other children, becoming involved in conflicts over toys. He has lashed out, biting one of his peers. Michael's observations show that he has engaged in a physical altercation with a peer or with you at least twice a day over the previous two weeks. Michael used to love playing in the construction corner building elaborate structures, but his concentration has decreased over the last two weeks and he will stay no longer than three minutes on any one activity. You have spoken with Michael's family about this change in behaviour and they agree that he is having a difficult two weeks. Michael's mum is expecting a baby at the end of the month and you wonder if this is causing Michael's distress.

OVER TO YOU

Have a look around your local community and find out whether there are any creative arts therapeutic services for Michael. What information would you need to find out about the therapy before you would suggest it to the family?

As we mentioned previously, the creative arts curriculum can hold the potential to give children a better understanding of the world around them and in turn help them make sense of any confusing or potentially unsettling life experiences. We will now look at some examples of how the creative arts curriculum can help children through any life transitions they may face.

Dramatic arts

The role play area in the early years environment provides children with a chance to act out situations they may not be comfortable with or try to answer questions they have about day-to-day life situations. If we look at the case study above and the prospective joyous occasion of the arrival of a new baby, Michael may have many questions such as: Where will they sleep? Will I have to leave when the baby comes? Will the

baby take my Mammy and Daddy? What's a big brother? Will I have to share my toys? These types of unforeseen and uncontrollable changes in a young child's life can be very distressing. Through close observations and relationships with both the children and families in the service the early years educator can keep their 'finger on the pulse' of any upcoming changes in the child's life and in turn provide materials and equipment which engage the child to enact these life questions through play.

OVER TO YOU

Look at the scenario in the case study below and think about what dramatic play materials and equipment the key worker can introduce into the environment for Tony's situation.

CASE STUDY

Tony is two years nine months old. He has started toilet training at home and his parents want to extend this into your service. His dad has described how when Tony is brought to the potty he is becomes 'distressed' and runs away. His dad has found Tony hiding under a bed in the family home. His parents have introduced stickers and star charts, which Tony enjoys looking at before the potty is introduced, but when the potty is in sight he becomes anxious.

Using the idea that role play can be used to navigate life stressors, look at the following situations that can happen in a child's life and think about how they could be accommodated in a developmentally mindful manner in the role play area:

- transitioning to primary school
- a family member leaving home
- moving house
- the death of a family pet
- bed time.

Professional therapeutic intervention

For young children there are two main role play-based therapies that can be used if children are finding life stressors particularly difficult: play therapy; and drama therapy.

- **Drama therapy:** Using a variety of expressive media such as movement, voice work, body language and speech, drama therapy aims to explore ideas, feelings and problems using drama-derived activities. This type of therapy also aids in developing an individual's spontaneity, imagination and creativity. It aims to improve self-image and self-confidence while developing social and relationship skills.
- **Play therapy:** This type of therapy is suitable for children as young as two and a half years. Using play, the specially trained therapist engages in scenarios with the child and helps them to release any needs, fears or wishes they may have. Play therapy also helps children to come to terms with emotional and behavioural difficulties in their lives.

Movement and dance

Physical fitness and exercise is a key ingredient for positive mental health. Dishman *et al.* (2013) highlight that exercise is a proven stress release and has been used as a treatment in anxiety and depression for young children. Children who engage in regular exercise have been noted to have higher self-esteem and a better outlook on life than children who are more sedentary. When you are planning your daily routine, see how much physical activity and large movement is offered to children throughout the day. A general rule of thumb should be that any quiet (sitting) activity such as mealtimes, rest time, story time, etc. should be followed by some form of movement activity. Movement activities can range from gentle to moderate to high-energy activities. (During all these activities plenty of drinking water should be available to ensure proper hydration.) Have a look at the following types of instructed and spontaneous movement activities and classify them as low-, moderate- or high-energy movement activities:

- running and catching games (e.g. You're It)
- throwing a ball
- yoga
- zumba
- climbing on steps, climbing frames or trees
- community walk
- head over heels/tumbling.

When planning for movement throughout the day, think of the following considerations:
- What are children's ability levels with movement?
- What activity will take place directly before the movement activity? For example, if the child has eaten a large meal would aerobics be suitable as a follow-on activity?
- What will take place directly after the movement activity? For example, if children generally nap at a certain time, would an activity such as running be suitable before their nap?
- How would you know if a child needed more physical activities in their daily routine?

The HSE initiative *Get Ireland Active* suggests that children should engage in a minimum of sixty minutes of moderate physical activities daily (HSE 2013). The European Commission-sponsored project known as IDEFICS (Identification and Prevention of Dietary- and Lifestyle- Induced Health Effects in Children and Infants) has suggested that to protect children from heart and blood circulation problems later in life, there should be a minimum of eighty minutes' exercise per day, twenty minutes of which should be vigorous. An infant's physical activities would focus on general gross motor movements. An important note to remember is that young children should never be forced to sit if they want to move: the child knows their body better than the adult. A general rule of thumb is to follow the child's lead.

OVER TO YOU

In pairs or a small groups plan an outline of a daily routine for the following age groups: birth–one year; one–two; two–three; three–four; and four–six. Focus on which low-, medium- and high-energy activities could be included in the day's events. Think about the reasons you want to include certain activities over others and how these activities could impact positively on a child's mental health.

Professional therapeutic intervention

Children can engage in dance movement therapy facilitated by a trained and registered therapist. This type of therapy aids in situations where children are blocked from expressing feelings, thoughts and concerns verbally. Through employing movement and dance creatively a person can explore their full range of emotions in an environment where they are safe from judgement and further harm.

Visual arts

Cole and Knowles (2011) propose that visual art activities can help children who display challenging behaviour, as these activities promote self-esteem. When a child receives praise and recognition for effort in completing their art it promotes what Cole and Knowles (2011) describe as 'positive psychological flow'. This occurs when children enjoy the activity they are engaged in, believe they can get better at it and achieve success in the area. The adult supports the child's expression of emotions through visual art when free-flowing conversation occurs in tandem with the artistic process. The case study below describes an interaction between Shauna (four years two months) and her key worker David.

CASE STUDY

Shauna is in the art area standing at the easel. David approaches Shauna and says, 'I see you chose to paint today, Shauna. Can I ask what is happening in the painting?' Shauna is placing lines of paint on the paper using different colours. Shauna says to David, 'It's the candles on the cake and it's not your birthday, you have to share birthdays, these are Jessica's candles and I'm not allowed blow them out, you'll get in big big trouble.'

David says, 'Oh, I see. Can I blow them out? One, two, three', and he pretends to blow the candles out. Shauna laughs and says, 'No, David, these are Jessica's candles. You have your own candles on your birthday.'

David responds by saying, 'Oh, okay, so what happens if I blow these candles out?' Shauna says, 'You'll be in big trouble, I warned you; no cake for you.' David then asks Shauna, 'Oh I see; have you ever seen anybody blowing out Jessica's candles before?'

Shauna, in a quieter tone of voice, says, 'Well, I had an accident and blew out Jessica's candles and Jessica cried and I got no cake and I was so sad and I said sorry to Jessica.' David responds, 'That sounds like a sad story on the happy birthday day. And you are painting the candles today?' Shauna says, 'For Jessica.'

> **QUESTIONS FOR REFLECTION**
> 1. Was this a planned or spontaneous activity?
> 2. How do you imagine Shauna planned to create this visual art piece?
> 3. What types of question did David use in the conversation – open or closed?
> 4. What types of emotions were conveyed through the process of completing this painting?
> 5. How might painting the candles help with any anxieties Shauna may be experiencing?
> 6. How could this activity be extended to help with Shauna's emotions?
> 7. How would you communicate the importance of this visual art piece to other people in Shauna's life, such as her peers (with Shauna's consent) or her family members?

When providing materials and equipment in the arts and crafts centre, be aware that different types of activity will evoke different memories and emotions. Have a look at the following activities and explore what types of emotion they might induce:
- finger painting
- clay sculpting
- cutting/tearing paper and pasting
- drawing with crayon
- play dough.

Professional therapeutic intervention

Art therapy is a popular form of treatment for children who are experiencing difficult life stressors. The old saying 'A picture is worth a thousand words' feeds into the premise of art therapy. In this therapy individuals express their innermost feelings and thoughts through a variety of visual artistic media. With a trained and registered therapist the client is able to reflect on their creations, linking images with words and feelings. The art therapist reflects with the client not only on the finished product but also on the process of making the piece.

Musical arts

Music has been used historically as a medium to relax and sooth people. Lullabies and humming ease infants to sleep; familiar rocking and nursery rhymes are used to comfort upset toddlers. Music is a universal and cross-cultural mental wellness tool. Harris (2009) reminds us that music has been used to express emotions, to communicate, in religious celebrations, to grieve, to entertain and to inform. Music can dramatically change energy levels in the room and the early years educator needs to be keenly aware of any music introduced into the environment. Music can be used with young children for a variety of purposes:

- to ease transitions, e.g. by singing the 'Tidy-up Song' between activities
- to create an awareness of routine, e.g. playing/singing certain songs at specific times of the day every day
- to help bodies rest, e.g. lullabies at sleep time
- to help raise energy levels, e.g. fast music before outside time.

The music people choose to listen to in a particular moment in time can give a fantastic insight into their emotions. In addition to this, the music we hear has a bearing on our mental wellness. Music is subjective, and different songs and compositions will have different meanings for the individual listening to them. Give children access to equipment to listen to music by themselves and with peers. Allow them the opportunity to hear the music they want to listen to. Support this individual choice through conversations, wondering with children about what songs mean, and help children to reflect on how songs make them feel.

Look at the following interaction and discuss how the conversation impacted on Henry's (three years ten months) emotional intelligence.

CASE STUDY

Henry is sitting with his key worker Maura at morning planning time.

Maura: Henry, do you know what you would like to do first this morning?

Henry: Listen to the sun song on the phones.

Maura: The sun song, in the music area, on the headphones?

Henry: Yeah.

Maura: It sounds like you have been thinking about this a lot, Henry. Pretend you are listening to the sun song now. [Maura puts her hands over her ears, pretending they are headphones.] Can you feel the song in your body?

Henry holds his hands at his ears and begins to smile.

> *Maura:* I can see the sun song makes your mouth smile, can you feel it anywhere else?
>
> Henry points to his chest.
>
> *Maura:* You can feel it in your heart too! It sounds like that song makes your body happy. That's a good thing to know if you ever feel sad. If you want to feel happy again you can listen to it.
>
> Henry walks over to the music area and puts on the headphones; Maura puts on the song 'Bring Me Sunshine' by Morecambe and Wise.

OVER TO YOU: SELF-REFLECTION

Take a pen and paper and write down the following emotions on a piece of paper. Beside the emotions write down a song that evokes this emotion in you. Think about how useful it can be to hear the song if you are feeling the emotion or if you want to change your mood:

- happy
- sad
- lonely
- jealous
- guilty
- excited
- angry.

Professional therapeutic intervention

Music therapy is a non-verbal intervention that uses sound as the medium of communication. When used with a trained and registered therapist it provides a safe space for self-expression. Music therapy uses a variety of musical instruments to develop the therapeutic relationship between client and therapist.

Chapter summary

The Aistear framework specifically includes mental wellbeing as an area for development with young children. This chapter explored how mental health can be defined as a state of wellbeing in which individuals realise their own potential, manage everyday stressors and are productive in their endeavours. This wellness can be encouraged in early education settings through the provision of free choice activities within the creative arts curriculum.

Using Maslow's hierarchy of needs we explored how individuals have in life a variety of needs or 'rights' to feel mentally well. The adult's role is to provide a balanced combination of physiological rights, safety rights, social rights, ego rights and growth rights to ensure that the early years setting is equipped to support a child's mental wellness.

Looking at the creative arts – dramatic arts, movement and dance, visual arts and music – we established that activities for mental wellbeing can be provided in the early years environment through a holistic and active play approach. In addition to day-to-day play, specialised creative arts therapies can be accommodated for children who are experiencing difficulties due to life stressors. Professional creative arts therapeutic interventions for young children include, but are not limited to, music therapy, drama therapy, play therapy, movement and dance therapy and art therapy.

OVER TO YOU

Reflect on this chapter and put together a hypothetical presentation for families entitled 'Promoting Mental Wellness in Young Children'. Your presentation can focus on any aspect of the chapter which you feel would be of most relevance to families or situations you might have encountered.

8
Unlocking the Adult's Creativity

This chapter explores aspects of the following Learning Outcomes:
- LO 3: Explore the role of the adult in creating an environment in which children feel secure and confident enough to take risks and explore new situations.
- LO 6: Explore challenges for adults in respecting choices and decisions of children.
- LO 8: Reflect on one's own role and responsibilities when engaging in creative arts activities with children, being mindful of health and safety.

This chapter aims to support the reader in unlocking their own creative process. When working in the field of early education the need for the adult to be able to tap into their own imagination cannot be underestimated. Saracho and Spodek (2002) identify that adult creativity is different from children's creativity. When adults display creativity it can be seen in an ability to invent something 'new', to problem solve in an innovative way and to produce artistic projects.

The Start Strong *Children 2020* report (Start Strong 2010) emphasises that the Irish early years sector needs to become professionalised in order to achieve high quality in the field. This report advocates that early years professionals should be skilled, motivated and well qualified. These three terms – skilled, motivated and well qualified – are deeply meaningful in personal autonomy. When working with young children one should endeavour to make every day a fun and exciting experience. This 'every day' approach is a fantastic self-motivator but can also lead to the educator becoming tired and burnt out if a professional ethos is not upheld in the service. This chapter will look at a number of key elements in keeping our professional approach creative and fun when working with young children. We will first address adult creativity, how it can be recognised in an early years professional and where it may be lost along one's life path. The chapter also offers some activities for the adult to unlock their own creative processes before turning to the Síolta Standard of Professional Practice and discussing how to stay fresh and creative when working in the field of early education.

Where is our creativity?

Adult creativity is a part of an individual's intelligence range and becomes visible in the behaviour of 'doing something'. You may have heard people saying, or you may have even said, 'I'm not creative', 'I'm not good at art', 'I can't sing' or 'I can't dance'. Creativity is not something that one person has and another does not. Creativity is an integral part of everybody. Some people can easily access their creativity and others may have difficulty tapping into it. Creative achievement is visible not only in the creative arts, but also in the field of science, in one's workplace, in the home, during recreation periods; it can be included in any aspect of daily life.

Each person can tap into their creativity in different ways. Often adults do not access their creative talents due to a lack of opportunity, a lack of encouragement and a lack of resources to develop their skills. When a person is given the chance to discover their creative talents it can have a positive impact on their self-esteem, self-perception and self-confidence.

It is a misrepresentation to believe that adult creativity can be 'unlocked' by simply letting go of inhibitions. Adult creativity is an active process in which skills, knowledge and resources are combined to problem-solve in innovative ways. The creative adult is able to use their acquired knowledge to control materials and ideas in a way that generates new concrete or conceptual achievements. Each person has a depth of creative talents to tap into. When discovering these creative talents they undergo a personal journey. The Northern Irish paper *Unlocking Creativity: A Strategy for Development* (DETI 2000) acknowledges that a number of factors can stunt a person's creative processes during the formative childhood years. Factors such as social disadvantage, turbulent parenting styles, difficult emotional life experiences and formal teaching methods that did not positively challenge the individual all contribute to a loss of creative confidence. These factors can result in adults becoming passive participants in their own lives rather than people who take risks, persevere at challenges and seek out answers that may be different to the social 'norm'.

The reflective early years educator has a responsibility to shift their thinking between the left and the right sides of the brain. The left side of the brain focuses on logic, memory and the academic skills we learn in school. The right side of the brain focuses on creating and trying something new. In today's society the analytical left side of the brain is given a higher priority than the risk-taking right side. Traditional schooling measures success through exams and point systems. Creative, 'outside the box' thinking is not currently assessed in the school system. In addition, scientific and business professionals have a higher monetary and social value than creative professionals, such as sculptors, poets or dancers. Look at the following aspects of creativity and think about how they are viewed in Irish society: are they promoted or discouraged?

- Trying and failing.
- Being 'different' or acting differently from other people.
- Discussing and showing feelings openly.
- Talking openly about one's success.
- Openly displaying one's creativity (e.g. showing visual art work, singing and dancing in public).
- Being reflective and taking time with plans and ideas.
- Questioning and challenging authority.

Both the left and right side of the brain are equally important when working with young children. The left side enables us to think rationally when approaching challenging situations; it gives us the ability to recall important details about young children and families and to complete critical daily tasks. The right side allows us to think about situations from different points of view, to imagine new ways of being and to see the world in a way that's individual only to you.

OVER TO YOU

Use the scale 0–10, with 0 being 'no creativity' and 10 being 'the most creative'. Draw out the scale and circle where you perceive your own creativity: 0, 1, 2, 3, 4, 5, 6, 7, 8, 9 or 10.

Looking at the number you circled, write down the answers to the following questions.

1. If you were to explain the reason you chose the number to a person you work with, how would you describe your creativity level?
2. Think of a person you know whom you would describe as 'very creative' (they might be at number eight or above on the scale). What is it about this person that allows them to access their creativity?
3. If you were to ask a person in your life who sees you as 'good' at working with children, where do you imagine they might rate you on the scale?
4. Are there some times when you are more creative than others?
5. Are there some activities in which you find your creativity increases or decreases?
6. If you wanted to increase your creative abilities, what would you need to do to move one step further on your scale?

Creative activities for adults

In this section we offer a range of adult activities that are designed to 'unlock' your creative abilities. These activities are best conducted in small groups in the following manner:
1   Begin with an 'icebreaker'.
2   Complete the activity (no more than three activities in a one-hour session).
3   Spend a few minutes completing a written individual reflection (using the questions below).
4   Finish with a group discussion on the creative process and your reflections.

During the activities you may experience emotions and automatic thoughts, which can also be referred to as your inner dialogue (what you tell yourself). After completing each activity, answer the following ten questions, recording these feelings and thoughts:
1   What did I find easy about the activity?
2   What did I find challenging about the activity?
3   Did I experience a recurring thought or emotion during the activity?
4   Was this a new thought or emotion or have I felt it somewhere before? If the latter, in what context did I feel it before?
5   Does this thought or emotion have a place in my life today as a creative professional? Why/why not?
6   What have I learned about myself after doing this activity?
7   How can I bring this learning into my work with children?
8   If I could have changed anything about what I did during the activity, what would that have been?
9   If I were to advise a colleague or friend how to complete the activity, what would I tell them?
10 If I were to extend this activity for my own personal development, what would be the next step in the activity?

Below are some icebreaker, dramatic arts, movement and dance, visual arts and musical arts activities for adults. It is a good idea to use this list as a starting point and add activities you feel might help you with your creative journey. It is important when completing these types of group activity to 'set the scene' to ensure that each individual engaging with the activity feels comfortable and supported throughout the process.

Think about the following themes that you could include in a 'group contract' when setting up a space for creative work with adults:
- confidentiality

- respecting each other's opinions
- timekeeping
- use of mobile phones and recording devices
- different personalities and abilities
- use of inclusive and respectful language and behaviours
- what happens if group contract is broken by individual(s).

> **OVER TO YOU**
>
> Design a 'group contract' for a group of adults that respects the values of the individuals in the group. Use the guiding points above as well as any additional points you may feel would be beneficial for a successful team experience.

Icebreaker activities

Icebreaker activities are designed to get people into the mindset of a creative activity. Icebreakers warm up the brain and body so that you can complete a group activity in a manner that promotes teamwork, communication and co-operation. The list of icebreaker activities below are commonly used to prepare the participant for the freedom of 'outside the box' thinking.

Human Bingo

The group facilitator designs a five by four grid on a piece of paper. Each box in the grid contains one of the statements below (or others, as appropriate). Everyone has a copy of the grid and a pen or pencil. Encourage the whole group to mix, talk and try to complete their card with as many names as possible. If one of the items listed on the bingo sheet relates to the person they are talking with, the person signs their name in that box. The group facilitator ends the activity after ten minutes and reviews some of the interesting facts the group has discovered about each other. If a group member completes their bingo sheet before the ten minutes they win a 'prize' of your choice. You can use the statements below or add your own statements to individualise them to your group.

- Has brown eyes.
- Tells great jokes.
- Has eaten sushi.
- Can swim.
- Is wearing purple.
- Speaks Spanish.

- Can write with their weaker hand.
- Plays the piano.
- Has two or more siblings.
- Had a coffee this morning.
- Lives a five-minute journey away.
- Can sing a song.
- Name begins with M.
- Had pizza in the last week.
- Loves to dance.
- Watches *The Big Bang Theory*.
- Has a hobby.
- Likes to get up early.
- Has tried an extreme sport.
- Is over six feet tall.

Shared Whispers

Arrange the group in a circle with a clear beginning and end. The person at the beginning of the circle thinks up a sentence with a minimum of four words in it and whispers this sentence to the person next to them. The sentence is passed through everyone until the last player announces the sentence to the entire group. As the sentence passes along the group it can only be stated once between participants and cannot be repeated! Remind the participants that there is no right or wrong, no winning or losing – the joy of this game is anticipating the message!

Fact or Fiction?

Ask everyone in the group to write on a piece of paper three things about themselves that other people in the group may not know. Two of the things they write are true and one is not. Taking turns, they read out the three 'facts' about themselves and the rest of the group votes which are true and which is false. Remind the group to keep the 'facts' fun and simple!

The Question Web

You need a spool of string or ball of wool for this activity and a list of twenty questions. Ask everyone to stand in a circle. The facilitator holds the end of the string and throws the ball/spool to one of the group to catch. They then choose one of the questions to answer. A list of twenty sample questions is given below and these can be adapted for the group. After each question is answered, the person throws the string to another member of the group. Eventually this throwing and answering process creates a web – and you should also learn some interesting things about each other! At the end of the game the facilitator comments that each member of the group all played a part in creating this unique web and if even one person had been substituted it would look different!

1. If you had a time machine that would work only once, what point in the future or in history would you visit?
2. If you could go anywhere in the universe, where would you go?
3. What three objects from your home would you take to a desert island?
4. If you could talk to any one person now living, who would it be and why?
5. If you could have a superpower, what would it be?
6. If you were a mammal, insect, fish, bird or arachnoid, what would you be and why?
7. If you could have a pet, real or imaginary, what would it be?
8. Name a present you will never forget.
9. Name one thing you are proud of.
10. What's your favourite thing to do in the winter?
11. Who's your favourite cartoon character and why?
12. What is your favourite dinner?
13. What is the hardest thing you have ever done?
14. If you were at a friend's house for dinner and you found a dead fly in your salad, what would you do?
15. What was the best thing that happened to you in the last month?
16. If you had the chance to live this week over again, name one thing you would do differently.
17. What is the first thing that comes to mind when you think about fish fingers?
18. What's the nicest thing you've ever eaten?
19. If you had the power to change one issue in the world today, what would it be?
20. What book, movie or TV show have you seen/read recently that you would like to be a character in?

Would You Rather ...?

Place a line of tape down the centre of a room. Ask the group to stand on the tape. As a group, ask and answer the following questions. Questions can range from the ridiculous to serious topics. When asked 'Would you rather ...?' the participants move to the left or right as indicated by the facilitator. Remember, when people have picked their answer, ask them the reason for their choice!

Would you rather...
- eat a spider or a caterpillar?
- own a talking dog or a flying pony?
- visit a beach or the top of a mountain?
- be a cucumber or a potato?
- be invisible or be able to read minds?
- be too hot or too cold?
- meet a really intelligent person or a really beautiful person?
- go without television or takeaway food for the rest of your life?
- eliminate hunger and disease or be able to bring lasting world peace?
- be stranded on a desert island alone or with someone you don't like?
- be the writer of a successful television show or the main actor in a successful television show?
- see the future or change the past?
- wrestle a lion or fight a shark?
- read a book or watch a movie?

Creative activities to unlock adults' dramatic talents

The following activities are designed to promote visualisation skills and imagination. When completing the following activities, remember that the process is more important than the end result. In addition to this, there are no rights and wrongs when completing the activities (keeping in mind the group contract).

Relax and daydream

Dim the lights in the room and arrange the seating in a way that gives each individual space. The facilitator invites the group into the space and ask them to sit on a chair, place their hands on their laps and when comfortable close their eyes. Participants may feel the urge to giggle or laugh. Gently encourage them to control the giggles themselves through deep breathing; if the giggles are uncontrollable the individual may need to step out of the room to regain self-control. Use the following visualisation introduction to encourage individuals to use their imagination.

Announce the following instructions to the group:

1. Sit comfortably with your back straight. Put one hand on your chest and the other on your stomach.
2. Breathe in through your nose. The hand on your stomach should rise. The hand on your chest should move very little.
3. Exhale through your mouth, pushing out as much air as you can while contracting your abdominal muscles. The hand on your stomach should move in as you exhale, but your other hand should move very little.
4. Continue to breathe in through your nose and out through your mouth. Try to inhale enough that your lower abdomen rises and falls. Count slowly as you exhale: one, two, three, four, five, six, seven, eight, nine, and ten.
5. Imagine you are sitting beside a waterfall. It is a summer's day and you can feel the sun on your face. There is a warm breeze in the air. You can see the water cascade into the stream below. In your mind you can see yourself stand up and walk slowly around the edge of the water. Notice the colours and textures around you. What do you see? What can you smell? What can you taste? What noises can you hear? What can you feel under your feet? Can you see the sun sparkling over the water? Can you hear the birds singing? Notice the smell of the trees. You place your toes in the stream and you can feel the cool water on your bare feet. You sit down beside the stream and you allow your thoughts to drift. Give yourself a moment to let yourself daydream in this space.
6. When you are ready, begin to bring your attention back to your breath. Sit comfortably with your back straight. Put one hand on your chest and the other on your stomach.
7. Breathe in through your nose. The hand on your stomach should rise. The hand on your chest should move very little.
8. Exhale through your mouth, pushing out as much air as you can while contracting your abdominal muscles. The hand on your stomach should move in as you exhale, but your other hand should move very little.
9. Continue to breathe in through your nose and out through your mouth. Try to inhale enough so that your lower abdomen rises and falls. Count slowly as you exhale; ten, nine, eight, seven, six, five, four, three, two, and one.
10. When you are ready, open your eyes.

Tell a story or write a poem

Telling a story or writing a poem that expresses something about your identity is an activity that can be done individually. Identify something about yourself that is part of your identity. Write a short story or a poem that represents this aspect of your identity. You can choose to share this story or poem with another individual, a small group or a large group. Remember, there is no right or wrong when completing this activity. You may feel an urge to compare your story or poem to other people's. Resist this urge and remind yourself that your story/poem is as individual as you are and cannot be measured.

Improvisation: Tall Stories

Arrange the group in a large circle. This activity can be recorded via audio or visual recording equipment. The group facilitator starts a story with a sentence that ends with 'suddenly ...' The person sitting next to the facilitator then has to add to the story with their own sentence that ends in 'suddenly ...' Continue the story until everyone has contributed. The story can become more ridiculous as each person adds their sentence. One it is recorded play it back to the group. Here are a few examples of starting sentences:

- 'I went to the zoo this morning and was passing the lion enclosure when suddenly ...'
- 'I went to collect my car from the garage when suddenly ...'
- 'Last Tuesday I turned on the TV when suddenly ...'
- 'When I saw you going into the hospital I tried to call you, but suddenly ...'

Mime

The facilitator divides groups into pairs or threes. This small group is supplied with a card/cards. They are asked to communicate the information on the card(s) to the large group without the using words. The members of the large group can speak when they are guessing the text on the cards. The group is required to guess the nature of the scene. Each scene should have at least three actions and have some degree of complexity. For example:

- putting on coat, leaving house, hailing a taxi
- opening an envelope, reading the letter, becoming excited with the content
- putting on arm bands, walking to the side of a swimming pool, jumping in
- calling your dog, putting on their lead, being dragged off by the dog
- drinking tea, checking your watch, jumping up shocked at the time.

Masks

For this activity you will need crayons or paints, markers, scissors and white card or paper. Give each member of the group a piece of white card or paper. Ask them to draw and cut out a life-sized shape of their face. Suggest to the group that they decorate the mask on both sides. One side represents what they think people see/know/believe about them, i.e. what is seen on the outside. The other side represents what they feel about themselves, i.e. things going on on the inside, what people do not necessarily know or see. Encourage people to use colour and shapes to describe feelings or emotions. Masks will not necessarily represent a human face as this activity is process-based.

Creative activities to unlock adults' movement and dance abilities

Adults are often self-conscious about movement and dance as this form of the creative arts is very visible to other people. Physical movement is a fantastic way to communicate messages to one another and this is done unconsciously every day through our body language. The following activities aim to link bodily movements with conscious thoughts and emotions.

Dancing

Divide people into groups using colours: Red, Blue, Yellow and Green. While everyone is sitting down, put on a piece of music that the whole group will enjoy. Encourage the group to move to the music while sitting. Turn the music up and suggest to the group to stand up, move round the room and dance. Now call out 'Red'. Everybody who is not in the red group should stand sill while the Red group continues dancing. Do the same with the 'Blue', 'Yellow' and 'Green' groups. Finish the activity by encouraging everyone from all the groups to dance again, with the facilitator joining in.

This activity can be extended to a pair or individual person dancing in a small group with others watching; or a pair or individual dancing in a stationary large group. You can choose to extend this further, with the group's permission, by recording the activity on a visual recording device and playing it back to the group.

Movement games

Movement games such as Duck Goose, Simon Says, Follow the Leader, Red Rover,

Hopscotch, Hide and Seek, Kick the Can, etc. can often be lost when we leave childhood. Give yourself space, ideally outside, and organise these games with the large group. Think of other traditional childhood games that could be used to encourage adult movement.

My Moves

Stand in a large circle and encourage each person to come up with a movement that has 'never been seen' by a human being before! There is no right or wrong in the movement, as the aim of this activity is to engage the right side of the brain to think creatively about movement. Encourage the members of your group to combine their moves with the 'new' moves being created around them.

Creative activities to unlock adults' visual arts talent

People often critique and compare visual art, especially if it is their own. Visual art work is subjective and represents an individual's own thoughts and feelings in a particular moment during a particular time. One common barrier for the adult when completing visual artwork is the  difficulty in translating the vision they see in their head to what they can create. Manage your own expectations of what you are able to create and be realistic about your own abilities. Feel secure in the knowledge that the image you have visualised is simply a guide; your finished piece will not look as you imagined it. One of the exciting aspects of creating visual art is that you will not know what it will look like until you decide it is finished!

Vision boards and action boards

Collect pictures and images from a variety of different places which represent two different concepts: Visions and Actions. On your Visions board collect images which represent dreams you have for your personal and professional life. On your Actions board organise images that represent the steps towards achieving your dreams. This art piece uses collage to visually represent individuals' hopes and dreams .

'All About Me' book

Take four sheets of paper, fold them each in half and secure together using twine or

staples. You can use any number of visual media to decorate your book.
- On the cover page, represent yourself with your name and your image, which can be a self portrait or a photograph that you take yourself.
- The first two pages represent you today, your life experiences in the world so far, your favourite things and your values.
- The next two pages represent your family, immediate and extended, where you live, your family 'motto' and cultures.
- The next two pages represent your friends, the experiences you have together, how you met and the reasons you enjoy each others' company.
- The last two pages are open to you to represent any aspect of your life that is unique to you.
- The back cover represents your future hopes and dreams in five, ten, fifteen, twenty years, etc.

Draw your neighbour

Using pencils, paint, or any other type of mark-making material sit opposite a person in your group. Employing any style you want (cubist, classic, impressionist, surrealist, etc.), depict your neighbour's image. When you have finished, frame the image and gift it to the person.

Pandora's box

Use card, wire, papier-mâché, etc. to sculpt your own Pandora's box. Legend says that this box held 'all the evils of the world', but your box can contain whatever you want it to. Use only 'junk' materials to create your sculpture and use the term 'box' loosely to mean any type of container you want your sculpture to look like!

Create a photography exhibition

Take a walk in your local community with the aim to find 'beauty in the mundane'. Take a variety of photographs and use technological aids such as Instagram, Picasa, Photoshop, etc. to adapt your image to your individual style. Print, frame and display your image in a gallery-style exhibition. Remember to give your image a title which you feel best represents the message of the piece.

Face painting

Split up into pairs or groups of three. Each person takes turns painting one other person's face and that person in turn paints somebody else's face. Think about how to display this art work and the process of completing it. Do you want to take photographs or a video recording of the process? Do you want to show your facial art work to your colleagues? How about bringing it outside the safety of the creative environment and take a walk outside with your painted face? How about going for a coffee with your face painted?

Creative activities to unlock adults' musical talents

Contemporary television shows such as *The X-Factor* and *The Voice* highlight society's value of music as a form of self-expression. These shows also highlight a darker aspect of society's view of music; that it can be criticised, sometimes quite harshly and through shaming techniques. Very few adults feel comfortable singing in public and the phrase, 'I'm a bad singer' is often heard from people who might be  asked to sing in a group. The following activities encourage adults to express their musical talents in a way that respects individuality and acknowledges difference in creative abilities. As with the other creative arts, music is as subjective to the creator as it is to its audience. It is important to remember that there are no rights or wrongs in the creation of music.

Song scramble

The facilitator writes out lines from several well-known songs, but writes down only one line on each piece of card. Make sure that only enough songs are used to cover the number of people present. The cards are then scattered on the floor. Once the game begins, each person grabs a card and tries to find the holders of the other cards that will complete the verse or section of the song. The winning group is the first one to correctly assemble and sing their song.

My song

Individually, in pairs or in a small group, compose your own song or piece of music that reflects anything about your day so far: your breakfast, your commute, the weather. When composing your song think about what musical instruments would accompany it. Perform your piece of music to the group using home-made or commercial musical instruments and find out whether they 'heard' your message through the music you composed!

Musical feeling

Listen to a variety of music (contemporary pop, rock, jazz, blues, traditional) and express in a creative way the feelings evoked by listening to this music. You might choose to represent your emotions through words in a story or poem, through a visual art piece, through a dramatic recreation or through composing a song or additional piece of music. Reflect on what it was about the different sounds, words and tempo that inspired you.

The adult's responsibility in the creative arts curriculum

A high-quality early years educator has a very unique personality. This person is able to love the children and families they work with, has a high level of patience and a never-ending amount of creative talents to tap into. The early years educator embodies many different roles:

- playmate
- friend
- anthropologist
- planner
- organiser
- tutor
- observer
- supervisor
- nutritionist
- manager
- security guard
- hygienist.

With each of these roles – as well as thousands of others – come varying degrees of opportunity for the adult to display their creative talents and ingenuity. Craft (2002) highlights a range of research that indicates that people who work with young children are noted as being 'caring' individuals who put the feelings of the children in their care above their own needs. These adults were generally observed to be hard-working and busy while engaging with young children. It was also acknowledged that an adult who chooses to work with children can sometimes feel 'selfish' if they choose to put their own needs over others in work and in their own personal lives.

Craft (2002) proposes that for the early years educator to be able to sustain the level of energy that is needed to be successful, and to remain creative, the practitioner should be 'nourished'. This 'nourishment' comes in a variety of forms: self-care, workplace supervision and continuing professional development. The first step the practitioner takes to ensure that they are adequately nourished is to complete training in their field. Saracho (2002) put forward the view that early childhood practitioners have a tremendous impact on society and throughout her research highlighted that the most important factor in a young child's education is the quality of the teacher. In Ireland the early years educator works in line with mandatory legislation such as the Child Care (Pre-School Services) (No. 2) Regulations (DoHC 2006a) and the Childcare Act (1991) among others. The Irish early years educator can also refer to Síolta and Aistear to use as a guide when implementing high-quality education and care in the early years service.

Looking at Síolta's Standard 11: Professional Practice, we can see that the training and ongoing development of the early years educator is of utmost importance in maintaining a high-quality service. Standard 11 states that 'practising in a professional manner requires that individuals have skills, knowledge, values and attitudes appropriate to their role and responsibility within the setting. In addition, it requires regular reflection upon practice and engagement in supported, on-going professional development.' When this standard is implemented with qualified staff who have in-depth practical knowledge of the pre-school regulations (DoHC 2006a), as well as personnel who put into practice the principles of Aistear, we can be assured that the foundations of a high-quality curriculum are firmly in place.

OVER TO YOU

Quiz yourself on the Child Care (Pre-School Services) (No. 2) Regulations (DoHC 2006a). Do you have the level of skills and knowledge required to meet national legislation?

Self-care and the creative arts

Working with young children is an incredibly rewarding job. Each day the educator gets the opportunity to watch young children grow and develop, to give and receive endless love and to see the joy on little faces when fun and creative experiences are provided. Craft (2002) describes how when an activity goes well the educator as well as the children feed off its energy and this stimulates the adult to persevere in their work. This level of constant energy can tire out even the most dedicated adult. Lougy et al. (2007) advise the educator to learn how to recognise when they are beginning to feel physically or psychologically tired and put in place the following strategies to manage workplace stress:

1. **Recognise how 'self-talk' can impact on your practice:** If you notice that your inner dialogue is problem-saturated, try to reframe the words you are telling yourself, for example instead of looking at challenging behaviour as a problem, describe it to yourself as an opportunity to plan a new activity.
2. **Prioritise issues or duties that need to be addressed:** Not everything needs to be resolved straightaway. Look at duties on a sliding scale and recognise what you are able to do now, what you can do next and what you are not able to do today.
3. **Ask for help:** If you need assistance, ask for it. Asking for help is sometimes seen as a negative. Reframe this negative thought by looking at asking for help as being astute and reflective with your resources today. Asking for help shows that you have ability to delegate as well as having keen time management skills.
4. **Link closely with families:** The parents/carers of the children in your care are the most important people in children's lives. Partner with parents as much as possible in your daily routine and develop a solid professional relationship with them.
5. **Acknowledge that only you can influence change in your life:** If you want something different in your daily routine, change it through actions as well as words. Kick that right side of your brain into gear and start thinking creatively about any problems in your day.
6. **See every little win as a success:** When you are influencing change, many little steps have to happen before you will see any big differences. Recognise what you can control and what you cannot control, and focus your energies on what you can change.
7. **Exercise your body and mind!** Aim to get your arms and legs moving during your break periods, on your walk into work and on your way home. If exercising with colleagues, put in a 'no shop talk' rule while on your breaks and put up signs in any break areas reminding staff of this. When talking with your colleagues, be mindful of the types of discussion that you are having. You do not want to burden people with problems during their rest times; and recognise and remove yourself if people are talking about stressful situations in your presence.
8. **Acknowledge if stresses from home have impacted on your work life:** Speak out loud to yourself if you react too quickly to a minor situation, for example 'I am over-reacting now because the traffic was bad this morning.' Give yourself space to leave your 'outside' problems outside.

Lougy *et al.* (2007) remind us that self-care is crucial when working with young children. If you feel that stress has become too difficult for you to handle by yourself, consult your workplace supervisor or your GP.

Workplace supervision

A high-quality early years service should provide accessible and ongoing supervision for staff. Supervision should be carried out by a member of staff who has completed training in this area and recognises that supervision consists of three main elements: support, learning and accountability. Sciarra and Dorsey (2001) maintain that the most effective supervision takes place when it is conducted by a well-established, trusted staff member who is an 'authority' figure. This person has an important role in developing a common culture within the service, outlining the programme of delivery and defining expectations for staff members. Research conducted by Caruso and Fawcett (2007) describes some expectations staff have about their workplace supervisor. These expectations include: honesty; offering constructive criticism; being able to spend time with staff; listening to staff; being knowledgeable; being able to accept criticism where appropriate; offering resources; offering space for self-reflection and evaluation; being trained; and being available to problem solve and resolve conflicts.

Workplace supervision can take a variety of forms:
- informal day-to-day conversations which build relationships and trust
- being available to talk about queries, concerns and achievements
- being available to resolve staff conflicts through mediation or other recognised forms of conflict resolution methods in line with service policy
- regular planned individual meetings to discuss plans, challenges and achievements to date
- regular staff appraisals
- full staff meetings
- in-service training
- planned out-of-service training.

OVER TO YOU

In a group, discuss how a well-maintained supervision schedule conducted by a well-trained and effective supervisor would impact on a practitioner's 'nourishment'.

Professional development

The need for early years practitioners to keep their skill base relevant through an on-going professional development schedule cannot be understated. Síolta Component 11.4 suggests a number of ways in which practitioners can keep their abilities fresh:
- attending conferences and workshops
- taking part in or organising cluster group meetings
- progressing one's education through third-level college courses and seminars

- completing online courses and employing internet resources
- compiling or consulting a resource library
- availing of and organising staff exchanges within and between services
- observing other practitioners/settings
- ongoing mentoring and coaching.

Partaking in regular and self-chosen professional development engages the adult and provides opportunities for new ideas in the education setting. Craft (2002) highlights a number of forms of professional development, or continuing professional development (CPD). In addition to the suggestions highlighted in Síolta Standard 11 she notes that CPD can be maintained through:
- action research
- self-directed study
- personal reflection
- experimental 'assignments'
- collaborative learning.

Craft (2002) outlines the following qualities needed in the early years professional for CPD to be a successful tool in nourishing one's creativity:
- **Openness:** The early years practitioner should be open to new ideas, concepts and ways of being in the environment. You may come across practitioners who have put together a 'yearly activity plan' and use it every year with every child they work with. This method of instructing can be stagnant and does not allow for new ideas, spontaneity and the individuality of a child-centred curriculum. Wake up each morning with the mind-set that you, the adult, can learn seven new things today. Watch out for this learning, record it and incorporate it into your instruction style.
- **Releasing the unconscious:** Give yourself space during your rest periods to daydream, visualise and give time to your hopes and dreams. At the end of each evening reflect on the creativity undertaken during the day and write down what you valued, what you wanted and what you need. Keep a dream journal beside your bed and write down what adventures your unconscious took you on while you slept.
- **Self-esteem and vision:** In adults as well as children self-esteem and self-worth must be valued in order for creativity to flourish. Engage in activities and relationships in your personal life which promote your vision of yourself. Remember, only you have the power to change how you view yourself!
- **Working with others:** You might spend your day surrounded by people, but working with children can be a very isolating position. Allow time to collaborate

with colleagues, to plan and reflect on activities together. Pair with professionals who have similar value systems to you and who will challenge you in a constructive and positive manner. Be mindful of dominant personalities when collaborating with others and keep confidence in your own abilities when working in a team.

- **Relationships:** There are many relationships to consider when fostering creativity: the relationships one has with oneself, with the children and families in one's care, with colleagues and supervisors, as well as the elusive and dynamic relationship an individual has with creativity itself! If you were to look at your relationship with creativity in terms of a Facebook status, would you be 'Single', 'It's complicated', 'In a relationship', 'Engaged' or 'Married'? Think of CPD as being like a visit to a creativity therapist with the aim of forging a happy, healthy and innovative future together!

OVER TO YOU

Craft (2002) acknowledges that the most successful CPD happens when it is initiated by the individual who will be engaging in it. Look at the examples of CPD mentioned above and undertake to complete one of them. Will you go on a workshop, visit a new early years setting, or undertake a piece of research, perhaps? Your local County Childcare Committee website, as well as Early Childhood Ireland, Activelink, The Wheel and many other online resources can provide you with a variety of opportunities for CPD.

Chapter summary

In this chapter we aimed to aid the reader to unlock their own creative processes. Adult creativity is different from the creativity found in children. When being creative the adult displays skills such as inventing new concepts and materials, problem-solving in innovative ways and producing artistic projects. As people move through life the creativity that comes with childhood may be diminished by a number of factors such as home life, school life, cultural expectations and a fear of failure. Adult creativity can be regained through an active process, giving over time to relearn skills, rediscover knowledge and make resources available to promote one's creative talents. Finding our creative 'selves' impacts not only on our professional abilities but also on our personal lives, as increased creativity results in higher self-esteem, self-worth and self-confidence in adults.

This chapter promotes adult creativity by highlighting different types of activity adults can engage with to give themselves space to explore their 'right brain' abilities.

The final section of this chapter looked at the role of the early years practitioner in maintaining a high level of creativity. To sustain the level of energy required for the many varied roles of the early years educator, one needs to nourish oneself through a process of self-care, workplace supervision and continuing professional development. Reflecting on Síolta Standard 11: Professional Practice, we can see that nourishment of the practitioner is key to maintaining a high-quality creative arts curriculum for young children.

9 Creative Safe Environments

This chapter explores aspects of the following Learning Outcomes:
- LO 2: Summarise the benefits of exploration and participation in creative arts for the child.
- LO 3: Explore the role of the adult in creating an environment in which children feel secure and confident enough to take risks and explore new situations.
- LO 6: Explore challenges for adults in respecting choices and decisions of children.
- LO 8: Reflect on one's own role and responsibilities when engaging in creative arts activities with children, being mindful of health and safety.

In this chapter we will explore how to facilitate creative play in the early years environment while working within the Childcare Act 1991, the Child Care (Pre-School Services) (No. 2) Regulations (DoHC 2006a), the Safety, Health and Welfare at Work Act 2005 and the Safety, Health and Welfare at Work (General Application) Regulations 2007. In addition, we will address the recommendations proposed for early years settings in Síolta Standard 9: Safety and Welfare.

You may notice that during play children are more likely to challenge their abilities, take risks and try new experiences. The adult has an important and difficult balance to maintain during play, as they must ensure that the child is safe while learning. Wilson (2012) describes how the adult's fear can be a barrier for young children's play. We fear that they will hurt themselves, that they will become frustrated, will fail in some way. The adult is a naturally cautious being and this caution sends messages to young children to protect themselves during play. Issues arise when our precautions are too strict and the child is prevented from engaging in a meaningful play experience.

Andrews (2012) discusses that risk during play is a necessary and integral part of children's overall development. Studies have shown that risky play is not only great fun but it also aids in children's brain development, helps them adapt to their environment and fosters the lifelong skill of resilience. The conscientious early years educator recognises that risky play is not only important for holistic growth, it is also an aspect of ensuring that children's rights are upheld. Ireland signed up to the United Nations Convention on the Rights of the Child in September 1990. In committing to the ethos of this document, the early years educator has a responsibility to ensure that children's rights are upheld in relation to how they choose to learn and play. Andrews (2012) asks the question, 'Who owns the play?'. When the adult influences the child's play frame due to a safety, health or welfare concern, the question should be asked, 'Who now owns the play?' Síolta Standard 1: Rights of the Child gives guidance around ownership and active learning experiences. In addition to Síolta, we can look to Hart's ladder of participation (1992) to guide us around the ownership dilemma. Rung number eight indicates the child holds full ownership whereas at rung one the adult 'owns' the activity.

Hart's 'rungs' are as follows:
- **8 Child-initiated shared decisions with adults:** Child-led activities in which decision making is shared between the child and adult working as equal partners.
- **7 Child-initiated and directed:** Child-led activity with little input from adults.
- **6 Adult-initiated shared decisions with child:** Child-led activities in which decision making is shared with child.
- **5 Consulted and informed:** Adult-led activities in which children are consulted and informed about how their input will be used and the outcomes of adult decisions.
- **4 Assigned, but informed:** Adult-led activities in which the child understands the purpose, the decision-making process, and has a role.
- **3 Tokenism:** Adult-led activities in which the child may be consulted, with minimal opportunity for feedback.
- **2 Decoration:** Adult-led activities in which the child understands the purpose, but has no input in how they are planned.
- **1 Manipulation:** Adult-led activities in which the children do as directed without understanding the purpose of the activities.

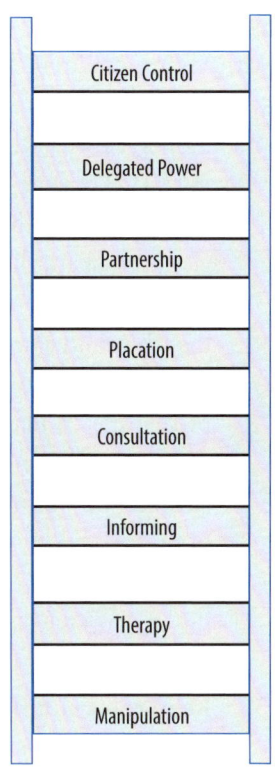

HART'S LADDER OF PARTICIPATION

> **OVER TO YOU**
>
> The idea of 'over-protection' is a concept put forward by Tim Gill (2007). He believes that the early years practitioner should move from the traditional philosophy of 'protection' to a more contemporary philosophy of 'resilience'.
>
> Using a large group format, divide into two teams and debate the positives and challenges of these two philosophies. Use the following terms as a guide for discussion: Safety, Challenge, Frustration, Risk, Hazard.

Rules and limits in the creative arts curriculum

In Chapter 2 we discussed Brown's 'fun, freedom and flexibility' (2003). When working with young children, freedom comes with limits as young children will be provided with consistent boundaries to ensure safety in play. There is a dilemma here for the practitioner; how can I impose rules when the child is exploring, creating and learning? Wilson (2012) outlines nine rules for creativity which can incorporate safety:

1. **Let the child lead the play:** Ensure that the child works at their own pace and is not rushed during activities. When facilitating active play experiences the practitioner can provide interesting and developmentally appropriate materials that the child can explore and investigate in new and interesting ways. This can be a difficult rule to follow as child-led play can get messy! The adult needs to have procedures in place to be able to ensure the safety of the child and other children within the 'mess', such as having a second adult to help with tidy-ups, a written cleaning programme, a routine in which children can tidy up, and having a 'work in progress' sign when deferring play.

2. **Children decide where to play:** This rule ensures that children move away from the traditional view of play that is solely at the table-top. The adult's role is to design the room for safe, supervised play.

3. **Keep rules simple:** It is important to have rules for children when they are playing. A common mistake of the adult is to impose unnecessary and complicated rules which children will not remember or understand. Once children reach the age of approximately three years they will be able to decide on the rules with you. Remember, for rules to work the adult must model them too!

4. **Keep 'helping' to a minimum:** When the adult is playing at the child's level the question 'Will you help me?' is often asked. Assess this question before responding and think; does the child need help or want help? Needing help may imply that the task at hand is too challenging for them at the moment and they may be

in danger if they attempt it on their own. Wanting help may mean that the child has a lack of confidence in their own abilities and your role here is to support the child through reassurance and gentle guidance so they can complete the task themselves.

5. **Praise the process rather than the results:** Rather than simply giving praise to the end result, we should offer encouragement to children's efforts. This 'process' reinforcement asks the adults to 'catch' the child engaging in learning.

6. **Respect the child's privacy:** Children should be given the opportunity to have their own space, thoughts and feelings. Provide safe spaces in the environment where children can go and be alone without interference from adults or peers. These spaces should still be visible by the adult and free from risk.

7. **Ensure the child feels safe:** For creative processes to happen children need to feel secure in their environment and have meaningful attachments with the adults in that space. Implementing the ethos of Maslow's hierarchy of needs, which we discussed in Chapter 7, we can aim to provide an atmosphere of security in the early years space.

8. **Treat children with respect:** When interacting with children, speak to them in the same way as you would a fellow professional. Children are more likely to follow rules and express themselves in a confident way if they know that you have respect for them. They will also feel respected when the adult provides a welcoming space which is filled with equipment and materials that are developmentally appropriate, clean, well maintained and fun!

9. **Creativity cannot be imposed:** When working with young children, never force them to engage in an activity they do not want to do. You may think the actiivity is a great opportunity for learning, but the child may find it scary or even repulsive. Always refer to the one golden rule and let the child lead the activity.

OVER TO YOU

Have a discussion about these rules and visualise how the early years practitioner would interact with children and families if they were following these guidelines.

Childcare Act 1991 and Child Care (Pre-School Services) (No. 2) Regulations

We have acknowledged the importance of risk taking in play for the progression of children's development and ensuring that children have ownership during play. We will now look at how these risks can be managed in a way that meets the requirements of the Childcare Act 1991 and the Child Care (Pre-School Services) (No. 2) Regulations (DoHC 2006a).

The Childcare Act 1991 names the Health Service Executive (HSE) as the body that is responsible for ensuring adequate health, safety and welfare of children aged under six years attending early years services (as opposed to a national school or equivalent). The 2006 Child Care (Pre-School Services) (No. 2) Regulations and accompanying 'Explanatory Guide to Requirements' is the tool used by the preschool inspectorate as well as early years practitioners to ensure that the ethos of the 1991 Childcare Act is upheld.

The 2006 Child Care (Pre-School Services) (No. 2) Regulations document is divided into six parts and has thirty-three individual regulations. We will now look specifically at a sample of the regulations that deal with health, safety and welfare in the early years environment.

Regulation 5: Health, welfare and development of the child

This regulation puts the duty on the practitioner to plan and implement developmentally and culturally appropriate activities for the children in their care. This regulation acknowledges play as a powerful vehicle for learning in the early years. There is an onus on the educator to provide 'opportunities, experiences, activities, interactions and materials' for the children attending the service and to acknowledge the importance of relationships in the facility, in line with the 'whole child' perspective outlined in the *National Children's Strategy* (DoHC 2000a). When planning creative activities, Regulation 5 guides the educator to be proactive in their approach to working with children, families and any relevant agencies that may be connected with the child.

Regulation 6: First aid

During daily events in early years services these will be need for first aid – common issues include scraped knees, bumps, etc. These first aid 'emergencies' are acknowledged in Regulation 6, which insists that within the early years service there must be suitably trained and certified adults in the field of first aid who have access to a suitably stocked first aid box. This regulation also highlights the need to have a trained first aider, with a well-stocked first aid kit, on outings with children.

Regulation 7: Medical assistance

Regulation 7 states that services must have detailed protocols (written policies) in place to address a situation in which children fall seriously ill while under the care of the early years service.

Regulation 8: Management and staffing

While children are in the service, strict child/adult ratios must be upheld. These ratios not only protect children's welfare but also make implementing daily routines and child-led activities possible. This regulation ensures that the service complies with a management system which is responsible for the implementation of the ratios as well as how children are grouped in the service. Regulation 8 is closely linked with Regulation 12, which outlines how many children can be catered for in an early years environment. The management is also responsible for recruiting suitable people into employment in the service. Any adults who have interaction with the children on the premises must be vetted by An Garda Síochána as well as having relevant and up-to-date references prior to beginning their work in the service.

Regulation 9: Behaviour management

When working with young children it is imperative that a consistent and positive behaviour management approach is in place. The behaviour management policy must be written, available to all stakeholders and be in line with the child protection guidelines *Children First* (DoCYA 2009) as well as the UN Convention on the Rights of the Child.

Regulation 18: Premises and facilities

This regulation deals specifically with the design and maintenance of the indoor environment. The practitioner is reminded to take the 'flow' of the space into account when organising interest and care areas as improper flow can lead to safety and health incidents/accidents. Stringent space ratios are outlined within this regulation which must be upheld to promote the welfare of children. This regulation also highlights the responsibility of the practitioner to ensure that children, families and staff feel welcome in the service to promote a high-quality care and learning facility.

Regulations 19, 20, 21: Heating, ventilation and lighting

These regulations combine to create a space where people feel comfortable. When rooms are adequately heated, ventilated and use as much natural light as possible the body can relax without feeling stuffy or tired.

Regulation 25: Equipment and materials

This regulation is especially important when planning safe creative activities. The practitioner has a responsibility to ensure that any materials and equipment employed in the service are non-toxic, are kept in a proper state of repair and are maintained in a hygienic manner through the use of recorded cleaning rotas. In addition, there must be a sufficient amount of materials and equipment available for the children, which are developmentally appropriate and suitable for purpose. This regulation specifically names items such as bedding, towels, spare clothes and child-sized furniture.

Regulation 26: Food and drink

Regulation 26 outlines specific requirements in the planning, preparation and serving of food and drinks to young children. Considerations such as range of food on offer, availability of meals, snacks and refreshments as well as food hygiene also need to be carefully noted when working with young children. This regulation names additional legislation that services must uphold when providing food on the premises.

Regulation 27: Safety measures

Within an early years environment the practitioner must be mindful of many dangers to young children, hidden and visible. This regulation names the following areas for ongoing assessment:
- safety of heating appliances
- safety of hot water
- preventing the spread of infection
- keeping children safe.

Regulation 28: Facilities for rest and play

When attending an early years service children must be offered suitable accommodation in which to rest and/or sleep. This regulation highlights safety measures during rest and sleep times, such as placement of the rest areas, hygiene considerations and recording procedures while children are sleeping. It also looks at outside play and suggests that children have daily access to the outdoors, 'weather permitting'. This section of Regulation 28 is closely linked with Regulation 27 in relation to safety considerations in the outside space.

Regulation 30: Insurance

Services are responsible for having public liability insurance (including cover when children are on outings) and for fire and theft insurance.

CREATIVE SAFE ENVIRONMENTS

OVER TO YOU
Look at a creative arts activity that you have planned in the past and assess its implementation in relation to the Pre-School Regulations. The HSE website has a full copy of the Pre-School Regulations available to download as well as other resources to ensure compliance under national legislation. Have a look at the regulations not mentioned in the section above and see how they relate to your planned activity.

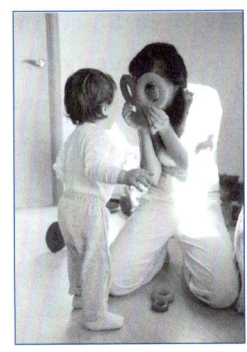

Health, Safety and Welfare at Work Acts

Safety is a real issue when working with young children and risk-taking is a natural aspect of children's play. Within the early years environment we must recognise that the safety of the adult must also be maintained. The Safety, Health and Welfare at Work Act 2005 and the Safety, Health and Welfare at Work (General Application) Regulations 2007 are two pieces of Irish legislation that aim to protect the adult in the workplace as well as the child. The Act and the Regulations are enforced under the guidance of the Health and Safety Authority (HSA) in line with Section 34 of the 2005 Act. This legislation looks at the following safety considerations:

- employers' duties
- employees' duties
- risk assessment and safety statements
- protective equipment and measures
- reporting accidents
- health and safety leave
- health and safety and young people
- violence in the workplace
- bullying
- harassment
- victimisation.

OVER TO YOU
Choose one of the topics listed above as outlined in the Safety, Health and Welfare at Work Act (2005) and prepare a short presentation that you could hypothetically give at a staff meeting in an early years environment. Use the following headings as a guide for your presentation:
- **definition of topic**
- **how the topic relates specifically to the early years environment**

- practical examples of where a workplace may not comply with the requirements
- practical examples to ensure topic is upheld under national standards
- how implementing the topic to a high standard would impact on the staff, children and families in an early years setting.

The legislation uses terms such as 'risk assessment' and 'safety statement'. Let us now look at these terms and apply them specifically to planning, implementing and assessing creative activities with young children.

Safety statement

The 2005 Act requires all employers to: identify hazards; carry out a risk assessment; and prepare a written safety statement. A safety statement is a written commitment which is prepared by an employer to safeguard the health and safety of employees while at work and also the health and safety of any other persons who may frequent the workplace, such as children and their families. In its *Guidelines on Risk Assessments and Safety Statements* (2006), the HSA outlines a six-step approach to follow when drawing up a safety statement:

1. Draw up a health and safety policy.
2. Identify the hazards.
3. Carry out a risk assessment.
4. Decide what precautions are needed.
5. Record the findings.
6. Review the programme and update as necessary.

OVER TO YOU

Purchase or download the HSA document *Guidelines on Risk Assessments and Safety Statements* (2006). Use this document to assess a safety statement you have access to, for example in an early years facility, in your own workplace, school, college or institute of education. Remember to make sure that the person who compiled the safety statement has given you permission to assess it. Following your investigation, feed back any comments, constructive criticisms or queries you have about the safety statement to the management of the company/service, etc.

Risk assessment

A risk assessment must be completed as part of the safety statement. It's important to be aware of the following terms when working safely in an early years environment.

Hazard

A hazard is anything that can cause harm, such as chemicals, a cracked step, broken toys, etc. Hazards can be organised into different categories: physical, chemical, biological, human and transport hazards. Examples of hazards are outlined in Chapter 3. The HSA also gives examples of additional 'health hazards':

- stress
- harmful noise
- harmful dust
- harmful lighting levels
- extreme temperatures
- injury through poor design of equipment, machinery or materials.

Risk

A risk is the possibility, large or small, that someone could be damaged by a hazard. Risks can be low, medium or high depending on the type of hazard, the number of people exposed to it and the measures of control in place. With risks we can use the word 'chance' as described by Andrews (2012), such as 'there is a chance Billy could fall off the swing'.

Risk assessment

A risk assessment is an ongoing and systematic process of identifying what could possibly cause harm to people in the environment. The employer/management needs to consider if they have taken enough measures to prevent harm or if they need to put more precautions in place.

Control

This term refers to controlling risk. In controlling risks the employer/management identifies, puts in place and documents practical approaches employed to minimise harm to people in the environment. Examples could include using radiator covers; installing temperature controls on hot water; outlining and monitoring equipment repair. 'Control' also refers to recording any injuries or incidents that take place within the environment using a standardised accident/incident report form.

As life happens, so will minor incidents and accidents, but we need to be aware that more serious injuries can also occur in the early years environment. The HSE reports that accidental injury is one of the biggest single causes of death in Ireland for children over the age of one. Kya deLongchamps, in her article 'Accidents just a splash away for

children' (2013), highlights that the risk of accidents increases when there is a change of routine for the child and adult. The early years educator has a weighty responsibility to keep children safe from danger and with this a distinction needs to be made between risks and hazards in the environment. Here are some examples of risks:
- allowing children to climb
- allowing children to engage in rough and tumble play
- exposing children to a variety of climates
- giving children the chance to try new things.

These risks can be managed by implementing appropriate precautions. On the other hand, hazards could include:
- poor supervision
- ill-maintained equipment
- developmentally inappropriate materials
- dangerous materials, e.g. toxic plants
- providing equipment that does not comply with safety standards
- allowing water to gather to a dangerous depth.

We can see in the risks and hazards above that the adult has an important role to play. High-quality planning and supervision are key elements in minimising harm in the early years setting. Think about how the practitioner could reduce dangers in the environment by introducing the following precautions:
- key worker systems
- closed-circuit television (CCTV)
- minimum space around equipment
- play surfaces which accord with general safety requirements
- safe hinges on any barrier gates
- daily written observations
- impact-absorbent surfaces under slides, swings, climbing frames/any equipment in which children can gain height
- regular meetings with parents/guardians
- non-toxic equipment and materials, including plants and flowers
- outside shelter for use during extreme weather
- ramps and handrails for high areas
- protection around refuse facilities and boilers.

> **OVER TO YOU**
>
> Design your own risk assessment for an indoor or outdoor space. Categorise features in the environment you choose as low risk, medium risk, or high risk and devise barriers to ensure that these risks can be managed safely. In addition, identify what hazards are in the area and describe how they can be removed or avoided. Think about how often the risks and hazards would need to be reviewed, amended and who would be responsible for safekeeping in a risky area.

Síolta Standard 9: Health and Welfare

The Síolta document incorporates the safety, health and welfare of children in elements of each of its sixteen standards. In this section we look specifically at Síolta Standard 9: Health and Welfare and discuss how it can be a useful guide when ensuring the safety of the child in the early years environment. Standard 9 highlights the adult's responsibility: 'promoting the health and welfare of the child requires protection from harm, provision of nutritious food, appropriate opportunities for rest, and secure relationships characterised by trust and respect'. To achieve this aim, the early years service is required to be mindful of the following components:

- **9.1:** The setting has implemented a full range of policies and procedures to prevent the spread of infectious diseases, reduce exposure to environmental hazards and stress, and deal effectively and efficiently with medical situations that may arise.
- **9.2:** The setting endeavours, through the implementation of a range of policies, procedures and actions, to promote the health of all children and adults.
- **9.3:** The setting has implemented the guidelines from *Children First* and *Our Duty to Care* in relation to child protection.
- **9.4:** The setting is proactive in supporting the development of healthy eating habits in children whilst supporting their enjoyment and appreciation of eating as a positive social experience.
- **9.5:** The setting has made significant efforts to ensure that children's need for rest, quiet time and privacy is appropriately catered for and respected.
- **9.6:** The setting has made provision to ensure that children can form and sustain secure relationships with adults, siblings, peers and other children.
- **9.7:** The setting ensures that all adults and children are prepared for emergency situations.

OVER TO YOU

These seven components combine to form a comprehensive framework for preventing harm to children and promoting best practice with regard to the welfare of young children in an early years setting. Using these components, look at the following case study and identify where the practitioner, Sandra, could use Standard 9 as a working guide in relation to Megan's safety, health and welfare.

CASE STUDY

Megan is fifteen months old and has been attending the early years service on a part-time basis from the age of six months. She is in the 'toddler room' with four other children aged between twelve months and twenty-four months. She has one key worker, Sandra, and an assistant, Michael, who helps during busy periods in the day.

Megan was recently diagnosed as having asthma, which is triggered by dust mites and pollen. In addition to this, Megan is lactose intolerant. Megan takes her nap at approximately one o'clock each day and might sleep for anything between forty and eighty minutes. Megan sleeps with her soother and her blanket, named 'dodo'. Megan enjoys playing with the dolls in the home corner, loves the water play area and the slide in the outside area. Megan does not like it if her hands get dirty and she dislikes sudden loud noises. Megan tends to play alongside another child named Jo. Megan's mum, Frances, has recently enquired about information on potty training and Megan's dad, Tom, has asked Sandra for the list of policies which might relate to practice promoting to the safety, health and welfare of Megan while she attends the service.

Chapter summary

In this chapter we looked at the delicate balance in the relationship between implementing the creative arts curriculum and the safety, health and welfare of the young child. In this chapter we saw that when children engage in active learning experiences risks are taken and children challenge their current capabilities. This can cause anxieties for the adult as they become cautious and fearful that a child may enter into behaviour that is outside safe parameters. We acknowledge in this chapter that this risky play is integral for children's overall development and should be encouraged. The dilemma for the practitioner is how to impose safety rules when the child is engaged in a creative play experience.

This chapter outlined safety regulations highlighted in the Childcare Act (1991) and the Child Care (Pre-School Services) (No. 2) Regulations (DoHC 2006a), namely

Regulations 5–9, 18–21, 25–28 and 30. This chapter also looked at the 2005 and 2007 Safety, Health and Welfare at Work Acts, discussing specifically safety statements and risk assessments in the early years setting. Here we noted the weighty responsibility the early years practitioner undertakes when caring for young children.

The chapter finally looked at Síolta Standard 9: Health and Welfare and outlined the seven components contained in it. An activity was offered to the reader which gives an opportunity to think about how an early years educator could put these safety components into practice.

10 Creative Arts Assessment

This chapter explores assessment in the Creative Arts for Early Childhood component which, when successfully completed, leads to an NFQ Level 5 award in Early Childhood Care and Education (awarded by QQI).

Let us first look at the learning objectives which have been discussed in this book:

- **LO 1:** Examine a variety of creative media opportunities with young children. Discussed in Chapters 4, 5, 6 and 7.
- **LO 2:** Summarise the benefits of exploration and participation in creative arts for the child. Discussed in Chapters 2, 4, 5, 6, 7 and 9.
- **LO 3:** Explore the role of the adult in creating an environment in which children feel secure and confident enough to take risks and explore new situations. Discussed in Chapters 2, 3, 4, 5, 6, 7, 8 and 9.
- **LO 4:** Plan opportunities for consultation with children to plan and engage in creative arts experiences. Discussed in Chapters 2, 3, 4, 5, 6 and 7.
- **LO 5:** Test open-ended materials and natural items for creative arts, in both indoor and outdoor environments, appropriate to different stages of children's development. Discussed in Chapters 4, 5, 6 and 7.
- **LO 6:** Explore challenges for adults in respecting choices and decisions of children. Discussed in Chapters 2, 5, 6, 7, 8 and 9.
- **LO 7:** Employ developmentally appropriate creative arts activities which promote the holistic development of the child. Discussed in Chapters 3, 4, 5, 6 and 7.
- **LO 8:** Reflect on one's own role and responsibilities when engaging in creative arts activities with children (being mindful of health and safety). Discussed in Chapters 3, 5, 6, 7, 8 and 9.

The adult learner has a responsibility to demonstrate in their assessment that they have achieved a particular standard in each of the eight Learning Outcomes outlined above. The two forms of assessment (Project and Collection of Work) are outlined in the programme designed for your adult education setting. The tutor of the

component award, Creative Arts for Early Childhood, has a responsibility to tailor the assessments and give the adult learner their 'assessment brief'.

It is important to note that what is written in this chapter is a guide for the learner to complete assessments. Pay close attention to the assessment brief given by your facilitator and follow instructions exactly. In your assessment brief you will notice a 'marking scheme'. Be vigilant to this scheme as each mark you gain will add up to your overall result at the end!

Collection of work

The collection of work is worth 60% of the total marks. This is quite a significant percentage. The collection of work assessment should be carried out over the duration of the course. This collection consists of ten pieces of work accompanied by supporting written documents.

In the collection of work the learner is required to provide evidence of the following Learning Outcomes:
- LO 1: Examine a variety of creative media opportunities with young children.
- LO 3: Explore the role of the adult in creating an environment in which children feel secure and confident enough to take risks and explore new situations.
- LO 6: Explore challenges for adults in respecting choices and decisions of children.
- LO 7: Employ developmentally appropriate creative arts activities which promote the holistic development of the child.
- LO 8: Reflect on one's own role and responsibilities when engaging in creative arts activities with children (being mindful of health and safety).

Adult art work

When demonstrating your learning you are required to present a selection of your own art, craft and design work that demonstrates a range of techniques, materials and equipment. In doing this, each learner is required to produce a minimum of five creative arts pieces for adults. It is important to remember that you are required to show your pieces of work during the external assessment period. When planning pieces of work, think about how they can best be displayed to the internal and external assessors.

Look at the following creative arts areas and examples of how adult arts pieces could be displayed for an internal and/or external assessor:
- **dramatic arts:** video/digital visual recordings, audio recordings, photography
- **movement and dance:** video/digital visual recordings, photography
- **visual arts:** original visual art pieces, video/digital recordings, photography
- **musical arts:** video/digital visual recordings, audio recordings.

Remember to save all your work during your Creative Arts for Early Childhood course. It is good practice to take photographs or video recordings as arts pieces are created, rather than just having a recording or example of the finished piece. It is the candidate's responsibility to ensure that any recordings, photographs, etc. are submitted to the assessor in a suitable, accessible format.

Each of the five adult pieces should be supported by a written/typed document which includes the following headings:

1. title of the piece
2. technique(s) used
3. list of the materials and equipment used
4. personal comment or response to the activity
5. recommendations
6. activities for children.

Let us look at some examples of how to address these headings:

1. **Title of the piece:** Put your own unique stamp on the piece by giving it a name.
2. **Technique(s) used:** Is it a dramatic piece, a movement and dance piece, a visual arts piece or a musical arts piece? What techniques did you use? Describe the reason you chose the technique(s) above any other medium and how the technique(s) suited your aim. Here are some examples of techniques you could use:
    - *Dramatic arts:* Mime, improvisation, acting out a prepared scene/story/theme, comedy, etc.
    - *Movement and dance:* Choreographed dance such as ballet, tango, waltz and salsa, freestyle such as disco or tap, etc.
    - *Visual arts:* Painting, printing, mosaic, sculpture, mark making, photography, etc.
    - *Musical arts:* Listening and responding, composition and/or performance of music such as jazz, classical, rap, rock, blues, soul, etc.
3. **List of the materials and equipment used:** Describe in detail what materials and equipment would be needed to recreate the activity. Add an extra dimension to this section by giving the approximate cost of the materials involved in the piece. Describe the reasons you decided to use these particular materials/equipment above others.
4. **Personal comment or response to the activity:** Think about answering the following questions when writing your personal comment. Aim to incorporate the Learning Outcomes mentioned above in your answers:
    - What did I aim to learn in completing the piece?
    - What did I find interesting in completing the piece?

- What did I find challenging in completing the piece?
- If I were to do the piece again, what would I do differently?
- How does research from literature inform my knowledge about the piece?

5 **Recommendations:** In this section think about:
- How could your learning have been further enhanced during the completion of the activity?
- If you were to extend/develop the activity for yourself, how could you do so?
- If you were to invite other adults to complete this activity, how would you change it to suit their individual skills and dispositions?

6 **Activities for children:** Think about how this activity could be adapted for:
- an individual child
- a small group (two to four children)
- a larger group (more than four children).

Also consider:
- How could you ensure Aistear learning goals for the children were met?
- Where in the early years environment would be best suited for the activity?
- How would the activity need to be adapted to suit individual children's abilities?
- What materials and equipment would need to be changed?
- How could you assess the learning during and after the activity?
- How might you extend/develop this activity for a group of children?
- What would the health and safety and legislative considerations be?
- What is the role of the adult in the activity?

Child art work

In addition to the five adult pieces candidates are also required to present a selection of creative activities suitable for use with children up to six years of age. You are required to produce a minimum of five pieces, which must display a range of techniques, materials and equipment across the creative arts field. Each piece must be supported by a document that includes the following headings:

1. title
2. technique(s) used
3. list of materials and equipment used
4. cost
5. age suitability
6. safety considerations
7. exploration of the role of the adult.

These might be addressed as follows:

1. **Title:** Give the piece a name; make it fun and child-friendly!
2. **Technique(s) used:** Is the piece a dramatic arts, movement and dance, visual arts or musical arts piece? Which techniques did you use? Describe the reason you chose the technique above any other medium. How did this technique best suit the overall aim of the piece? The following are examples that could be used in child activities:
    - *Dramatic arts:* Socio-dramatic play, storytelling, poetry, puppets, imaginative/fantasy play, etc.
    - *Movement and dance:* Freestyle movement, themed movement (animals, clouds, fireworks, etc.), movement with accessories such as costumes, ribbons, noise makers, etc.
    - *Visual arts:* Mark making, painting, printing, mosaics, collages, photography, 3D sculpture, junk art, etc.
    - *Musical arts:* Musical appreciation, composition, performance across the various genres such as classical and contemporary children's music, lullabies, rock, rap, jazz, soul, blues, folk, etc.
3. **List of materials and equipment used:** Make a list of all materials and equipment needed. Be detailed in this section and outline where in the early years environment it would be best to carry out the activity.
4. **Cost:** Detail how much this activity would cost to prepare, implement and assess per child and per group. Take into consideration how you could put into place cost saving measures such as using recycled materials, etc.
5. **Age suitability:** Think about which age group this activity would be most suited to. What abilities would a child need to have gained before being able to complete the activity? Is the activity flexible enough to be adapted for children with different abilities? How does this activity link with the four themes of Aistear to ensure that a holistic developmental framework is being nurtured?
6. **Safety considerations:** Looking at the Child Care (Pre-School Services) (No. 2) Regulations as well as the Safety, Health and Welfare at Work Acts, highlight what you need to consider in order to ensure children's welfare when undertaking this activity.
7. **Exploration of the role of the adult:** Think about the following stages of an activity and detail the adult's role and responsibilities at each stage:
    - *planning the activity*
    - *implementing the activity*

CREATIVE ARTS ASSESSMENT

OVER TO YOU

Using your own ideas or the examples of adult creative arts activities in Chapter 8 and children's creative arts activities in chapters 4, 5 and 6, design a plan of ten 'collection of work' pieces. Think about the following:

- How can I best divide the pieces to display my creative abilities as well as addressing the Learning Outcomes?
- In my supporting document, how can I show that I have incorporated my own reflections, linked my learning from work-based practice and included appropriate research in the form of books, internet-based research, journal articles, etc.?
- How will I display both the process of creating this piece and the finished product? Will I use photographs, digital/video/audio recordings, the original work or a mixture of all these formats?
- How will this collection of work be exclusively 'mine' and reflect my creative journey as opposed to that of another learner in my group? What can I do to ensure that my work is original and authentic?
- Looking at the brief that has been distributed to your group, how are the marks being assigned? Does my work match up with the marking scheme? If I were to objectively look at my 'Collection of Work', what marks would I give it? Where would I take marks away? How can I improve my work to increase the possibility of marks? Do I need to be more reflective/add more links to practice/add more links to theory?

Project

The second part of the assessment is a project, which is worth 40% of the total marks. It is advised that this piece of work is completed over a period of six to eight weeks. In completing this project the candidate is required to provide evidence of Learning Outcomes two, four and five:

- **LO 2:** Summarise the benefits of exploration and participation in creative arts for the child.
- **LO 4:** Plan opportunities for consultation with children to plan and engage in creative arts experiences.
- **LO 5:** Test open-ended materials and natural items for creative arts, in both indoor and outdoor environments, appropriate to different stages of children's development.

This project requires each candidate to prepare a lesson plan for a creative art activity suitable for a group of children in the age range nought to six years. Guidelines suggest that the candidate includes:
1. age suitability for the activity
2. overall rationale for completing the activity
3. benefits of exploration and participation in the activity
4. specific learning objectives for the activity
5. a brief description of the activity.

We will now look at an example of how to put together a Creative Arts for Early Childhood project using a four-part approach. Remember that for the project to be effective the activity implemented should meet the following criteria:
- follows the component tutor's instructions for completion
- is a creative arts activity
- is process-based and open-ended
- is child-centred
- works in line with the Child Care (Pre-School Services) (No. 2) Regulations and ideally the Aistear principles and themes
- employs play as the learning tool.

Completing the project

Section 1: The formalities

Include the following documents in section one:
- the official marking sheet (supplied by your component facilitator)
- a copy of the assignment brief with marking scheme (supplied by component facilitator)
- cover page: with your name, the date, title of assessment and component name. You can also include a declaration which states that the assessment is your own work in line with plagiarism guidelines. Ensure that your cover sheet and brief meet the standard outlined by your educational facilitator.

Section 2: Introduction

Introduction: Answer the questions below in a considered and comprehensive manner. Try to imagine that the person reading your finished project has no understanding about planning a creative arts activity and you are trying to explain it to them.
1. What is the purpose/rationale of an early years professional engaging young children in the creative arts in general?

2   What is your creative art activity called?
3   How would you (briefly) describe your activity?
4   What are your reasons for planning this activity?
5   Who do you want this activity to be for?
6   How did you gain the views of the children, their families and key workers in planning this activity?
7   How will we see the views of the child being respected during the implementation of this activity?
8   What materials will be needed for the activity? (Include costing.)
9   What equipment will be needed for the activity?
10 Where in the early years environment will the activity take place?
11 How long is the activity planned to take and how does this tie in with children's developmental abilities?
12 What are the health and safety considerations in line with best practice and national legislation?
13 What are the equal opportunities considerations?
14 What is the role of the adult during this activity?

Aim of assessment: Write one sentence about what you hope to achieve in completing this assessment, for example: 'The aim of this project is to plan, implement and assess a visual arts activity for four children aged between three and four years of age.'

Objectives: Objectives are checklists of goals which you need to complete before your aim is reached. Your set of objectives will depend on the activity planned.

Creative arts activity chosen: Spend some time detailing the creative arts medium which will be used in the activity, the technique and the theme of your implemented activity. It is important to reference books, internet research, journal articles, etc. in this section. Use the following key points as a guide:
- Describe what a dramatic, movement and dance, visual or music activity is and discuss the general benefits for children engaging with this particular art form.
- Describe what specific technique you are planning to implement and how this can benefit a child's holistic development.
- If your activity is based around a theme, describe this theme in detail and how the creative arts activity suits this theme. For example, a theme could be a cultural celebration, a colour, a texture, a sound, a time of year, a taste, a place, etc.

Group of children: Describe the demographics of the group of children who will be partaking in the planned activity: how many children, their ages, gender(s), interests, abilities; and how these differences could influence each child's learning experience.

When describing specific children it is best to use pseudo-names (false names) rather than the children's real names to protect confidentiality. Use false names rather than codes/initials such as TC, as these codes can sometimes seem cold or clinical.

Links to national legislation and Aistear: Emphasise how your planned activity links with the 2006 Child Care (Pre-School Services) (No. 2) Regulations and describe how it links with the four Aistear Themes: Communication, Exploring and Thinking, Wellbeing, and Identity and Belonging. How might this activity be assessed using the Aistear approach? You can also link your activity to Síolta here.

Section 3: Implementation

'A picture is worth a thousand words.' Include a copy of your implemented activity using an observation, photographic/digitally recorded evidence and a sample of work taken from the activity. Ensure that any observations/images/samples of work that are used in this assessment are in line with the early childhood service's confidentiality standards as well as privacy standards outlined by your educational facilitator.

If your activity is a visual arts piece you could choose to include a photograph or sketch of the display you employed.

Section 4: Evaluation

In this section you are assessing the impact of the activity. Consider the following questions:
- What was positive overall about the implementation of the activity from the perspectives of the children, the children's family and myself?
- What was challenging overall about the implementation of the activity from the perspectives of the children, the children's family and myself?
- What could I have improved from the perspectives of the children, the children's family and myself?
- What learning took place from the perspective of the children, the service and myself?
- How could this activity be developed/ extended?
- Reflecting on the activity, what literature research best informed my practice and why?

Conclusion

In your conclusion you should summarise your overall assignment (Sections 2, 3 and 4). It is often observed that learners become complacent about completing the conclusion and make it too brief and sparse. Remember: there are marks to be gained in your conclusion. Look at the following questions and aim to answer them to build a well-rounded conclusion to your project:

1. What did your research say was useful about creative arts for young children?
2. What were your aim and objectives and how did you meet them?
3. What was your planned activity? How, when and with whom did you implement it?
4. How did your activity link with national legalisation and the Aistear framework?
5. What did the group of children learn from the activity?
6. What did you learn about yourself from doing the activity?
7. What did you learn from your literature research?
8. What did you learn from the children after implementing the activity?
9. If you were to plan the activity again, what would you do differently?
10. If you were to give a co-worker advice on planning an activity, what three things would you highlight?
11. If you were to extend the activity, how would you do this?
12. If you were to plan a brand new creative arts activity, what would it be?
13. How are Learning Objectives 2, 4 and 5 demonstrated throughout the project?

Reference list

Throughout your project you will have used a variety of sources to help you in your research. It is important to acknowledge any ideas you have taken from books, websites, magazines, newspapers, documentaries, photos, charts and graphs, etc. Unreferenced work is regarded as plagiarism. In your reference list include all the sources (books, websites, etc.) used in your project. Check with your educational facilitator about the system of referencing used in your place of learning.

Appendix

Your appendix might include original observations, confidentiality forms, additional photographic materials, graphs, charts or other visual aids that could enhance your project.

OVER TO YOU

Complete a 'trial run' project. Using the template above, choose a theme, a creative arts activity and an imaginary group of children. Plan, implement and evaluate this hypothetical activity. Reflect on what you could have improved upon (timekeeping, research, consultation with stakeholders, etc.) and give yourself some practice in planning, implementing and reviewing an activity before you are formally assessed.

References and Resources

References

Alexander, S. (2013) *Guide to Growing Vegetables*, 6th edn, Dublin: Teagasc.
Andrews, M. (2012) *Exploring Play for Early Childhood Studies*, London: Sage.
Barnes, R. (1987) *Teaching Art to Young Children, 4–9*, New South Wales: Allen & Unwin.
Beaver, M., Brewster, J., Jones, P., Keene, A., Neaum, S. and Tallack, J. (2001) *Babies and Young Children: Diploma in Child Care and Education*, 2nd edn, Cheltenham: Nelson Thornes.
Beckerleg, T. (2008) *Fun with Messy Play: Ideas and Activities for Children with Special Needs*, London: Jessica Kingsley.
Brown, F. (2003) 'Compound Flexibility: The Role of Playwork in Child Development' in F. Brown (ed.) *Playwork: Theory and Practice*, Open University Press, pp. 51–65.
Bruce, C. (2010) *Emotional Literacy in the Early Years*, London: Sage.
Bruce, T. (1991) *Time to Play: In Early Childhood Education*, London: Hodder & Stoughton Educational.
— (2004) *Developing Learning in Early Childhood 0–8 Years*, London: Sage.
Bryce, T.G.K. and Humes, W.M. (2003) *Scottish Education: Post-devolution*, Edinburgh: Edinburgh University Press.
Burnham, J. (1993) 'Systemic supervision: the evolution of reflexivity in the context of the supervisory relationship', *Human Systems* 4:349–81.
Campbell, C. and Jobling, W. (2012) *Science in Early Childhood*, New York: Cambridge University Press.
Cannella, G.S. and Viruru, R. (1997) 'Privileging child-centred, play-based instruction' in G.S. Cannella, *Deconstructing Early Childhood Education: Social Justice and Revolution*, New York: Lang, pp. 117–36.
Caruso, J.J and Fawcett, M. T. (2007) *Supervision in Early Childhood Education: A Developmental Perspective*, Teachers' College, Columbia University.
CECDE (Centre for Early Childhood Development and Education) (2006) *Síolta: The National Quality Framework for Early Childhood Education*, Dublin: CECDE.
— (2007) *Síolta Research Digests*, Dublin: CECDE <http://www.siolta.ie/media/pdfs/siolta_research_digests.pdf>.
Clarke, A. and Moss, P. (2001) *Listening to Young Children: The Mosaic Approach*, London: National Children's Bureau and Joseph Rowntree Foundation.
Cole, T. and Knowles, B. (2011) *How to Help Children and Young People with Complex Behavioural Difficulties*, London: Jessica Kingsley.
Craft, A. (2002) *Creativity and Early Years Education: A Lifewide Foundation*, London: Continuum.
Curtis, A. and O'Hagan, M. (2003) *Care and Education in Early Childhood: A Student's Guide to Theory and Practice*, London: Routledge Falmer.

Deiner, P. (2011) *Inclusive Early Childhood Education: Development, Resources, and Practice*, New York: Cengage Advantage Books.

deLongchamps, K. (2013) 'Accidents just a splash away for children', *Irish Examiner*, 30 June.

DoCYA (Department of Children and Youth Affairs) (2009) *Children First: National Guidance for the Protection and Welfare of Children*, Dublin: Stationery Office.

— (2012) *The State of the Nation's Children: Ireland 2012*, Dublin: Stationery Office.

DES (Department of Education and Science) (1999) *The Irish Primary School Curriculum*, Dublin: Stationery Office.

DETI (Department of Enterprise, Trade and Investment (Northern Ireland)) (2000) *Unlocking Creativity: A Strategy for Development*, Northern Ireland: Government Publications Office.

DoHC (Department of Health and Children) (1991) *Childcare Act*, Dublin: Stationery Office.

— (2000a) *National Children's Strategy*, Dublin: Stationery Office.

— (2000b) *National Health Promotion Strategy 2000–2005*, Dublin: Stationery Office.

— (2005) *We Like This Place: Guidelines for Best Practice in the Design of Childcare Facilities*, Dublin: Stationery Office.

— (2006a) *Child Care (Pre-School Services) (No. 2) Regulations 2006*, Dublin: Stationery Office.

— (2006b) *Food and Nutrition Guidelines for Pre-School Services*, Dublin: Stationery Office.

— (2006c) *The State of the Nation's Children: Ireland 2006*, Dublin: Stationery Office.

Dishman R., O'Connor, P. and Tomporowski, P. (2013) *Exercise Psychology*, Illinois: Human Kinetics Inc.

Dodds, S. and Jarvis, P. (2008) *Perspectives on Play: Learning for Life*, Essex: Pearson Education.

Donaldson, J. and Scheffler, A. (2011) *The Stickman*, London: Alison Green Books.

Drew, W.F. and Rankin, B. (2004) 'Promoting creativity for life using open-ended materials', *Young Children*, 59(4): 38–45.

Essa, E. (2010) *Introduction to Early Childhood Education*, Belmount CA: Cengage Learning.

Flora, S.B. (2006) *Fine Motor Fun: Hundreds of Developmentally Age-appropriate Activities Designed to Improve Fine Motor Skills*, Minnesota: Key Education.

Fox, J.E. and Schirrmacher, R. (2010) *Art and Creative Development for Young Children*, USA: Wadsworth.

French, G. and Murphy, P. (2005) *Once in a Lifetime: Early Childhood Care and Education for Children from Birth to Three*, Dublin: Barnardos' National Children's Resource Centre.

Fumoto H., Robson S., Greenfield S. and Hargreaves, D.J. (2012) *Young Children's Creative Thinking*, London: Sage.

Gardner, H. (1983) *Frames of Mind: The Theory of Multiple Intelligences*, New York: Basic Books.

Gascoyne, S. (2012) *Treasure Baskets and Beyond: Realizing the Potential of Sensory-rich Play*, Berkshire: Open University Press.

Gill, T. (2007) *No Fear: Growing Up in a Risk Averse Society*, UK: Calouste Gulbenkian Foundation.

Gillham, A.K. (2011) 'Let those angels get dirty faces', *Irish Times Health Supplement*, 7 July.

Goldschmied, E. and Jackson, S. (2004) *People Under Three: Young Children in Day Care*, 2nd edn, London: Routledge.

Greenland, S.K. (2010) *The Mindful Child: How to Help Your Kid Manage Stress and Become Happier and More Compassionate*, New York: Free Press.

Greenman, J. (2005) 'Beyond the journal', *Young Children on the Web*, May, 1–8.

Griffiths, F. (2012) *Supporting Children's Creativity through Music, Dance, Drama and Art: Creative Conversations in the Early Years*, Oxford: Routledge.

Harris, M. (2009) *Music and the Young Mind: Enhancing Brain Development and Engaging Learning*, Plymouth: MENC: National Association for Music Education.

Hart, R. (1992) *Children's Participation from Tokenism to Citizenship*, Florence: UNICEF Innocenti Research Centre.

Herr, J. (2000) *Creative Learning Activities for Young Children*, USA: Delmar Thompson Learning.

Holland, P. (2003) *We Don't Play with Guns Here: War Weapon and Super Hero Play in the Early Years*, Berkshire: Open University Press.

HSA (Health and Safety Authority) (2005) *The Safety, Health and Welfare at Work Act*, Dublin: Stationery Office.

— (2006) *Guidelines on Risk Assessments and Safety Statements*, Dublin: Stationery Office.

— (2007) *Safety, Health and Welfare at Work (General Application) Regulations*, Dublin: Stationery Office.

HSE (Health Service Executive) (2013) *National Guidelines on Physical Activity for Ireland: Get Ireland Active*, Dublin: Stationery Office.

Hughes, A.M. (2010) *Developing Play for the Under 3s: The Treasure Basket and Heuristic Play*, 2nd edn, New York: Routledge.

Hutt, J.R. (1979), cited in J.R. Hutt, S. Tyler, C. Hutt and H. Christopherson (1989) *Play, Exploration and Learning: A Natural History of Pre-School*, London: Routledge.

Hyson M. (2004) *The Emotional Development of Young Children: Building an Emotion-Centred Curriculum*, New York: Teachers' College Press.

Isbell, R.T. and Raines, S.C. (2007) *Creativity and the Arts with Young Children*, 3rd edn, New York: Cengage Learning.

Jasmine, G. (2004) *Preschool Arts and Crafts*, California: Teacher Created Resources.

Jones, J. (2012) 'A little more talk about mental health. Please', *Irish Times* Tuesday 9 October.

Lougy, R.A., DeRuvo, S.L. and Rosenthal, D. (2007) *Teaching Young Children with ADHD: Successful Strategies and Practical Interventions for PreK-3*, California: Corwin Press.

Martin, C.L. and Fabes, R.A. (2009) *Discovering Child Development*, 2nd edn, Boston MA: Houghton Mifflin.

Maslow, A.H. (1943) 'A theory of human motivation', *Psychological Review* 50(4), 370–96.

Mayesky M. (2009) *Creative Activities for Young Children*, 10th edn, New York: Cengage Advantage Books.

Morrow, L.M.(2007) *Developing Literacy in Preschool*, New York: Guilford Press.

NCCA (National Council for Curriculum and Assessment) (2004) *Towards a Framework of Early Learning: A Consultative Document*, Dublin: Stationery Office.

— (2009) *Aistear: The Early Childhood Curriculum Framework*, Dublin: Stationery Office < http://www.ncca.ie/en/Curriculum_and_Assessment/Early_Childhood_and_Primary_Education/Early_Childhood_Education/Framework_for_early_learning/>

New, R.S. and Cochran, M. (2007) *Early Childhood Education: A–D*, USA: Praeger.

Odegard, N. (2012) 'When matter comes to matter – working pedagogically with junk materials', *Education Inquiry*, 3(3), September, 387–400.

OECD (Organisation for Economic Co-operation and Development) (2004) *Thematic Review of Early Childhood Education and Care Policy in Ireland*, Dublin: Stationery Office.

Riley, J. (2007) *Learning in the Early Years 3–7*, 2nd edn, London: Sage.
Ronsen, M. (2010) 'Foreword' in C. Tims, *Born Creative* <http://www.demos.co.uk/publications/born-creative->
Rose, D.H. and Meyer, A. (2006) *A Practical Reader in Universal Design for Learning*, Boston MA: Harvard Education Press.
Saracho, O. (1990) *Cognitive Style and Education*, New York: Gordon and Breach.
— (1992) 'The relationship between preschool children's cognitive style and play: implications for creativity', *Creativity Research Journal*, 5(1), 35–47.
— (ed.) (2012) *Contemporary Perspectives on Research in Creativity in Early Childhood Education*, USA: Information Age Publishing.
Saracho, O. and Spodek, B. (2002) *Contemporary Perspectives in Literacy in Early Childhood Education*, USA: Information Age Publishing.
Schmid, T. (2006) *Promoting Health through Creativity: For Professionals in Health, Arts and Education*, London: John Wiley & Sons.
Sciarra, D.J. and Dorsey, A.G. (2001) *Leaders and Supervisors in Child Care Programs*, New York: Cengage Learning.
Start Strong (2010) *Children 2020: Planning Now, for the Future – Children's Early Care and Education in Ireland*, Dublin: Start Strong.
UN (United Nations) (1989) United Nations Convention on the Rights of the Child, adopted by the UN General Assembly on 20 November.
Vygotsky, L.S. (1978) *Mind in Society: The Development of Higher Psychological Processes*, Cambridge MA: Harvard University Press.
White, J. (2008) *Playing and Learning Outdoors: Making Provision for High-quality Experiences in the Outdoor Environment*, London: Routledge.
— (2011) *Outdoor Provision in the Early Years*, London: Sage.
Wilson, R. (2012) *Nature and Young Children: Encouraging Creative Play and Learning in Natural Environments*, London: Routledge.
Wright, S. (2010) *Understanding Creativity in Early Childhood: Meaning-Making and Children's Drawing*, London: Sage.

Resources
Online resources
Early Childhood Ireland – www.earlychildhoodireland.ie
Facebook
Farmville
Further Education and Training Awards Council – www.fetac.ie
Hanen Centre (Early Language Programmes) – http://www.hanen.org
Instagram
Irish Association of Creative Arts Therapists – http://www.iacat.ie/
Irish Play Therapy Association — http://www.ipta.ie
Photoshop
Picasa
Pinterest

Síolta – http://www.siolta.ie/
Robinson, Sir Ken (February 2006) TED talk – 'Schools Kill Creativity'
Watts, Alan: lecture, available on YouTube – 'What If Money Didn't Matter?'

Music and songs

'All I Want is You' (Barry Louis Polisar)
'Alphabet Song'
'Baa Baa Black Sheep'
Beethoven's Symphony No. 6 (used in Disney's *Fantasia*)
'Better Git it in Your Soul' (Charles Mingus)
'Bob the Builder '
'Bring Me Sunshine' (Morecambe and Wise)
'Colours of the Wind' (from Disney's *Pocahontas*)
'Diddle Diddle Dumpling'
'Dingle Dangle Scarecrow'
'The Duck Song' (Bryant Oden)
'The Farmer in the Dell'
'Five Little Ducks went Swimming One Day '
'Five Little Monkeys'
Flight of the Bumblebee (Rimsky-Korsakov)
Four Seasons (Vivaldi)
'The Grand old Duke of York'
'Happy Birthday To You'
'Happy Silly Song' (Mark Andrew Hanson)
'Heads, Shoulders, Knees and Toes'
'He's Got the Whole World in His Hands'
'The Hippopotamus Song' – 'Mud, Mud, Glorious Mud' (Flanders and Swann)
'Hot Cross Buns '
'Hound Dog' (Elvis Presley)
'How Much is that Doggie in the Window?'
'Humpty Dumpty'
'If All the Raindrops' (Barney)
'If You're Happy and You Know it, Clap Your Hands'
'I'll Tell Me Ma'
'I'm a Little Teapot'
'Incey Wincey Spider'
'It's My Party' (Lesley Gore)
'It's Oh So Quiet' (Björk)
'London Bridge is Falling Down'
'Mahna Mahna' (*Muppet Show*)
'Me and You' (Barry Louis Polisar)
Moonlight Sonata (Beethoven)
'My Bonnie Lies Over the Ocean'
'Nellie the Elephant '
'Old McDonald had a Farm'
'Once I Caught a Fish Alive'
'Pat-a-Cake'
'Polly Had a Dolly'
Prelude in E minor (Chopin)
Requiem (Verdi)
'Ring a Ring a Rosie'
'Rock a Bye Baby'
'Row, Row, Row Your Boat'
'Rupert and the Frog' (Paul McCartney)
'Sing a Song of Sixpence'
'Sir Duke' (Stevie Wonder)
'Slippery Fish'
'Take a Chance on Me' (ABBA)
'Teddy Bears' Picnic'
'The Trolley Song' (Judy Garland)
'Twinkle, Twinkle, Little Star'
'Under the Sea' (Disney's *The Little Mermaid*)
William Tell Overture (Rossini)
'You Are My Sunshine' (Elizabeth Mitchell)

Children's books

Ahlberg, A. and Ahlberg, J. (1985) *Peepo!* UK: Puffin Books.
Asquith, R. (2003) *Babies*, New York: Simon & Schuster Children's Publishing.
Briggs, R. (1986) *The Snowman*, California: Dragonfly Books.
Brown, M.W. (1947), *Good Night Moon*, UK: Harper Collins.

Carle, E. (1969) *The Hungry Caterpillar*, New York: Philomel Books.
Donaldson, J. (2001) *Room on the Broom*, New York: Puffin.
— (2006) *The Snail and the Whale*, UK: Puffin Books.
— (2008) *A Squash and a Squeeze*, London: Macmillan Children's Books.
McBratney, S. (2006) *Guess How Much I Love You*, Massachusetts: Candlewick Press.
— (2006) *I'm Sorry*, Hong Kong: Harper Collins.
Newcombe, Z. (2003) *Five Little Monkeys*, UK: Walker Books.
Postgate, D. (2009) *The Hairy Toe*, UK: Walker Books.
Roddie, S. and Cort, B. (2010) *Colour Me Happy!*, London: Macmillan.
Rosen, M. and Oxenbury, H. (2009) *We're Going on a Bear Hunt*, UK: Little Simon.
Sendak, M. (2012) *Where the Wild Things Are* (25th anniversary edn), Hong Kong: Harper Collins.
Seuss, Dr (1957) *The Cat in the Hat*, London: Random House.

Children's stories

Cinderella
Five Little Ducks
Goldilocks and the Three Bears
Humpty Dumpty
Little Red Riding Hood
Old McDonald
There Was an Old Woman who Swallowed a Fly
The Three Little Pigs
Three Billy Goats Gruff

Index

A Squash and a Squeeze, 80
accidents, 23, 134, 218, 219, 221, 223–4
   see also risk assessment
action boards, 204
active learning, 3–4, 34, 153, 183, 215, 226
active research, 20, 154
activities, creative arts
   aims and objectives, 21–2
   assessment, 27–30
   implementation, 26–7
   planning, 19–24, 27, 30
   resources *see* resources, creative arts activities
adult/child ratios, 22, 121, 160, 219
Aistear: The Early Childhood Curriculum Framework
   assessment, 27–8, 29
   communication, 124–5, 128, 132–3, 136–7, 139, 144, 149
   exploring and thinking, 123–4, 127–8, 131–2, 135–6, 138–9, 143, 148–9
   identity and belonging, 125–6, 128, 133, 137, 140, 144–5, 149–50
   mental health/wellbeing, 174–5, 181
   outdoor movement and music area, 122–6
   principles, themes and guidelines, 4, 11, 33–4
   wellbeing, 122–3, 127, 130–1, 134–5, 138, 142–3, 147–8, 181
alternative materials, 150–7
Andrews, M., 214–15, 223
animals, 103, 107
art galleries, 92–3, 137
art therapy, 189
arts and crafts centre
   indoor, 86–95
   outdoor, 133–7
assessment
   of creative arts activities, 27–30
   for Creative Arts for Early Childhood award, 228–37
attachment, 34–5, 38–9, 175
audio equipment, 111

babies, 34–9, 82, 175, 242
Barnes, R., 106
behaviour management, 55, 219
book corner, 74–82
books, 37, 74–82, 242–3
brain, in creativity, 194, 195
Brown, F., 10, 17, 18
Brown, Margaret Wise, 81, 82
Bruce, C., 144
Bruce, T., 3, 138

career education, 171
Caruso, J.J., 210
chemical hazards, 23, 90
Child Care (Pre-School Services) (No.2) Regulations
   adult/child ratios, 22, 121, 160, 219

   behaviour management, 55
   hygiene, 83
   observations, 28
   outdoor play, 118
   planning activities, 20
   practitioner skills and knowledge, 208
   project assessment, 234, 236
   rest and sleep facilities, 177
   safe environments, 217–21, 232
Childcare Act 1991, 208, 217–18
children
   child protection, 219, 225
   rights, 14, 177–80, 215
   stages of play *see* developmental stages, play during
Children 2020: Planning Now, for the Future – Children's Early Care and Education in Ireland, 193
Children First, 219, 225
Clarke, A., 56, 133
co-operative play, 45, 50–1, 54, 55
Cole, T., 188
collection of work, Creative Arts for Early Childhood award (NFQ Level 5), 229–33
colour, 14, 35, 36, 38, 42, 61, 85, 86–7
colouring books, 89
comfort toys, 145
communication
   Aistear, 124–5, 128, 132–3, 136–7, 139, 144, 149
   non-verbal, 69, 87, 123, 124–5, 132, 149
community involvement, 158, 167
construction area, 70–4
construction play, 47, 71, 146, 148–9
consultation, 21, 133, 159, 215
continuing professional development (CPD), 208, 210–12, 213
course assessment, 228–37
CPD (continuing professional development), 208, 210–12, 213
Craft, A., 207–8, 211–12
creative arts activities *see* activities
Creative Arts for Early Childhood (NFQ Level 5 award)
   collection of work, 229–33
   learning outcomes, v, 9, 19, 32, 61, 117, 174, 193, 214, 228, 229, 233
   project, 233–7
creative environments, 14–15
creative learning, 1, 14
creative play, 1, 3, 14
creativity
   in children, 1–2, 4–5, 194
   importance for practitioners, 193
   promoting creativity in adults, 196–207
   rules, 216–17
culinary art activities, 97–8
curriculum *see Aistear: The Early Childhood Curriculum Framework*
Curtis, A., 9–10, 71

dance *see* movement and dance
deficiency needs, 175–6
deLongchamps, Kya, 223–4
developmental stages, play during
    birth to one year, 34–9
    one to two years, 39–44
    two to three years, 44–9
    three to four years, 50–4
    four to six years, 54–9
discovery area/gardening centre
    indoor, 106–10
    outdoor, 126–9
Dishman, R., 186
Dodds, S., 102
Donaldson, Julia, 80
Dorsey, A.G, 210
drama therapy, 186
dramatic arts
    for babies, 37
    for one to two year olds, 41
    for two to three year olds, 47
    for three to four year olds, 51–2
    for four to six year olds, 54–5, 56
    in arts and crafts centre, 90–1
    in book corner, 78–9
    in construction area, 72–3
    in discovery area, 108
    in home corner, 64
    in messy play area, 84
    in music centre, 112–13
    in small world area, 103–4
    in table top area, 98–9
    in writing centre, 67–8
    alternative materials, 150–7
    and mental wellbeing, 185–6
    outings, 167–9
    promoting skills in adults, 200–3
    visitors, 171–2
dramatic play, 5
dress-up, 63
Drew, W.F., 150, 153–4

Early Childhood Arts and Culture (NFQ award), v–vi
early years practitioners
    continuing professional development, 210–12
    roles, 207
    self-care, 208–9
    workplace supervision, 210
education system, Irish, 3–4
ego rights, 178–80
emergencies, 225
emotional environments, 15–17
emotional literacy, 144
empathy, 128, 146
environmental awareness, 128
epistemic play, 36, 40
exercise, 118, 122, 186, 187, 209
    see also movement and dance
exploring and thinking (Aistear), 123–4, 127–8, 131–2, 135–6, 138–9, 143, 148–9

face painting, 205–6
fact or fiction, 198
Fawcett, M.T., 210
Fighting Words, 81
first aid, 218
flexibility, 18
Food and Nutrition Guidelines for Pre-School Services, 177
food hygiene, 220
Fox, J.E., 87
freedom, 17–18
Froebel, Friedrich, 3, 119
Fumoto, H., 1
fun, 17, 26
functional play, 40

galleries, art, 92–3, 137
games, 41, 54, 118, 196–207
games with rules stage, 54, 132
garden area *see* discovery area/gardening centre
Gardner, H., 60–1
gender roles, 63
Gillham, A.K., 118
Goodnight Moon, 81
Google, 20, 110
Greenman, J., 142
Griffiths, F., 105
growth rights, 180
Guidelines on Risk Assessments and Safety Statements, 222
gun play, 103

Harris, M., 110, 114, 115–16, 189–90
Hart's ladder of participation, 215
hazards, 22–3, 90, 223, 225
    see also accidents; risk assessment
health, 225–6
    see also mental wellbeing; safety; Safety, Health and Welfare at Work Acts; wellbeing
Health and Safety Authority (HSA), 221, 222, 223
Health Service Executive (HSE), 187, 218, 221
healthy eating, 127, 225
heart problems, 187
herbs, growing, 127
Herr, J., 89, 123
heterotopia, 152
hierarchy of needs, 175–6
High/Scope, 20, 62, 144, 150, 181–3
Holland, P., 103
home corner, 28, 41, 62–6
HSA (Health and Safety Authority), 221, 222, 223
HSE (Health Service Executive), 187, 218, 221
human bingo, 197–8
hygiene, 22–3, 83, 220
Hyson, M., 15–17

icebreaker activities, 197–200
identity and belonging
    Aistear, 125–6, 128, 133, 137, 140, 144–5, 149–50
    Síolta, 16, 140
imagination, 4–5
imaginative play, 44, 47, 56
    see also dramatic arts

infectious diseases, 225
injuries, 166–7
instruments, musical, 38, 43, 58, 65–6, 101–2, 110, 111, 114, 122
insurance, 22, 160, 220
intellectual environments, 13–14
intelligence *see* emotional literacy; multiple intelligence theory
interest areas, 60–1, 121–2
   see also outdoor play; play areas
Irish Association of Creative Arts Therapists, 184
Irish Play Therapy Association, 184
Isbell, R.T., 3, 4

Jarvis, P., 102
Jones, Dr Jacky, 175
Junior Certificate, 3
junk materials *see* alternative materials

key workers, 15, 144, 153, 165, 177
Knowles, B., 188

ladder of participation, Hart's, 215
language, development *see* writing centre
learning, creative, 1, 14
learning outcomes (Creative Arts for Early Childhood award, NFQ Level 5), v, 9, 19, 32, 61, 117, 174, 193, 214, 228, 229, 233
learning product, 3
learning styles, 61
leaves, 135
legislation *see* Child Care (Pre-School Services) (No.2) Regulations; Childcare Act 1991; Safety, Health and Welfare at Work Acts
libraries, 168
literacy, 66–8, 153
lost child procedures, 165–6
Lougy, R.A., 208–9
love, 178
low-load environments, 142–3
ludic play, 44, 50

masks, 203
Maslow, Abraham, 175–6
mathematical concepts, 127
mathematical materials, 97
Mayesky, M., 60–1
meals and snacks, 132–3
medical assistance, 218
mental health *see* mental wellbeing
mental wellbeing
   children's rights, 177–80
   children's wellbeing, 174–6
   dramatic arts, 185–6
movement and dance, 186–8
musical arts, 189–91
   therapeutic benefits of creative arts, 180–4
   visual arts, 188–9
messy play area
   indoor, 82–6

   outdoor, 137–40
Meyer, A., 61
mime, 202
Montessori, 3, 150
mosaic approach, 56, 133
Moss, P., 56, 133
mouthing, 35, 38
movement and dance
   for early years, 6
   for babies, 37–8
   for one to two year olds, 41
   for two to three year olds, 47
   for three to four year olds, 52
   for four to six year olds, 56–7
   in arts and crafts centre, 91
   in book corner, 80
   in construction area, 73
   in discovery area, 108–9
   in home corner, 64–5
   in messy play area, 84
   in music centre, 114
   in small world area, 104
   in table top area, 99–100
   in writing centre, 68–9
   alternative materials, 155–6
   and mental wellbeing, 186–8
   outings, 169
   promoting skills in adults, 203–4
   visitors, 172
multiple intelligence theory, 60–1
music therapy, 191
musical arts
   for early years, 7–8
   for babies, 38
   for one to two year olds, 42–3
   for two to three year olds, 48–9
   for three to four year olds, 53
   for four to six year olds, 58
   in arts and crafts centre, 93–5
   in book corner, 81–2
   in construction area, 74
   in discovery area, 110
   in home corner, 65–6
   in messy play area, 86
   in music centre/outdoor music and movement area, 110–16, 122–6
   in small world area, 105
   in table top area, 101–2
   in writing centre, 70
   alternative materials, 157
   instruments, 38, 43, 58, 65–6, 101–2, 110, 111, 114, 122
   and mental wellbeing, 189–91
musical concepts, 115–16
   outings, 170
   promoting skills in adults, 206–7
   resources, 242
   visitors, 172–3
my song, 206

National Children's Strategy, 218
National Council for Curriculum and Assessment (NCCA), 28, 29–30, 34, 183
  see also Aistear: The Early Childhood Curriculum Framework
National Health Promotion Strategy 2000-2005, 181
nature, 16, 19, 93, 106–10, 126–9, 133–4, 143
NCCA (National Council for Curriculum and Assessment), 28, 29–30, 34, 183
non-verbal communication, 69, 87, 123, 124–5, 132, 149
numeracy, 66–8, 153
nutrition, 177

observations, 28
observe, wait and listen (OWL), 94–5
O'Hagan, M., 9–10, 71
online resources, 118, 241–2
open-ended play, 87, 140, 150, 152–4, 179, 182
outdoor play
  arts and crafts centre, 133–7
  assessment, 121
  benefits, 118–19
  Child Care (Pre-School Services) (No.2) Regulations, 220
  discovery area/gardening centre, 126–9
  materials, 150–7
  messy play area, 137–40
  music and movement area, 122–6
  outings *see* outings
  planning, 119–21
  quiet area, 140–5
  role play area, 146–50
  table-top area, 129–33
outings
  assessment, 167
  examples, 167–71
  planning, 11, 22–3, 158–67
  safety, 159, 165–7
OWL (observe, wait and listen), 94–5

painting *see* visual arts
parallel play, 39, 41, 44
parents and families, 13, 21, 28
peer interaction, 179
Perry Preschool Project, 182–3
personal growth, 180
Personal Learning Plans (PLPs), 30
Pestalozzi, 119
pets, 41, 67, 107
physical environments, 12–13, 110
physiological rights, 177
planning, creative arts activities, 19–24, 27, 30
play
  areas *see* play areas
  creative, 1, 3, 14
  outdoor *see* outdoor play
  partnerships, 21, 179
  stages *see* developmental stages, play during
  therapy, 184, 186

play areas
  arts and crafts centre, 86–95, 133–7
  book corner, 74–82
  construction area, 70–4
  discovery area, 106–10, 126–9
  home corner, 28, 41, 62–6
  messy play area, 82–6, 137–40
  music centre, 110–16, 122–6
  outdoor *see* outdoor play
  small world area, 102–6
  table-top activities, 95–102, 129–33
  writing centre, 66–70
poems, 202
practitioners, early years *see* early years practitioners
praise, 58
pretend play, 44, 50
process-based education, 3–4
professional development (CPD), 208, 210–12, 213
project, Creative Arts for Early Childhood award (NFQ Level 5), 233–7
puzzles, 95, 96

question web, 199
quiet areas
  indoor, 74, 90, 100
  outdoor, 140–5

Raines, S.C., 3, 4
Rankin, Baji, 150, 153–4
recycled materials *see* alternative materials
Reggio Emilia, 4, 144, 150, 153–4, 167
relax and daydream exercise, 200–1
resilience, 175, 183, 214, 216
resources, creative arts activities
  books, 242–3
  music and songs, 242
  online, 118, 241–2
  stories, 243
  types, 22–4
rest and sleep facilities, 177, 220, 225
rights, children's, 14, 177–80, 215
risk assessment, 159, 214–15, 217, 222–5
  see also safety
Robinson, Sir Ken, 4–5
role play, 44, 45, 72, 90, 146–50, 185–6
  see also dramatic arts
Ronsen, M., 1
Rose, Colin, 61
Rousseau, 3, 119
rules, 17, 49, 51, 53–4, 55, 216

safety
  arts and crafts centre, 89–90
  children's rights, 215
  legislation *see* Child Care (Pre-School Services) (No.2) Regulations; Childcare Act 1991; Safety, Health and Welfare at Work Acts
  outings, 159, 165–7
  risk assessment, 159, 214–15, 217, 222–5
  rules, 216–17

safety, *continued*
    safe environments, 9–10, 22–3, 217–21, 232
    safety rights, 177
    safety statements, 222
Safety, Health and Welfare at Work Acts, 214, 221–5, 232
Saracho, O., 14, 18, 193, 208
Schirrmacher, R., 87
Schmid, T., 180
Sciarra, D.J., 210
self-actualisation, 176
self-care, 208–9
self-esteem, 176, 178–80, 181, 211
sensorial play, 34–6, 131
shared whispers, 198
sharing, 45–6
singing, 48–9, 70, 82, 115–16, 206–7, 242
    see also musical arts; songs
Síolta: The National Quality Framework for Early Childhood Education
    children's rights, 14, 215
    community involvement, 158, 167
    consultation, 21, 133
    curriculum, 14, 20
    environments, 11, 12, 13, 16, 110, 130
    health, safety and welfare, 225–6
    identity and belonging, 16, 140
    legislation, 20
    parents and families, 13, 21, 28
    planning and evaluation, 20, 21, 27
    professional development, 208, 210–11, 213
    wellbeing, 130
small world area, 102–6, 146–7, 148
smart, 61
social environments, 10–11, 14, 16, 130
social learning theory, 40, 44
social rights, 178
socio-dramatic play, 5, 64, 102, 103, 146, 147–8
solitary play, 39
songs, 41, 70, 82, 190–1, 206–7, 242
    see also musical arts; singing
SPICE framework, 10, 17
Spodek, B., 193
Start Strong, 193
The State of the Nation's Children, 180–1
Steiner, Rudolf, 3, 144, 150
stories, 56, 61, 77–81, 91, 202, 243
stranger danger, 166
stress, 208–9, 225
supervision
    children, 43, 49, 54, 90, 125, 180, 224
    workplace supervision, 210
symbolic representation, 50, 71

table-top area
    indoor, 95–102
    outdoor, 129–33
templates, 100–1
The Cat in the Hat, 81
The Snowman, 80

throwaway materials *see* alternative materials
tidy-up time, 26–7
Towards a Framework of Early Learning: A Consultative Document, 183
trauma, 184
treasure baskets, 36–7, 131–2, 150–1
trees, 106

United Nations Convention on the Rights of the Child, 215
Unlocking Creativity: A Strategy for Development, 194

vegetables, growing, 127
virtual play, 118
vision boards, 204
visitors, 171–3
visual arts
    for babies, 37–8
    for one to two year olds, 42
    for two to three year olds, 48
    for three to four year olds, 52–3
    for four to six year olds, 57–8
    in arts and crafts centre, 91–3
    in book corner, 80–1
    in construction area, 73
    in discovery area, 109–10
    in home corner, 65
    in messy play area, 85
    in music centre, 114–15
    in small world area, 104–5
    in table top area, 100–1
    in writing centre, 69
    alternative materials, 156–7
    benefits for children, 6–7
    displaying work, 92–3
    and mental wellbeing, 188–9
    outings, 169–70
    promoting skills in adults, 204–6
visitors, 172
visualisation, 200–1
Vygotsky, I.S., 34, 123, 153, 179

water activities, 138–9
weather, 119–20
wellbeing
    Aistear, 122–3, 127, 130–1, 134–5, 138, 142–3, 147–8, 181
    Síolta, 130
    see also mental wellbeing
White, J., 128, 137
whole child approach, 174, 218
Wilson, R., 214, 216–17
wooden blocks, 73
workbooks, 100–1
workplace supervision, 210
World Health Organization (WHO), 175, 181
writing centre, 66–70